# An Introduction to the UK Economy

*A Companion for*
*Positive Economics*

# An Introduction to the UK Economy

*A Companion for Positive Economics*

**Colin Harbury**
Professor of Economics
The City University
London

**Richard G Lipsey**
Professor of Economics
Queen's University
Kingston, Ontario

**Pitman**

PITMAN PUBLISHING LIMITED
128 Long Acre, London WC2E 9AN

*Associated Companies*
Pitman Publishing Pty Ltd, Melbourne
Pitman Publishing New Zealand Ltd, Wellington

© C D Harbury & R G Lipsey 1983

First published in Great Britain 1983
Reprinted 1983

Diagram artwork by Len Huxter and Lindsey Heppell

ISBN 0 273 01957 0

Text set in 9½ on 12 pt Linotron 202 Bembo,
printed in Great Britain at The Pitman Press, Bath

development; trade union strength; trade union structure; collective bargaining; disputes; other factors of production; rent; risk.

houses; finance houses; building societies; insurance companies; pension funds; the monetary sector as a whole; the Bank of England; the Issue Department; the Banking Department; liabilities; assets.

# List of illustrations

# Preface

Economic theory is only useful if it is understood in the context of the real world. Each of us is the author of a book which emphasises either theory or descriptive economics. We have been in the habit of recommending students to read each other's book, as well as our own, and we have now jointly written what be believe is a real companion to *An Introduction to Positive Economics*[1]. We hope, however, that our book will go equally well with any other theory text[2].

Readers familar with *Descriptive Economics*[3] will recognise material which has been updated and adapted. Much of the more elementary material there has been dropped, but there is a great deal which is new and needed to illustrate economic theory.

This book is primarily intended for students beginning to learn economic theory on A-level or first year courses in universities, polytechnics and other institutions of further education, as well as for those preparing for professional examinations in accountancy, banking, etc. Full details of the material covered are listed in the contents. They include those aspects of the UK economy, both micro and macro, which we regard as important for understanding the relevance of economic theory.

We have gone out of our way not to clutter either our text with endless tables of indigestible statistics or our charts with numbers calculated to decimal-place accuracy. We believe that all a student can, or should, take away from a book such as this is an outline view of the economy's institutions and functions and its chief orders of magnitude, which date far less quickly than the detailed statistics.

Our illustrations have been designed to help our readers retain visually most of the more important quantitative features of the UK economy. To this end we have deliberately employed a variety of diagrammatic styles and types, including straightforward graphs, pie charts, histograms and bar

1 *An Introduction to Positive Economics*, Richard G Lipsey, 6th edition, Weidenfeld & Nicolson, 1983.
2 Students who would like a briefer overview of economic theory before tackling a detailed book such as *Positive Economics* may find it helpful to read first *Economic Behaviour: An Introduction*, Colin Harbury, Allen & Unwin, 1980.
3 *Descriptive Economics*, Colin Harbury, 6th edition, Pitman, 1981.

charts in two and three dimensions. We hope that they, together with the text, will assist readers to gain a general knowledge of the economic forest without having to try to absorb the detailed structure of every sectoral tree.

There are no special reasons for students to read this *Introduction to the UK Economy* before starting work on economic theory, though the material should be quite intelligible for anyone wishing to read it first. Within the text we have given liberal cross references to the 6th edition of *An Introduction to Positive Economics* (referred to throughout as Lipsey) and we imagine that the two books are best read in parallel.

Among the many people whom we should like to thank, we would like to single out both our publishers who have supported the venture—especially Weidenfeld & Nicolson for their goodwill over a book in which they have no commercial interest.

Colin Harbury
Richard Lipsey
1983

# 1 The economy in outline[1]

Our modern economy is complex. The purpose of this introductory chapter is to outline its distinctive features, which will then be described in greater detail later in the book.

The features to which we shall draw attention are:

- **Resources**—land, labour and capital
- **Production**—primary, secondary and tertiary
- **Foreign trade**—exports and imports of goods and services
- **Economic growth** and living standards
- **Unemployment**
- **The monetary system**—financial institutions and the price level
- **Government**—the economic role of the state

**Resources**

The resources of a society consist not only of the free gifts of nature, such as land, forests and minerals, but also of human capacity, both mental and physical, and of man-made aids to further production, such as tools, machinery and buildings. It is sometimes useful to divide these resources into three main groups—**land**, **labour** and **capital**—known as **factors of production**.

Land

The United Kingdom is a country where land is very scarce relative to the population. Fig 1 shows the uses made of it. Of the $24\frac{1}{2}$ million hectares, 2 million are covered with forest and another quarter of a million are inland water; 3 million hectares are classed as urban, ie used for houses, factories and the like. Even the 19 million which remain can by no stretch of the imagination be called good agricultural land. About a third is either so mountainous or has such poor soil that it is beyond the margin of cultivation and is called 'rough grazing'. Scotland has two-thirds of the total for Britain, and much of Welsh agriculture is on land of this type.

The remainder of the land, about 12 million hectares, is used for the cultivation of tillage crops and grasses. Most of the latter is permanent pastureland, but up to a third is for temporary grazing or mowing in rotation with other crops.

1 For an introductory outline which includes the relevant theoretical concepts see Chapters 4, 5 and 6 in *An Introduction to Positive Economics*, Richard G Lipsey, Weidenfeld & Nicolson, 6th edition, 1983, hereafter referred to as Lipsey.

*Fig 1* Land use 1980; relative importance of different uses
Source: *Annual Abstract of Statistics*

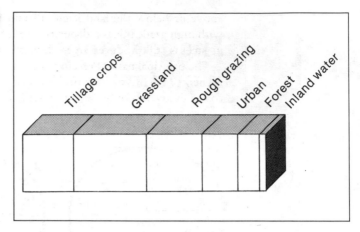

The use made of the 5 million hectares devoted to tillage crops is shown in Fig 2. Over three-quarters is devoted to cereal production, both for human and livestock consumption. Barley replaced oats as the foremost grain crop around 1960 and something like 10 per cent of the available area is used for sugar beet, potatoes and vegetables, the principal 'other' categories being fruit and flowers, hops and rape grown for oilseeds.

*Fig 2* Land under tillage crops 1980; relative importance of major crops
Source: *Annual Abstract of Statistics*

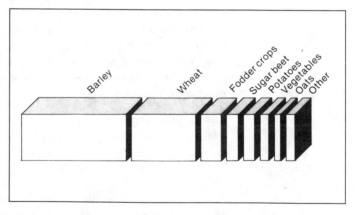

The shortage of good land suitable for arable cultivation makes the livestock population of the country a vitally important part of its agriculture for, by and large, livestock can thrive on poorer soils than growing crops like cereals and vegetables. In 1980 there were over 100 million chickens, 30 million sheep, half that number of head of cattle and about 8 million pigs on farms in the country.

The term land, as used by economists, conventionally includes those free gifts of nature commonly called natural resources, such as minerals and other raw materials lying above or below the land itself. Britain is not well endowed with high grade mineral deposits, though about 10 per cent of its steel is still produced from domestic iron ore.

The principal natural resource in Britain at the present time is energy. For a very long time the main source of energy was coal. Discoveries of North Sea gas and oil in the 1970s has led,

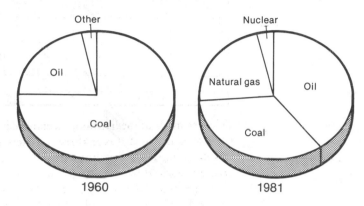

*Fig 3* Inland energy consumption 1960 and 1981
Source: *Monthly Digest of Statistics*, May 1982

as Fig 3 shows, to the displacement of coal from its position as the major supplier of energy consumed in the UK. Britain is currently self-sufficient in energy supplies. Estimates of the unexploited reserves of oil and natural gas are understandably imprecise and vary with new discoveries. Coal reserves are, however, substantial and the coal industry is capable of resuming a primary role when North Sea reserves run out.

## Labour

The supply of human resources is referred to by economists as labour—another factor of production. The amount that is available is called the **labour force** and depends, in the first instance, on the size of the population.

In 1801, when the first census was taken, the total population of Britain was roughly 12 million. Thereafter it grew at an astonishing rate. As Fig 4 shows, it doubled in 60 years, and by 1861 there were over 24 million people. It had more than doubled again by 1951, when the population was over 50 million. It had mounted still further 20 years later to about 56 million, at which figure it has, at least temporarily, more or less stabilised.

The population of Britain is by no means evenly spread over the whole country. It is clear from Fig 4 that England, Wales, Scotland and Northern Ireland have very unequal shares of the total population. If the population of each of these countries is related to its size, however, the inequality is

*Fig 4* Population since
1801
Source: *Annual
Abstract of Statistics*

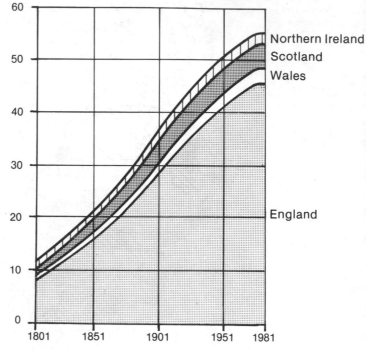

even greater, since England has over four-fifths of the people
and only just over half the land, whilst Scotland has a third of
the land but only about a tenth of the people. Wales has a tenth
of the land but only a twentieth of the people and Northern
Ireland has a twentieth of the land but a mere 3 per cent of the
population. We can express these facts in another way by
saying that in England there are about 900 people per square
mile, in Wales about 350, in Northern Ireland less than 300
and in Scotland only about 175.

The reasons for these very unequal densities of population
are to be found partly in differences in climatic conditions, but
the overwhelming causes are economic. For all but a very
select few of the population, where to live is decided for them
by the whereabouts of the farms, factories, shops or offices at
which they work to earn their living. When Britain was an
agricultural country the population was fairly evenly spread
over the good farming land. With the growth of industry
the siting of factories became the predominant influence. We

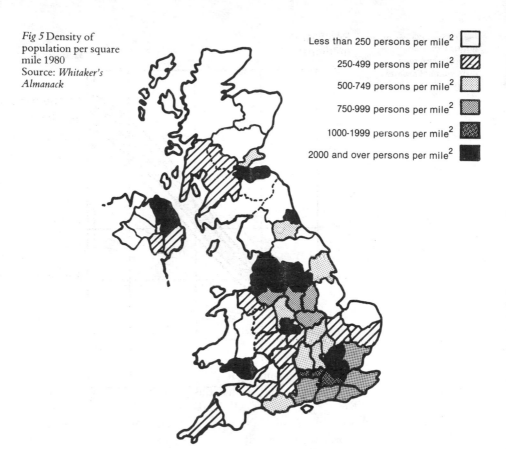

*Fig 5* Density of
population per square
mile 1980
Source: *Whitaker's
Almanack*

Less than 250 persons per mile$^2$

250-499 persons per mile$^2$

500-749 persons per mile$^2$

750-999 persons per mile$^2$

1000-1999 persons per mile$^2$

2000 and over persons per mile$^2$

shall examine further aspects of the regional distribution of
industry in Chapter 3.

The map (Fig 5) reveals the main features of the geographical distribution of the population and shows the concentrations around the principal cities. At present something
like four-fifths of the entire population live in urban areas and
only one-fifth in the country. Even a good many of the latter
work in towns. To emphasise the extent of urbanisation,
notice that in 1980 there were nearly 20 cities in Britain with
more than a quarter of a million inhabitants, and seven
conurbations (Birmingham, Clydeside, Leeds, Liverpool,
London, Manchester and Newcastle) which together occu-
pied about 3 per cent of the land but housed a third of the
people.

The regional distribution of the population is continually
changing. Rural depopulation and the growth of cities began
with the industrial revolution, but not all urban areas have
grown at the same rate. Fig 6 brings out the main changes in

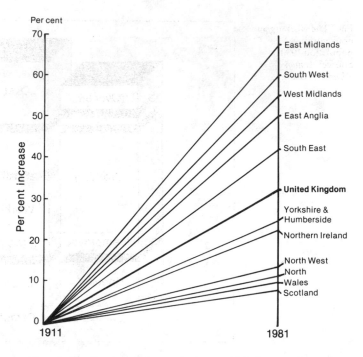

*Fig 6* Regional population changes 1911–81; percentage increase in population
Source: *Annual Abstract of Statistics*

Per cent

Per cent increase

70 — East Midlands
60 — South West — West Midlands
50 — East Anglia
40 — South East
30 — **United Kingdom**
20 — Yorkshire & Humberside — Northern Ireland
10 — North West — North — Wales — Scotland
0

1911                    1981

regional distribution of population which have taken place since 1911. It shows that the greatest increase in population has occurred in the Midlands, South West, East Anglia and South East England, while Scotland, Wales, Northern and North West England have experienced *relative* declines. These changes are the result of internal migration of workers and their families, attracted by employment opportunities in the areas involved, and natural increases of the populations themselves.

A fairly recent tendency, not observable from Fig 6, is for people to choose to live in outlying suburbs rather than in the centres of large cities. In the interwar years this led to the sprawling conurbations mentioned previously. In order to prevent further erosion of the countryside, the government introduced a policy of designating 'green belts' of land, usually several kilometres wide, around larger cities, where urban building was virtually prohibited. With similar objectives in mind, 32 'new towns', now with a combined population of over 2 million, have been created under legislation passed in 1946.

We started our discussion of labour as a factor of production by looking at the size of the population. However, only about half of the total community can be regarded as being available for work in the ordinary sense of the word. How then do the remainder spend their time? Fig 7 helps to provide the answer.

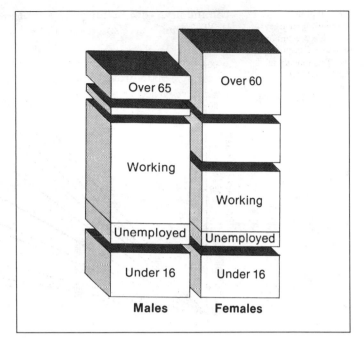

First, about half are growing up; the school-leaving age ensures that the 13½ million boys and girls under 16 shall not undertake full-time work and they must therefore be excluded from the labour force. At the other end of the scale there is a similar, though smaller, group of women over 60 and men over 65 (the ages of entitlement to retirement pensions). The remainder includes housewives, students, the infirm, convicts and others. They are excluded from the working population, not because they do not work, but because they are not paid a wage for doing so. True, housewives may be given housekeeping allowances by their spouses, but by no stretch of the imagination can they be thought of as being employed by them!

Capital

The third and last factor of production consists of all those man-made aids to further production, such as tools, machinery, plant and equipment, which are not consumed for their own sake but are used to make other goods and services, ie capital.

The value of the nation's capital stock is very large, at the beginning of the 1980s running to a figure with nine noughts. It is difficult to appreciate the significance of such a magnitude. One way of putting it into perspective is to consider that it represents something like the total output of the entire economy for 4 to 5 years.

Fig 8 shows the breakdown of the tangible assets of the

community, with buildings as the largest item. Notice also that dwellings account for nearly a third of the total assets. These, it is true, are not capital goods of the kind we described. However, they are long-lasting and, in the sense that they help to provide for enjoyment in the future, they are usually regarded as part of the nation's capital resources.

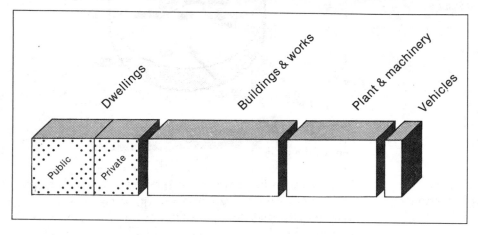

Tangible assets are not the only components of the national wealth. Some assets are locked up, for example, in the skills acquired by education and training. Such intangible assets are hard to evaluate in money terms and they are not included in Fig 8.

**Production**

We have looked at the available resources. We now continue our overview of the British economy by looking at how these resources are used in the production of goods and services.

We first use a well-established distinction which categorises production into three types, known as **primary**, **secondary** and **tertiary production**. Fig 9 shows the relative importance of the three types of production in present day Britain, according to the number of workers employed.

Primary production

This consists of all economic activity which is a first step in the productive process, ie the harvesting of the natural resources of the world, especially agricultural crops and minerals, which provide the foodstuffs and basic raw materials upon which other production depends. At the present time less than 5 per cent of the labour force works in agriculture and mining.

Secondary production

This is concerned with the later stages in the production of finished goods. It therefore comprises all of what is called

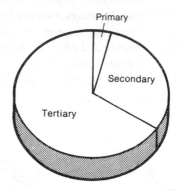

*Fig 9* Types of industrial activity 1981; percentage of total labour force engaged in primary, secondary and tertiary production
Source: *Monthly Digest of Statistics*

manufacturing industry, though today that is less than 30 per cent of the total.

**Tertiary production**

This involves the provision of **services** which either help other producers to do their jobs, eg transport, or satisfy consumer demands for such things as entertainment or hairdressing. As can be seen in Fig 9, all tertiary services employ about two-thirds of the working population. They include workers in transport, retailing, commerce, finance, government and the professions.

The fact that secondary and tertiary employment account for such a high proportion of the total is one indication of the advanced state of industrial organisation in Britain. This is clearly illustrated if we compare the situation today with that in the past. The proportion of the labour force engaged in primary production 100 years ago was about 25 per cent. Were reliable figures available for, say, 300 years ago the contrast would be even more striking. At that time agriculture was almost the only important industry, and the proportion of the labour force engaged in primary production was correspondingly high. Manufacturing business was still rare and, in those days before railways and cars, transport was difficult and the numbers in government service and the professions were much fewer.

Employment in secondary production was the first to increase with the industrial revolution. Then, as technical advances raised productivity in industrial production, resources were released for the tertiary sector, while the output of manufactured goods was maintained and even raised. The relative importance of the services sector increased, gaining ground from secondary production. Indeed, in the last 20 years or so the decline in employment in manufacturing industry has accelerated. The process has become known as **de-industrialisation** and is not confined to the UK. The causes of this trend are not fully understood, but it is certainly partly a result of the growth of technology in manufacturing. Whether it is a natural stage in economic development or a matter of grave concern remains controversial.

*Fig 10* Employment in the main industrial sectors 1981
Source: *Monthly Digest of Statistics*

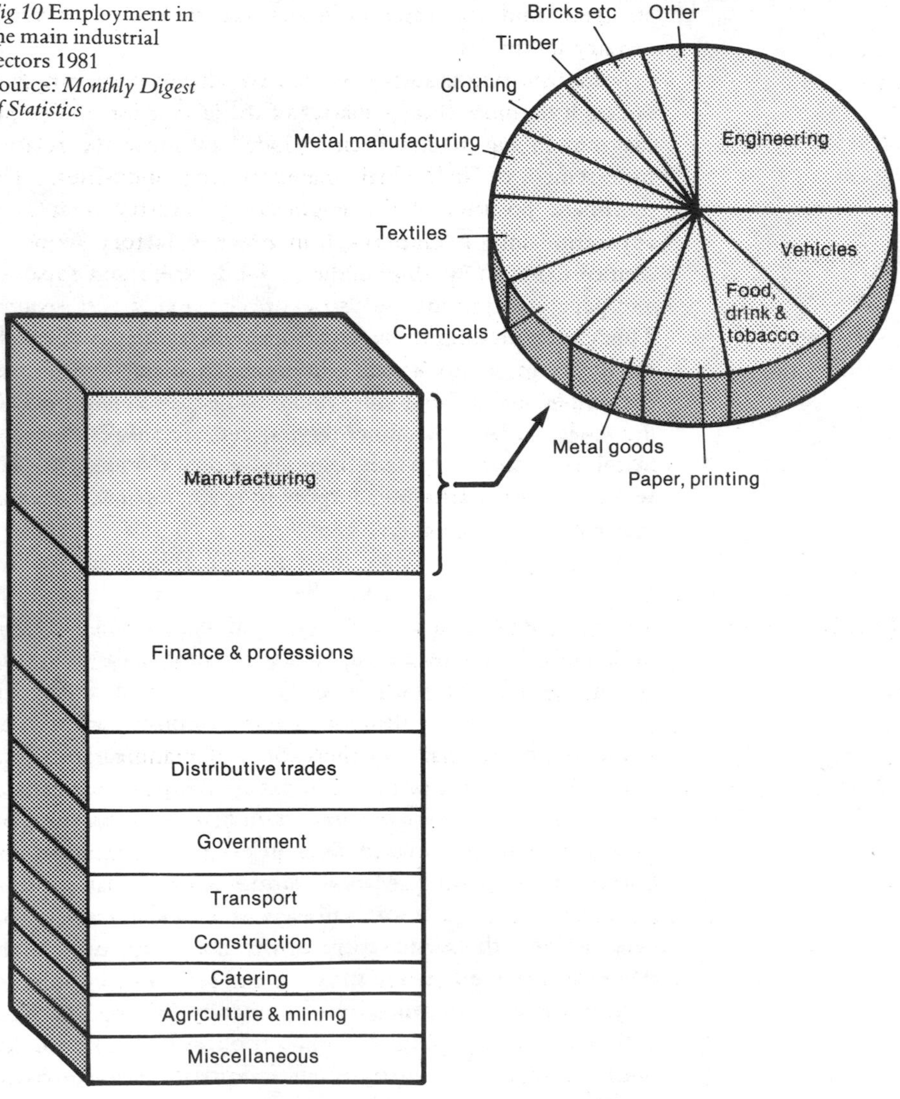

### The pattern of production

Fig 10 will help us to probe a little further into the detailed distribution of the labour force. The main block in the diagram shows the chief sectors of tertiary activity. Finance and the professions employ about 5 million people, almost a quarter of the total. About 1 person in 8 works in the distributive trades and 1 in 15 in government. This last figure relates only to those directly employed by central and local government. It excludes others who work for the state, eg in schools, nationalised industries and the health service. The relative importance of the state in the economy as a whole is a different matter, which is discussed later. Transport, construction and the catering trades are the other principal tertiary industries.

Manufacturing industry, as we have already seen, employs only a little more than a quarter of the labour force. The pie diagram in Fig 10 has been included to show the relative importance of individual manufacturing industries. The dominant position of the engineering industry is at once apparent, since it employs 1 in every 4 factory workers. Vehicles (including shipbuilding), food, drink and tobacco, and paper and printing industries are the next largest groups. Together with engineering, these industries account for the employment of over half the manufacturing workforce. Among others, metal goods (a miscellaneous category including tools, cutlery, metal containers, etc), chemicals, textiles, metal manufacture (mainly iron and steel), clothing, timber and bricks are sufficiently important to be separately distinguished.

**Foreign trade**

The United Kingdom is far from being an isolated self-sufficient country; instead it engages in a substantial amount of trade with the rest of the world.

In the last century Britain held a dominant position in world trade, especially in the export of manufactured products. A 100 years ago Britain supplied almost 40 per cent of such world exports, compared with less than 10 per cent today—Britain now takes fifth place after Germany, the United States, Japan and France. Britain is also the fifth largest importer in the world. More relevant in some ways, however, is the role imports play in the UK economy. Somewhere around a quarter of all goods and services consumed in Britain are made up, directly or indirectly, of imports. This underlines the key place of foreign trade in the economic life of the country and may be contrasted with the situation in the USA or Japan, for example, where imported goods comprise notably lower proportions of the national income. (There are, of course, countries where the proportion of imports to national income is higher than in the UK, eg Belgium and the Netherlands—see page 96.)

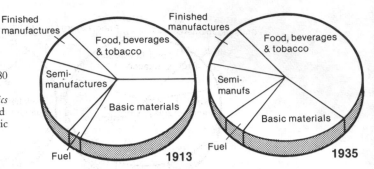

*Fig 11* UK imports; commodity composition in selected years 1913–80 Sources: *The British Economy, Key Statistics 1900–70,* London and Cambridge Economic Service, and *Annual Abstract of Statistics*

**1913** — Finished manufactures; Food, beverages & tobacco; Semi-manufactures; Basic materials; Fuel

**1935** — Finished manufactures; Food, beverages & tobacco; Semi-manufs; Basic materials; Fuel

## Commodity composition

The traditional picture of Britain in the world economy in the past was characterised by her great dependence upon foreign sources of supply for essential raw materials and foodstuffs, paid for by the export of manufactured products. This is no longer the case. The importance of primary products in the import bill has greatly diminished as a result of many factors, including the development of synthetics and the decline of some raw material using industries, such as textiles.

Figs 11 and 12 show the major changes that have taken place in the composition of British foreign trade since 1913. It can be seen that food, beverages and basic materials accounted for about three-quarters of total imports before the First World War, but for only about a fifth by 1980. The only material to have increased significantly has been fuel, though, thanks largely to North Sea oil, the UK had become a *net* fuel exporter by the 1980s. The corollary of the decline in imports of primary products, also seen in Fig 11, is the great rise in the importance of manufactures and semi-manufactures, which

*Fig 12* UK exports; commodity composition in selected years 1913–80 Sources: *The British Economy, Key Statistics 1900–70,* London and Cambridge Economic Service, and *Annual Abstract of Statistics*

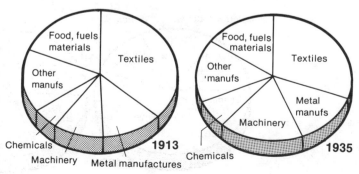

**1913** — Food, fuels materials; Textiles; Other manufs; Chemicals; Machinery; Metal manufactures

**1935** — Food, fuels materials; Textiles; Other manufs; Metal manufs; Machinery; Chemicals

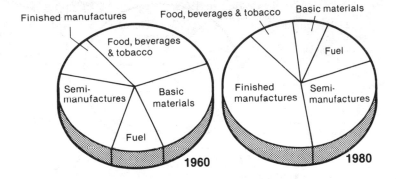

**1960**     **1980**

nowadays account for about two-thirds of total imports. Since UK exports have remained mainly of manufactured goods (see Fig 12), British overseas trade is best characterised as consisting predominantly of the exchange of manufactured goods with other countries. There have, however, been substantial changes in the relative importance of different kinds of manufactured goods which are exported. To a substantial extent these reflect shifts in the structure of industrial production.

**Geographical distribution**

The geographical distribution of UK trade has also shifted very substantially from that of former times. Before the Second World War, the countries of the Commonwealth were Britain's major trading partners. Now, however, on both the import and export side, the countries of Europe occupy the dominant position, accounting for roughly half the total. By far the most important of these countries are the members of the European Economic Community (EEC), which Britain

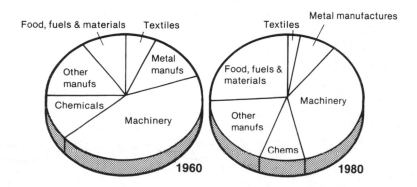

**1960**     **1980**

joined in 1972. The sources of imports and destinations of exports are shown in Fig 13.

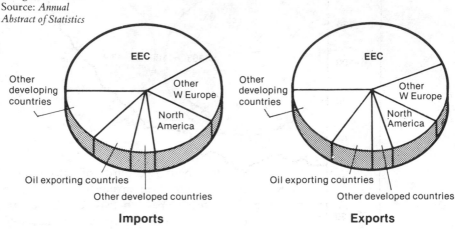

**Imports**                    **Exports**

Invisible trade

We should not leave the subject of overseas trade without mentioning that the UK engages in a considerable amount of exchange of services. Such trade is known as **'invisible' trade**, in contrast with the **'visible' trade** in exports and imports of goods with which we have so far been concerned. Invisible earnings from the services of financial institutions, in the form of returns on overseas investments and from other sources, have played an important part in paying for the UK's excess in the value of imports over exports of goods.

**Economic growth**

Economic growth has been one of the dominant forces for industrial nations over the last 200 years. It has raised living standards to levels where goods and services, such as cars and foreign travel, have come within the reach of the mass of the population in countries such as Britain.

Fig 14 shows how real output has grown in the UK during the present century. It can be seen that progress has not been entirely steady. In some years growth rates have been high—up to 8 per cent. In others the rate has actually been negative, output falling by almost as much as it rose in the good years. However, the long-term trend has been unequivocally upwards. Since the end of the Second World War output has grown by about $2\frac{1}{2}$ per cent per annum, on average. This figure may seem low by comparison with some other countries, eg Germany, Japan and France, in the postwar years, but it is substantially higher than the average rate of growth in Britain earlier in the century, which was about 1 per cent before the First World War and 2 per cent in the interwar

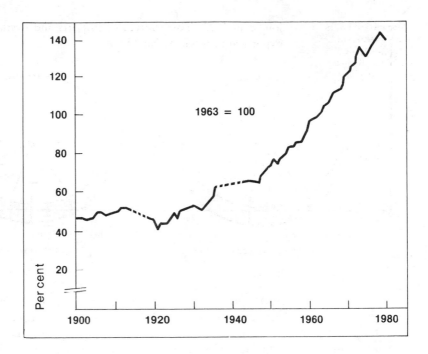

140 —
120 —
100 —
80 —
60 —
40 —
20 —

1963 = 100

Per cent

1900    1920    1940    1960    1980

*Fig 14* Real output
1900–80
Sources: *The British
Economy, Key Statistics
1900–70*, London and
Cambridge Economic
Service, and *Annual
Abstract of Statistics*

period. Moreover, the cumulative workings of compound interest can lead to rather startling results; a growth rate of 2 per cent per year, if continued for a century, will lead to more than a sevenfold increase in real national income. Britain's achieved rate of $2\frac{1}{2}$ per cent causes output to double within a generation, as can be seen by inspection of the levels of output in 1950 and 1980 in Fig 14. Material living standards rose by almost the same extent. Only *almost* because the population, among whom output needs to be divided, rose by about 10 per cent so that income *per head* rose by rather less than gross output.

**Unemployment**

The account of economic growth in the previous section has been of *achieved* output, not maximum *potential* output. We know that the latter has been considerably greater than the former in some years because not all the country's productive capacity has been fully utilised. In so far as all workers are not fully employed, output is less than the maximum that is technically possible.

Fig 15 traces the history of unemployment during the present century, as depicted by the percentage of the labour force out of work. In the 19th century there was a reasonably regular trade cycle of booms and slumps lasting 8–10 years. The level of unemployment varied continuously; there were

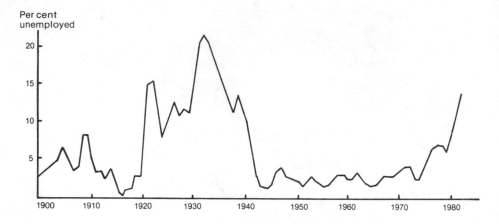

Fig 15 Percentage
unemployment
1900–82 (figures for
1900–26 relate to the
unionised labour
force; subsequent
figures relate to the
total registered
working population)
Sources: *The British
Economy, Key Statistics
1900–70*, London and
Cambridge Economic
Service, and *Annual
Abstract of Statistics*

no *prolonged* periods either of full employment or of heavy unemployment.

The period between the two world wars presents a dismal picture of heavy unemployment. The unemployment of the 1920s was an isolated British phenomenon associated with the long-term decline in some of Britain's staple export industries. The high British unemployment rate was not matched elsewhere in the world in that decade; in the United States, for example, the mid-1920s was a period of boom. The 1930s, however, saw heavy unemployment throughout the world. At the worst point in the Great Depression one person in four was unemployed in the United Kingdom. A similar situation ruled in America and in many other industrialised countries.

During the Second World War unemployment fell to an extremely low level indeed. After the war unemployment still fluctuated, but from 1945 until the early 1970s the fluctuations were over a much narrower range than in the 19th century. Even with all possible allowances for changes in the definitions of the unemployment figures, the period following 1945 showed a substantial reduction in the average level of unemployment.

In 1974 the world entered the worst recession since the Great Depression of the 1930s. Unemployment in the UK began a steady upward climb that took it from 2½ per cent in 1974 to 6 per cent in 1977. Unemployment then fell slightly but began to rise rapidly in 1980, reaching 11 per cent in 1981 and 14 per cent in 1982.

## The monetary system

So far this chapter has discussed the *real* parts of the economy, that is to say the supply of the real resources of land, labour and capital and the production of real goods and services. However, the economy has another side to it, a *monetary* one, which reflects the fact that resources and goods are measured in terms of their prices or monetary values.

Money has traditionally been defined as anything that is generally accepted by virtually everyone in exchange for goods and services. It includes notes and coins, but the most important means of making payments today is through banks. Bank deposits, the sums standing to the credit of customers, are the prime constituent of what is regarded as money in the UK, though there are several alternative definitions of the money supply which will be discussed in Chapter 8, pages 174–6.

The business of banking is mainly in the hands of the four large so-called **clearing banks**—Barclays, Lloyds, Midland and National Westminster. Against their deposit liabilities they hold a variety of financial assets, ranging from notes and coins in the vaults, through securities, to the loans and advances they make to customers, often by granting them overdraft facilities. It is the last of these which are of major importance in determining the quantity of money in existence.

The monetary sector of the economy, however, includes a great many other financial institutions, for example merchant banks, accepting and discount houses, building societies and insurance companies, which will be considered in Chapter 8. All deal in monetary assets of one form or another. Their activities may affect key economic variables, especially the general level of prices, output and employment levels. Since the banks and other financial institutions can play important roles in these matters, the government often tries to influence them in pursuit of its policy objectives. The state has many ways of doing so. Several are carried out through the central bank—in the UK, the Bank of England—which is owned by the government and is its instrument of monetary policy.

The Bank of England can exert influence on the supply of money by pressuring the banks to alter their lending policies. It can freeze and unfreeze their cash reserves and in other ways affect the banks' liquidity (the proportion of cash and other assets to total deposits). The Bank can also influence the level of interest rates, ie the prices paid by borrowers or received by lenders of money, and in that way influence spending and thereby also the price level, output and employment.

Inflation

Changes in the general level of prices affect real output. The strength and duration of this effect are controversial, but governments throughout the world have been worried by inflation. Moreover, recent years have witnessed a rather remarkable and, in a sence, novel movement in the general level of prices. This is the persistence of inflation, which hardly needs describing to anyone alive today.

Fig 16 shows the course of the *average* level of retail prices in

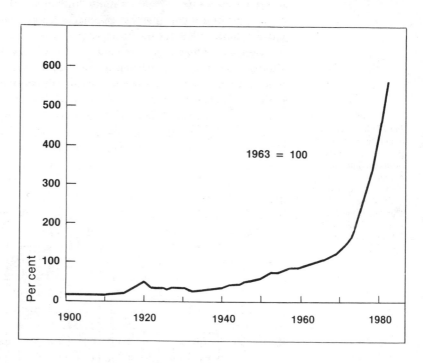

*Fig 16* Index of retail prices 1900–81
Sources: *The British Economy, Key Statistics 1900–70*, London and Cambridge Economic Service, *Annual Abstract of Statistics*, and *Monthly Digest of Statistics*

the UK since 1900. It demonstrates that, apart from a very few years after the First World War and in the early 1930s, the general trend has been decidedly upwards. Indeed, by 1981 prices were approximately 30 times their 1900 levels—put another way, £1 in 1982 would buy the same amount that could be bought for little more than 3 pence in 1900.

The modern age of inflation is, however, largely a postwar one. The first 20 years after the Second World War were those of a fairly steady, if slow, rate of increase in the level of prices—2 to 3 per cent per annum on average. Towards the end of the 1960s inflation started to accelerate and first reached double figures in the early 1970s. In 1974 the rate topped 20 per cent and the following year prices rose by more than 25 per cent in 12 months. There was some reduction in the rate of inflation towards the end of the 1970s, but in 1980 it rose once more above 20 per cent. Subsequently the rate has fallen (we shall discuss this in more detail in Chapter 9).

**Government**

The UK is a **mixed economy**. A great many decisions are taken by private individuals in markets where the forces of supply and demand work relatively free from government interference. However, there are important sectors where the state enters directly or indirectly into decision-making on the allocation of resources.

Fig 17 shows the size of government activity as measured by the proportion of public expenditure to total national income since 1900 (government expenditure here excludes expenditure by the nationalised industries). This is only one of a number of indicators that can be used for the same purpose; indeed, the precise percentages obtained are sensitive to which indicator is chosen. However, there is no danger in drawing

*Fig 17* Government expenditure as a percentage of GNP Sources: *The Growth of Public Expenditure in the UK*, A T Peacock and J Wiseman, 2nd edition, Allen & Unwin, 1967, and *National Income and Expenditure*

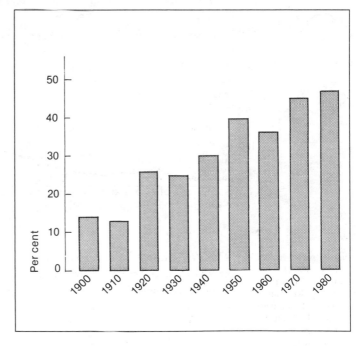

the general conclusion that the trend is of substantial growth in government expenditure. While not much more than 10 per cent of the national income passed through the government's hands at the beginning of the century, by 1980 the proportion had risen to almost half. Similar trends have been experienced by other countries.

There are many explanations for the growth of public expenditure which, of course, carried with it growing government income from taxation. They include major changes in the public's attitude to the role of the state in the provision of social services (the Welfare State) and decisions to take certain important industries into public ownership (nationalisation), especially after the Second World War.

There is also a technical reason why the public sector tends to grow relative to the rest of the economy. It is known as the **relative price effect**. Put simply, the reason is that productivity in government services rises more slowly than in manufacturing industry because of the small scope for mechanisation and, therefore, for economies of large-scale production. The prices of government services tend to rise in consequence *relative* to those of the rest of the economy (this is why it is called the *relative* price effect). Since the output of the public and private sectors is valued by reference to their prices (or costs), the size of the former has a natural tendency to increase relative to that of the latter. This is not, of course, an iron law. Governments can exercise control over the total expenditure from the public purse. The Conservative administration which took office in 1979 was committed to a reduction in the scope of the public sector, and set out to put its policy into effect by transferring certain activities into private hands (known as 'privatisation') and by other devices.

State intervention in the economic life of the country takes a wide variety of forms and is carried out, both directly and indirectly, by many agencies of central and local government and by other bodies. It is difficult to classify them because some activities can be placed in more than one category, but some idea of their extensive nature may be gleaned from the following, far from comprehensive, list.

*Social services*

The government provides public education in schools and institutions of further education, including universities and polytechnics. It also runs the national health service and supplies a substantial amount of public housing.

*Redistribution of income and wealth*

The state tries to affect the distribution of income and wealth in many ways, including the provision of benefits such as free education and subsidised housing. Additionally there are two instruments for redistribution which are of prime importance:

a the levying of taxes, especially on income and capital earned and owned by individuals
b providing so-called transfer benefits in cash to individuals, eg retirement pensions, unemployment benefit, and family income supplements

| | |
|---|---|
| *Control of the general level of economic activity* | The government takes responsibility for the achievement of certain major goals of economic policy. Chief among these are the rate of economic growth, the level of unemployment and the rate of inflation. |
| *Intervention in the private sector* | Some state activity is designed to affect resource allocation in the private sector of the economy. The measures in this category are especially varied. They include the use of taxes and subsidies to influence the regional location of industry and to help particular industries in need of special assistance, eg agriculture. There are state agencies to help settle industrial disputes between management and workers, and laws have been passed to control pollution, to prevent racial or sex discrimination in employment, to limit the powers of monopolies, to monitor commercial advertising, etc. |
| *Provision of goods and services* | In addition to the social services, the government is responsible for providing many goods and services which might not be provided in sufficient quantities or of adequate quality if at all, by private enterprise, eg roads, defence and the police. Some of these services may be provided directly by the state, while others may simply be paid for out of government funds. |
| The nationalised industries | There are certain industries which possess some of the characteristics of commercial enterprises but which are, for special reasons, controlled by the state. These are the nationalised industries. |

The nationalised industries employ about 8 per cent of the working population. Fig 18 shows their relative size according to the number of their employees.

They are run by what are known as **public corporations** and have a considerable degree of independence. Although the members of the boards of management of the corporations are appointed by the appropriate minister, eg Secretary of State for Industry, the corporations are free from day to day interference in their affairs. They are regarded as running commercial enterprises, although sometimes with special social responsibilities as well. They generally charge for their services and are set financial targets, though they sometimes receive subsidies from public funds.

The first appearance of nationalised industries can be traced to well before the Second World War, but the major period of extension of public ownership of industry in Britain occurred during the period 1945–51 when the Labour Party first held a majority of seats in the House of Commons. Nationalisation is, of course, a political as well as an economic matter,

*Fig 18* Employment in
the major nationalised
industries 1981
Sources: Reports of
the boards of the
nationalised industries
(The National
Freight Corporation
became the National
Freight Co when
bought up by its staff
in May 1981.)

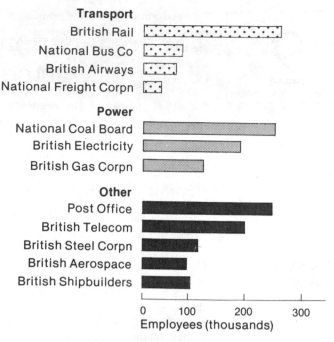

Transport
British Rail
National Bus Co
British Airways
National Freight Corpn

Power
National Coal Board
British Electricity
British Gas Corpn

Other
Post Office
British Telecom
British Steel Corpn
British Aerospace
British Shipbuilders

0    100    200    300
Employees (thousands)

although the opposition parties were not wholly opposed to
the nationalisation measures during this period. Conservative
governments since then have, however, made arrangements
for the return of certain parts of the public sector to private
hands from time to time, and a major drive for privatisation
was part of the election platform of the Conservative government which took office in 1979. Since then a variety of
measures have been brought forward for the introduction of
private capital and competition into the nationalised industries. Some assets have been, or are planned to be, sold to private
buyers, eg 52 per cent of British Aerospace was sold in 1981.

Not included as nationalised industries in the sense in which
that term is conventionally employed are a number of
businesses which have come to be owned by the state. Public
ownership in these instances has come about as a result of the
establishment in 1975 of the National Enterprise Board
(NEB), with responsibility for improving industrial efficiency, especially in areas of high technology, in regions of high
unemployment and for small firms. The NEB was also given
the power to buy shares in private businesses. The intention
was that these should be profitable enterprises, though in
practice not all have been, and the government has acquired
something of a reputation for rescuing such 'lame ducks' as
British Leyland and Rolls Royce when these companies were
in serious financial circumstances.

# 2 | The organisation of business activity[1]

Economists theorise about business decisions and generally agree that such decisions are affected by the institutional arrangements within which they are taken. In this chapter and the next we deal with these matters and describe the structure of industry in the UK. This structure has resulted from the operation of market forces as well as intervention by the government.

**Forms of business organisation**

We start with an explanation of the organisational features of modern firms. There are four main forms of private business organisation in Britain:

- Single proprietorships
- Partnerships
- Cooperatives
- Joint stock companies (called corporations in North America)

The single proprietorship

The oldest and simplest form of business organisation is the one man concern. The distinguishing feature of this type of enterprise is not that all the work is necessarily done by one man, though this may be the case, but that the business is *owned* by one individual. Such businesses are easy to set up and the owner can easily maintain full control. However, the size of the firm is limited by the amount of capital that the owner can raise for himself and he is, moreover, personally responsible in law for all the debts incurred by the firm. It is not surprising to find, therefore, that the single proprietorship is not now of much importance in the UK, although it still flourishes in a few sectors such as farming and shopkeeping.

Partnerships

More common than the one man concern is the partnership. Whenever a sole operator feels that the burden of his business is too great, the alternative of going into partnership with one or more other people may be attractive.

1 This chapter deals with material relevant to the theories discussed in Lipsey Parts 2–4.

Partners may have complementary contributions to make. For example, an inventor may go into partnership with an accountant. However, a major reason for seeking a business partner is often that the capital needed for operations is more than a single owner can provide. In such circumstances a partnership with others who contribute shares of the capital and take out proportionate shares of any profits may be a suitable form of business organisation.

Partnerships, however, suffer in the same way as do single proprietorships in that each partner is legally liable for all the debts of the firm, even if they have been incurred by the activity of another partner. There is no limit to this liability, which extends to the whole of a firm's debts, regardless of the amount of capital which the individual partners have originally contributed. Thus, for example, in a two man partnership where one partner supplies £20 000 of the original capital and the other only £1000, if the partnership incurs net debts to the extent of £5000 and the first partner becomes bankrupt and unable to meet any of the debt, the partner who put down only £1000 in the first place may have to meet the whole of the £5000, even if it means selling his house and any other property in order to do so.

The risk of being in partnership with people who prove to be unreliable, unscrupulous or even merely inefficient is consequently great and partnerships persist only in relatively small numbers—often in family businesses, where mutual confidence is strong, and in certain professions where the form is traditional and in which their survival is aided by what are called **limited partnerships**. In these, certain partners enjoy liability only to the extent to which they have invested money in the firm, provided they take no part in the running of the business.

Cooperatives

The third type of private business organisation to be considered is the cooperative society, which is mainly of importance in the retail trade.

The origins of the cooperative movement are political and are associated with the name of Robert Owen. The first successful experiment was in Rochdale in 1844, cooperation in retailing expanding greatly after that. Today there are about 200 retail societies, although their number is gradually being reduced by amalgamations.

The distinctive feature of cooperative societies lies in their ownership. While other shops belong to individuals or are joint stock companies (see opposite), cooperatives are, in a sense, 'owned' by those of their customers who pay a minimum deposit on a share in the business. The cooperatives sell to the general public but part, at least, of the capital comes from members, most of whom contribute only small sums, and there is an upper limit on the amount of share capital which may be held by any individual. Most districts have their own local 'coop'; the members elect a committee of management from among themselves who decide upon the general policy of the store and appoint a manager and full-time staff to do the work.

The principle on which cooperative societies grew up was one whereby goods were sold at normal retail prices. At the end of each half year the profits, in the form of a 'dividend' of so many pence per pound of purchases, were distributed to members in proportion to their purchases during the period. In recent years, most have adopted a policy of giving trading stamps at the point of sale instead. In so far as stamps are offered to all customers this naturally reduces the incentive to join the coop, but some societies give a bonus to members, though the less profitable societies have abandoned giving trading stamps altogether. The size of the dividend, or the exchange value of the stamps, depends not only on the amount spent at the store but also on the size of the profits. The profits vary, of course, from society to society according to the efficiency of their operations. It should also be mentioned that coops have still retained some of the ideals of their founders and some funds are devoted to the provision of scholarships for members and employees, and other social aims.

**Joint stock companies**

The fourth and last type of business organisation, the joint stock company, is so important that we shall discuss it at much greater length.

Public prejudice against the joint stock form of organisation in the 18th and 19th centuries was strongly influenced by the abuses of company promoters at the time of the South Sea Bubble, and it was not until 1855 that the great privilege of **limited liability** was made generally available. Limited liability arises from the fact that companies are regarded in law as entities separate from the individuals who own them. A company can enter into contracts, it can sue and be sued, it can own property, it can contract debts, and its obligations are not those of its owners. Companies have a continuity of life unaffected, therefore, by changes in ownership, and they have become the most important form of business enterprise in Britain.

Such companies must include the word 'Limited' (or 'Ltd') in their name so that outsiders may know that the liability to meet the debts of the company is limited for every individual owner of the business (known as a **shareholder**) to the extent of the amount of capital that he or she has contributed or promised to contribute. The advantages of this privilege are very substantial; two, in particular, are of outstanding importance.

*Large amounts of capital become much easier to raise*   This follows from the reduced risk to the individual investor, who knows from the outset the maximum amount of money he or she can lose, should the worst come to the worst. He will no longer be so afraid of venturing into business with other people whose names he may not even know. In fact, in many large companies there are thousands and even hundreds of thousands of shareholders, the vast majority of whom contribute only a minute proportion of the total capital of the business.

*Transfer of ownership can take place with a minimum of formality*   Limited liability removes the need for each shareholder to know every other shareholder personally. Consequently a shareholder can sell his shares to anyone else. In other words, there is a distinct advantage, absent from a partnership, that the shares can always be sold quickly if one is in urgent need of cash. The great importance of this transferability of shares has given rise to the appearance of a specialised market place where shares are bought and sold. It is called the **Stock Exchange** (see pages 32–4).

The advantages which limited liability bestows on an individual company are matched, to some extent, by an increased risk to others, especially to companies and individuals who do business with it, and to minority shareholders whose interests may be lost sight of in very large companies. There is also a risk that unscrupulous company promoters may fraudulently try to raise funds for their own ends from the public. In an attempt to safeguard the community from such risks, a number of Companies Acts have been passed, mainly requiring publication of information about the state of the firm and its management.

There are two principal types of company, **public** and **private**. The latter must restrict their shareholders to 50 and are not permitted to offer their shares for sale to the general public. For these reasons private companies are not obliged to publish as much information about their affairs as are public companies, which, by EEC law, must describe themselves as public limited companies (**plc**s). They are greatly outnumbered by private companies but tend to be much larger.

There are approximately half a million companies in existence, but only about 3 per cent are public companies. On the other hand, the great majority of large businesses in Britain are organised as public companies. Some indication of the importance of giant companies is given by the fact that the 100 largest groups of joint stock companies in manufacturing produce over 40 per cent of total output. (See pages 56ff for a discussion of business concentration.)

Business accounts

The most important information that companies are required to publish is contained in their balance sheet and profit and loss account.

The **balance sheet** consists of a statement of the value of the business's assets together with its liabilities, or claims on them. There are two kinds of assets:

- **fixed assets** such as land, buildings, machinery and equipment
- **current assets**, which are the result of business operations and include stocks of raw materials and finished products, debts due to the company from its customers and cash

There is also a special kind of asset called **goodwill**, which is an estimate of the benefit deriving from a firm's reputation.

The **liabilities** of the company are financial claims on its assets. Since all assets must be owned by someone they must be equal to the total liabilities. There are two classes of liabilities:

- liabilities to the owners of the business, ie the shareholders
- liabilities to other creditors, including customers and those who have made loans to the company

It should be realised, too, that balance sheet valuations of assets are not necessarily as precise as they may appear. Assets are not all put up for sale continually, so that assessments of their value may be somewhat arbitrary. This can make comparisons of profit rates on capital difficult, both among companies and over time within the same company. A simplified balance sheet of a typical company is shown on page 28.

Balance sheet as at 31 December 19–0

| Capital and liabilities | £ | £ | Assets | £ | £ |
|---|---|---|---|---|---|
| Issued capital | | | Fixed assets | | |
|   Ordinary shares | x | |   Land, buildings | x | |
|   Preference shares | x | x |   Machinery, equipment | x | |
| Loan from XYZ Bank Ltd | | x |   Goodwill | x | x |
| Current liabilities | | | Current assets | | |
|   Sundry creditors | | x |   Stocks of raw materials | x | |
| | | |   Stocks of finished products | x | |
| | | |   Current debtors | x | |
| | | |   Cash at bank | x | x |
| | | £x | | | £x |

A single balance sheet gives a picture of the financial state of a business at the time it is drawn up. To appreciate a company's prospects, however, it is necessary to compare balance sheets over a run of years and to observe the progress that has occurred in the growth or depletion of the assets. A company's financial state may be best studied, however, with the help of the **profit and loss account**. Whereas a balance sheet relates to the financial position of a company at a particular *point of time*, the profit and loss account is a record of a company's operations over a stated *period of time*, such as a year. It is a statement of the residual profit or loss achieved by a company in the period, derived by taking the total revenue earned by a firm and subtracting all costs incurred in earning it.

Profit and loss account for the year ending 31 December 19–0

| Expenditure | £ | £ | Income | £ |
|---|---|---|---|---|
| Fixed costs | | | Revenue from sales | x |
|   Rent | x | | | |
|   Research & development | x | | | |
|   Managerial salaries | x | | | |
|   Interest on bank loan | x | | | |
|   Depreciation allowance | x | x | | |
| Variable costs | | | | |
|   Wages | x | | | |
|   Fuel used | x | | | |
|   Raw materials used | x | x | | |
| (Net profit for year | | x) | (Net loss for year | x) |
| | | £x | | £x |

A typical profit and loss account is shown on page 28. Note the distinction, important in the theory of the firm, between **fixed** (or **overhead**) **costs** and **variable** (**prime**, or **direct**) **costs**. Only the latter change as output changes, though the longer the period of time under consideration the more types of costs tend to be variable rather than fixed.

An important deduction from the *gross* profit of a business is usually made to allow for the **depreciation** of its assets, which are subject to wear and tear and to obsolescence. Depreciation allowances are provided for in the accounts and must be subtracted from the revenue to arrive at the *net* profit. These depreciation provisions represent the value of capital equipment used up in the process of production. They must be deducted from the market value of current production in order to discover whether or not such production is profitable. It should be added that depreciation allowances are only estimates, which may be difficult to make in the face of uncertainty, especially about the future rate of inflation and hence about the future value of capital equipment. //

*Frank wood*

**The financing of the modern firm**

Firms obtain finance for their operations in four ways:

- by selling **shares** in the business to buyers, who then become owners
- by borrowing through the sale of **bonds**
- by **borrowing** from banks and other financial institutions
- by **reinvesting** the firm's profits

**Types of shares**

There are two main groups of shares: preference shares and ordinary shares or equities.

**Preference shares**, as their name implies, entitle their holders to shares in the firm's profits before other shareholders. The money they receive is known as a **dividend** and is usually fixed as a percentage of the capital invested. Pye of Cambridge, for example, issued a $5\frac{1}{2}$ per cent preference share which yields £5.50 for every £100 of shares held. So long as the company makes sufficient profit to meet the dividends of the preference shareholders, they all receive their dividends in full. Of course, if the company makes no profit at all no dividends are paid (the dividend is then said to be 'passed'), but even if the company has a phenomenally profitable year, preference shareholders get no more than their fixed rate of dividend.

It is usually presumed, unless stated to the contrary, that preference shares are **cumulative**, ie when a dividend is passed shareholders have the deficiency made good in a later year if profits recover. Often the right is evidenced by the word 'cumulative' being included in the name of the shares, eg those of Courtaulds plc. There may also be more than one class of preference share and, occasionally, participating preference shares are issued which allow the holders a share in profits over and above the stipulated figure, eg Trianco's 6 per cent cumulative participating preference shares.

Preference shareholders may or may not be allowed a vote at company meetings, but they rarely have much power.

Holders of **ordinary shares** (or **equities**) usually do have voting rights and a residual claim on the company profits. Their dividend is not guaranteed, but is decided on a year to year basis when the profit position is known. The rate of dividend is declared as a percentage of the *nominal* value of the shares. It does not represent the profit rate for all sharehol-ders—this depends upon the price paid for the shares. Tate and Lyle, for example, paid a dividend in 1982 of 16.4 pence on each of their £1 ordinary shares. Thus, a person who bought 100 shares at £1 each received £16.40. It is, however, unlikely that many shareholders paid exactly £100 for 100 shares. For them the rate of profit is not 16.4 per cent. In mid-1982, for instance, the price of one of these shares was £1.82, so someone buying then would receive a dividend **yield** of about 9 per cent (£16.40 as a percentage of £182).

The income received by equityholders is liable to fluctuate from year to year, so that equities are generally regarded as risky investments. For an individual shareholder, however, a portfolio consisting of a range of shares in different companies reduces the risk. On the other hand, someone wanting to speculate in the hope of a high return can choose to invest in companies in risky lines of business, eg mine exploration. The risk attaching to shares depends, too, on the relative import-ance of equity to other issued capital carrying a fixed rate of interest (the 'gearing' ratio, see page 31).

*Bonds*

Some part of a company's capital may be issued in the form of **debentures** (or loan stock) known as **bonds**. Bondholders are sometimes confused with preference shareholders, with whom they have some common features, but a **debenture** is essentially different from a share of any kind. It may most properly be regarded as a kind of IOU which the company gives to a person in return for a loan. The rate of interest on debentures is fixed in advance, such as the United Biscuit Company's 8 per cent debentures, holders of which have the prior right to receive this interest before any dividends are paid on preference or ordinary shares.

In the event of the company going into liquidation, ie being wound up, debendure holders, as creditors of the company, have the first claim (together with any other trade creditors) to the return of their capital; their holding may even be secured by pledges attached to specific assets belonging to the company. The disadvantage of raising capital in the form of bonds is that the company must pay out interest even if there are no profits. Many a firm has been forced out of business because it could not meet its obligations in the form of fixed interest payments.

*Gearing*

The riskiness of any ordinary shares is liable to be affected by the ratio of equities to total capital. This is known as the **gearing ratio**, which is said to be high if the proportion of bonds and other fixed interest debt to equities is large (and vice versa).

The companies HIG plc and LOW plc in the example below illustrate this point. Both have the same profits available for distribution in each of 2 years and the same total issued capital, but they have different gearing ratios. HIG plc is highly geared, with 80 per cent of its capital in the form of 5 per cent debentures. When profits double in a good year from £5000 to £10000 it would be possible to raise the dividend on ordinary shares six fold from 5 to 30 per cent, after meeting the obligations to debenture holders. LOW plc, on the other hand, is low geared, with only 20 per cent of its capital in 5 per cent debentures. The same doubling of profits would only permit a rise from 5 to 11¼ per cent for the ordinary shareholders.

|  |  | HIG plc | | LOW plc | |
|---|---|---|---|---|---|
|  | £ | | £ | | £ |
| Capital | 100 000 | 5 per cent debentures | 80 000 | 5 per cent debentures | 20 000 |
|  |  | Ordinary shares | 20 000 | Ordinary shares | 80 000 |

| | Dividends | | | | | | | |
|---|---|---|---|---|---|---|---|---|
| | Allocation of profits | | Dividend rate per cent | | Allocation of profits | | Dividend rate per cent | |
| | Year 1 | Year 2 | Year 1 | Year 2 | Year 1 | Year 2 | Year 1 | Year 2 |
| | £ | £ | % | % | £ | £ | % | % |
| *Capital* | | | | | | | | |
| Debentures | 4 000 | 4 000 | 5 | 5 | 1 000 | 1 000 | 5 | 5 |
| Ordinary shares | 1 000 | 6 000 | 5 | 30 | 4 000 | 9 000 | 5 | 11¼ |
| Total | 5 000 | 10 000 | | | 5 000 | 10 000 | | |

A real example of a very low geared company is Dowty (an engineering group) with less than 10 per cent of its capital needing to be serviced by fixed interest securities. It is difficult to find a very highly geared company, for the reason given above. Fodens, the commercial vehicle manufacturer, was so highly geared in 1979, with over a third of its capital in fixed interest debt, that it underwent severe financial problems, ending in its being taken over in 1980.

*New issues*

Companies wishing to raise new capital have a choice of methods.

1 They may opt for a **public issue** of shares to the general public. This is often done in cooperation with a specialist financial institution such as a merchant bank or an issuing house. Such issues are commonly guaranteed by 'underwriters' who agree to buy any unsold shares at a price fixed in advance.
2 A second method is the **offer for sale**, where the new shares are sold to an issuing house which then disposes of them to the public.
3 Another alternative is a **placing**, whereby particularly small issues of shares are sold by arrangement, privately, to investors.
4 Lastly, shares may be offered to the company's existing shareholders in what is called a **rights issue**. This method tends to keep the costs of the issue down, but the shares normally have to be offered on favourable terms.

*Reinvested profits*

We stated earlier that a major source of capital for new investment comes from **ploughing back profits** into the business. This is one of the easiest ways for the controllers of a firm to raise money. It implies holding back dividend payments in the short term, but it can lead to larger earnings for shareholders later. It is also by far the most important means, quantitatively speaking, of expanding businesses. Fig 19 shows that undistributed profits far exceed other uses of company profits. ('Other interest' is to banks and other lenders.)

The Stock
Exchange

One of the great advantages of the joint stock form of organisation mentioned earlier is that shares can be bought and sold with relative ease. The existence of the specialised market place, called a **stock exchange**, helps greatly in this respect.

The London Stock Exchange is an institution primarily concerned not with raising new capital for companies, but

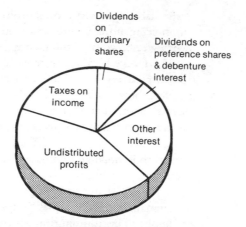

*Fig 19* Allocation of company income 1981 Source: *National Income and Expenditure*

Dividends on ordinary shares

Dividends on preference shares & debenture interest

Taxes on income

Other interest

Undistributed profits

with purchases and sales of *existing* shares. However, it is not an open market but one restricted to dealings by its members, of whom there are more than 4000, who elect a governing Council. There are two classes of members; brokers and jobbers. **Brokers** act as agents for the public; jobbers are middlemen who buy and sell to brokers (and to each other).

Imagine an investor who wishes to buy 1000 shares of the Wheel Cheetew plc. He gets in touch with a broker and tells him of his intentions. The broker then goes in search of jobbers who deal in the shares of this company. Approaching the jobbers in turn, the broker asks them the price of the shares, without saying whether he wishes to buy or to sell. The jobber quotes him a two-way price, such as 75p–80p, which means that the jobber is prepared to buy shares at 75p or to sell them at 80p. The difference between the two prices is the jobber's 'turn' or profit. Having asked the prices of several jobbers, the broker returns to the one who offered the lowest price and, if the quotation has not risen in the meantime, reveals that he wishes to buy 1000 shares. The deal is then noted by both parties.

All types of shares and bonds of some 10 000 quoted public companies are dealt with on the Stock Exchange. So, too, are securities issued by the British government, local authorities and foreign governments. The first of these are known as **gilt-edged** because the likelihood of bankruptcy is virtually nil.

Investors who wish to minimise risk can buy shares in investment trust companies which carry a range of shares. Alternatively they can buy units in a **unit trust**. This is an organisation which holds a portfolio of securities, so that the purchaser of a unit participates in the benefits and risks attaching to all the shares in the portfolio. These units are especially attractive to small savers and can be bought and sold in small denominations and with a minimum of formality without necessarily going through the Stock Exchange.

Many investors intend to hold on to shares that they buy for a relatively long time. Others are speculators, known as 'bulls', 'bears' and 'stags'. **Bulls** expect a price rise; they buy shares now, hoping for the price to increase later. **Bears** expect a price fall; they agree on a price now at which they are to sell shares in the future. They do not own the shares at this point, but hope to buy them at a lower price before the contract to deliver becomes due. **Stags** expect the market price of *new* shares to be higher than the price at which they are initially offered for sale. They contract to buy forthcoming issues of shares, hoping to sell them at a profit after trading begins on the market.

## The control of joint stock companies

The standard theory of the firm is based on the assumption that businesses seek to maximise their profits. The proposition has some intuitive appeal in the case of small firms, where the owners run their businesses, but a major criticism of the theory centres around the question of who actually controls the firm.

Companies are owned by their shareholders, with whom ultimate control therefore lies. However, this is something of an oversimplification. In order to discover where effective control really lies, it is necessary to consider three important issues:

- the power of personal and institutional investors
- the role of company managers
- the size distribution of share ownership

## *The power of personal and institutional investors*

The capitalist system grew up on the basis of the purchase of shares by private individuals. However, as the economy developed, joint stock companies began to assume a major role in the financial as well as the industrial sectors with the appearance of large-scale financial institutions, such as insurance companies, merchant banks and building societies (see pages 181ff).

In recent years—partly, it has been suggested, because of high rates of taxation—the private investor has come to play a much diminished role in the finance of British companies. The relative importance of private individuals in the ownership of shares in 1963 and 1980 is shown in Fig 20. Between the two years the proportion of the total value of ordinary shares owned by persons fell from well over 50 per cent to

*Fig 20* The ownership of shares in companies 1963 and 1980 Sources: *The Ownership of Company Shares*, Central Statistical Office, 1979, and *Shareholder Analysis, A Supplement to the Stock Exchange Factbook 1980*

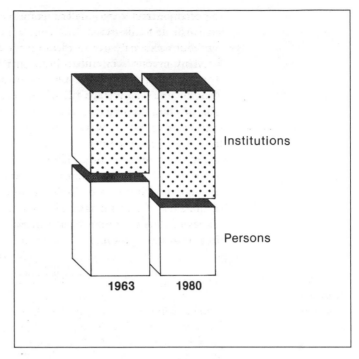

under 40 per cent, while that of institutions rose accordingly. The most important of such institutions, in quantitative terms, are insurance companies and pension funds (operated for employees), many of which are managed by banks.

The dominant position of financial institutions in the ownership of capital does not, of course, preclude private individuals from benefiting from the profitability of British companies. They merely benefit indirectly rather than directly. It is, however, important to realise that such institutional shareholders are often large and, although individually they may not own very substantial proportions of the shares in a company, they may have a greater power than this would suggest because they may all act collectively.

The question of the control of companies as distinct from their ownership will be discussed shortly. First we need to see how joint stock companies make day to day management decisions.

*Company management*

Shareholders of large companies are generally remote from the company business. They rarely know enough about the affairs of the company to be involved in day to day decision-making, which is the concern of the board of directors. **Directors** are officials of a company, nominally appointed by shareholders at the **annual general meeting**, although they may often be (and for public companies are required by law to be) shareholders as well.

The power that shareholders are able to exercise over directors depends very much on the particular circumstances of a company. Often the power may be slight. This is especially the case where the distribution of shares is very wide and there are no really large shareholders. It is also the result of small attendances at company meetings. Absentee shareholders have the right to appoint 'proxies', or agents, to vote for them at the meeting, but as directors are in by far the best position to secure proxies, they themselves may be armed with an overwhelming number of votes and be able to control the decisions of the meeting.

The directors elect one of their number to be chairman and titular head of the company, and another (sometimes the same person) to be managing director, who is personally responsible to the board of directors for running the company. The managing director is nearly always a full-time appointment, and it is usually he or she who appoints senior staff—works manager, sales manager and the other heads of department— each of whom is responsible to the board. Some of the other directors meet only infrequently, and many of them may be directors of several companies at the same time.

*Share ownership and control*[1]

Effective control of a joint stock company lies in the ownership of the voting shares. Industrial democracy is based on the principle of one vote for every voting share held. Whoever can raise a majority of votes at company meetings can, therefore, control the meetings.

There is no general rule concerning the minimum percentage of total voting shares which qualify for a controlling interest. It is rare, except in small companies, that as much as 51 per cent is necessary. If ownership is widely diffused and the majority of small shareholders are absent from a company meeting (as is often the case), the proportion of votes needed for effective control could be as little as 10 per cent. It would be an oversimplification to associate control of a company with a single individual. Groups of shareholders may act collectively, whether related by family or by common interests, as in the case of institutional shareholders.

It is thought, not unreasonably, that companies whose boards of directors collectively control a large number of voting shares may to some extent ignore the wishes of outside shareholders. They may, for example, be less concerned with

1 The importance for economic theory of the issues of ownership and control is discussed in Lipsey Chapter 24.

trying to maximise profits for shareholders than with aiming for expansion of the firm which will protect their jobs and raise their own remuneration. Some interest attaches, therefore, to identifying director-controlled and owner-controlled, ie shareholder-controlled, companies. Such a distinction is not easily established, partly because full information on share ownership is not available.

Some shares are held by 'nominees', concealing the true beneficial ownership. Fig 21 has, however, been drawn up with the use of data collected in the course of recent research. It shows the percentage of voting shares in the hands of the board of directors (or their families) for a number of companies in 1976. All the companies are large ones—in the top 250 in Britain ranked by the value of their net assets or sales in the year in question.

*Fig 21* Director shareholdings in selected companies 1976; percentage of voting shares owned by directors or their families (the percentage for each company is measured separately clockwise from the 12 o'clock origin)
Source: data supplied by Professor A Silberston

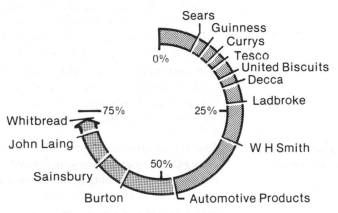

The diagram shows a wide variation in the shareholdings of directors in this selection of companies. It must be emphasised, however, that they are not intended to be representative of British industry as a whole. In particular, they exclude large companies such as ICI and Shell, where directors' holdings are too small to be represented. The point of the diagram is to indicate that there are some companies where directors appear to exercise control. It is no easy matter to identify exactly which they are. Much depends on how diffused non-directors' shareholdings are, how many proxy votes the board acquires, the precise identity of the chairman and managing director (including his relationship to the founder of the firm and his family), and other matters. Moreover, it must not be thought that, even where the directors are able to assemble enough votes to control meetings, they can necessarily ignore the views of other shareholders, particularly with regard to the level of profits. This may be true for companies where a single firm or institution holds more than 50 per cent of the voting shares, but it is rare with large public companies.

Boardroom battles can take place indicating that even the directors are not all of the same mind regarding policy. Ultimately, if the directors fail to operate a company effectively they have to face the risk that outside interests (individuals, institutions or other companies) may try to acquire sufficient shares to give them a controlling interest and enable them to unseat the existing directors. Such **takeover bids** for the control of a company may be orchestrated in so-called 'dawn raids', involving the transfer of very large blocks of shares in a matter of minutes. In so far as they involve mergers or amalgamations between companies, this is discussed in Chapter 3, pages 59 to 66.

## Public sector business organisation[1]

The government engages in a great deal of economic activity. Much of this is carried out directly by, or through, central and local government departments. However there are certain industries which possess some of the characteristics of commercial enterprises which are, for special reasons, owned by the state. They are particularly important in transport and power supplies, as well as in communications, steel and other industries. The organisational structures of the nationalised industries vary in detail, for example in the degree to which they are centralised, but they have a number of common features.

## The public corporation

Nationalised industries in Britain are run by what are known as **public corporations**. The form and functions of these bodies differ somewhat from case to case, but in all there is a close resemblance to the boards of directors of joint stock companies. The chairmen and members of the corporations are appointed by the appropriate minister, eg Secretary of State for Energy, Secretary of State for Industry, but the corporations are otherwise free from day to day interference in the management of their affairs. Many members of the boards of nationalised industries come from private industry and, since 1978, have included civil servants and employee representatives. The major appointments are generally made for a fixed period of years, and matters of wages and conditions of service for the staff are generally determined independently from those in the Civil Service.

1 Issues of nationalised and publicly regulated industries are discussed in Lipsey Chapter 23 for pricing policy, and Chapter 33 for more general issues.

| The control of nationalised industries | Since public corporations are to a certain extent independent bodies which do not have to face a shareholders' meeting every year, it is clearly important that they should have to submit to some control from outside. This happens in three main ways. |

Since public corporations are to a certain extent independent bodies which do not have to face a shareholders' meeting every year, it is clearly important that they should have to submit to some control from outside. This happens in three main ways.

In the first place, each nationalised industry is subject to a considerable measure of control from the appropriate minister. As already mentioned, he appoints the members of the boards of the corporations. He can also dismiss them. The minister has general powers of direction and can call for statistical, financial or any other information required. Ministerial powers over specific matters are written into the individual Acts of nationalisation.

While ministers are not responsible to Parliament for the day to day administration of the nationalised industries, parliamentary control can be exercised through the normal procedures. Particularly important in this connection are debates on the annual reports of the corporations, and the work of the House of Commons Select Committee on the Nationalised Industries, which was formed in 1957 especially to examine their reports and accounts.

Finally, provision is usually made for the establishment of **consumer councils**, eg for the Post Office, railways, gas and electricity. These are intended as vehicles for the consuming public to voice their satisfaction or dissatisfaction with the way in which things are run. Some cover the whole of the country, eg the National Gas Consumers' Council, but in many cases there are area councils to deal with local issues.

**Financial obligations of nationalised industries**

Nationalised industries resemble commercial enterprises in several respects. Unlike many other government activities, they are not intended to be financed mainly, if at all, from taxation; they are expected to cover all or part of their costs by charging for their services. Some of the nationalised industries, however, have certain recognised social obligations, eg to provide electricity, telephone services and rail transport to rural areas at less than full cost. Some, too, enjoy a monopoly position which can be exploited.

The financial obligations imposed on the nationalised industries have changed significantly over the years as a result of an increasing awareness of the commercial side of their operations and of a desire to compare their performance with that of companies in the private sector of the economy. Capital for development, over and above the capital generated internally, is borrowed from the National Loans Fund operated by the central government, which, in turn, borrows from the market in order to obtain the best terms.

The terms of the original Acts of Parliament setting up the early corporations called for each industry to break even over an average of good and bad years. A substantial change in policy, however, followed the publication of two White Papers in 1961 and 1967. The second of these was the more important from the viewpoint of the conduct of the internal affairs of the nationalised industries. Whilst recognising the existence of certain social obligations, it emphasised the commercial side of their operations and recommended that prices should be set to reflect long run marginal costs, subject to the industry being able to cover its full costs of operation and to meeting its financial targets (see page 41).

The application of marginal cost pricing follows conclusions drawn from economic theory on optimal resource allocation. This policy has been adopted in many cases, including in the gas industry where it resulted in the (unpopular) earning of substantial short run profits, justifiable in terms of the need to conserve an energy source, expected to be in short supply towards the end of the century. The pricing policy for the nationalised industries has not, however, always been strictly applied but has been allowed to lapse when it interfered with the government's overall economic strategy, especially for the control of inflation.

Marginal cost pricing was intended to establish a system whereby consumers of particular products pay for the cost of providing each product. This avoids any cross-subsidisation, so that profits made in one line of activity are not used to allow another to be carried on at a loss. However, this does still happen, for example, the charge for posting a letter is the same regardless of whether it is from Lands End to John O'Groats or from one house in Little Puddlecombe to another. There are two reasons for marginal cost pricing not being applied in such cases:

a the desire to subsidise certain classes of individual, eg those living in rural areas, or
b the need to keep down administrative costs

As far as investment policy is concerned, the earlier of the White Papers led to the setting of target rates of return on capital for each nationalised industry. The targets were arrived at after consideration of the social obligations of the different industries and their financial histories. They varied from $12\frac{1}{2}$ per cent for electricity to a break-even formula for coal.

The 1967 White Paper was more concerned with *new* investment than with the average rate of return on capital employed. The main innovation at this time was the introduction of a so-called **test discount rate** (**TDR**), intended as a measure of the real cost of using capital in the public sector of the economy. It could be changed from time to time, reflecting changes in the cost of raising capital. It was set at 8 per cent, but later was raised to 10 per cent.

The most recent developments in investment policy followed the publication of yet another White Paper in 1978, which endorsed the general commercial approach of its predecessors. The policy recommendations of the 1978 White Paper were for the setting of financial targets for 3 to 5 years ahead and the adoption of a **required rate of return** (**RRR**) of 5 per cent. The RRR, allowing for inflation, would reflect the real cost of capital in the economy and form the basis for targets for individual industries. A further measure of control introduced was the so-called **external financing limit** (**EFL**), which can be used to limit the cash outflow from year to year.

## Nationalisation and denationalisation

It must not be thought that the public and private sectors of the economy are totally separate. The government contracts out much work to private businesses while making the major decisions on spending itself, eg on road construction. From time to time industries have also been added to or removed from the list of those nationalised. By and large it has been Labour governments that have been in favour of nationalisation and Conservative governments against. The former were responsible for the major extension of state ownership during the period of office of the first majority Labour administration immediately after the Second World War.

## Privatisation

Recently, the Conservative government elected in 1979 adopted a policy of increasing competition in the public sector which has come to be called **privatisation**. Measures proposed under this head are of several kinds. Some have been for straightforward denationalisation by selling off assets to private buyers, eg Thomas Cook and British Aerospace, or for the introduction of private capital, eg the shares of the British National Oil Corporation were transferred to a new company called Britoil in 1982, after which 51 per cent of Britoil shares were offered for sale to the public. Others have involved the relaxation of controls underpinning monopoly powers, eg postal services and gas appliances. Not all of these measures have been proceeded with at once. The proposal for the sale of shares in British Airways, made possible by the Civil Aviation Act of 1980, for instance, was delayed by the unprofitability of the company.

## Market structures[1]

This chapter has dealt mainly with the legal and institutional framework within which private and public sector businesses make decisions. Economic theory tells us, however, that the behaviour of a firm is affected also by the kind of market in which it operates, and in particular by the number of firms in the industry and the type of product sold, both of which influence the degree of **competition**.

We shall look at the size and concentration of firms in Chapter 3, but it must be admitted now that it is not easy to generalise about the degree of competition. The power that a firm can exercise over price, however, *can* be associated with market structure. Some structures allow the firm to set its own price while others make the firm a mere price taker, responding to prices set by the impersonal forces of market supply and demand. Fig 22 shows two contrasting products which typify the extreme cases. The graph shows the course of prices for a motor car and for a primary product, copper.

The car industry is not perfectly competitive. Each manufacturer enjoys some degree of monopoly power arising from the special features of its model, whether real or imagined by buyers. Within limits, therefore, it is able to set prices for itself. Such **administered pricing**, as it is called, can be contrasted with the behaviour of suppliers of many primary products, where the material is homogeneous and there are many producers. One such product is copper, the world price of which is set daily on the London Metal Exchange. Fig 22 shows how much more volatile is the price of copper than that of the administratively set Ford Escort.

It should be added that the power of individual manufacturers may extend beyond fixing their *own* selling prices to setting minimum prices below which their customers may not *resell* their products[2]. This applies in particular to the retail trade. Such price setting can be attractive to shopkeepers in so far as it protects them from cut-price competition from competing shops. It is not surprising, therefore, that many manufacturers, acting partly in their own interests and partly

1 The theoretical issues involved in market structure distinctions are discussed in Lipsey Chapter 19.
2 Problems of price setting and non-price competition are discussed in Lipsey Chapter 21.

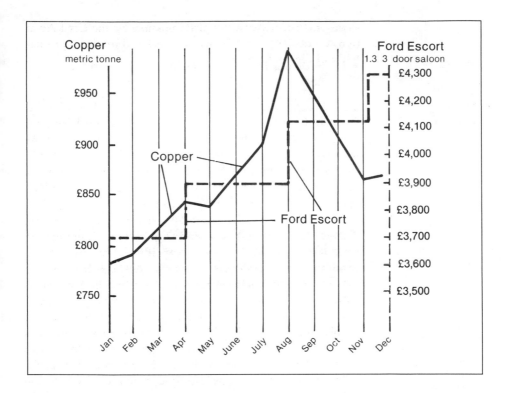

**Copper**
metric tonne

£950

£900

£850

£800

£750

Copper

Ford Escort

**Ford Escort**
1.3 3 door saloon

£4,300

£4,200

£4,100

£4,000

£3,900

£3,800

£3,700

£3,600

£3,500

Jan Feb Mar Apr May June July Aug Sep Oct Nov Dec

*Fig 22* Average monthly prices of cars (Ford Escort) and of copper 1981 Sources: *Monthly Bulletin of Statistics,* United Nations, and *The Motor*

in response to requests from retailers, long ago took steps to ensure that their products were sold everywhere at the same price. General conformity to such fixed prices frequently used to be maintained by collective agreements between the appropriate trade associations of manufacturers and distributors, involving such effective methods as 'blacklisting' retailers who cut prices below those agreed and withholding further supplies from them.

This practice of **resale price maintenance** (**RPM**) is estimated to have applied to goods accounting for about a third of total consumer expenditure shortly after the end of the Second World War. Since the effect of RPM is to restrict the scope for price competition, which might benefit consumers, the government introduced legislation in the 1960s outlawing the practice in almost all cases (see page 135). Manufacturers may still attach a recommended retail price (MRP) to their goods, but this can be, and often is, ignored by retailers.

**Non-price competition**

Competition between firms is not restricted to prices but may take a variety of other forms. The most important type of non-price competition is related to the nature of the product

and is associated with **advertising**, which can increase sales in two ways:

- by spreading information about the existence of a commodity
- by persuading people that an article is worth buying

The way in which persuasion is achieved is not important from the point of view of the advertiser. Whether you are induced to buy a particular brand of toothpaste because you are told it contains a substance which has been 'proved' to reduce tooth decay or whether it is because you have seen a picture of a pretty girl using it, the effect on sales of that toothpaste is the same. The tendency to emphasise persuasion is at the back of much of the criticism continually levelled at advertising. On the other hand, it is argued that the provision of information, especially about new products, is valuable and may help to build up sales to the point where costs begin to fall.

*Fig 23* Advertising expenditure 1980 Source: *Marketing Manual of the UK*, Mirror Group Newspapers

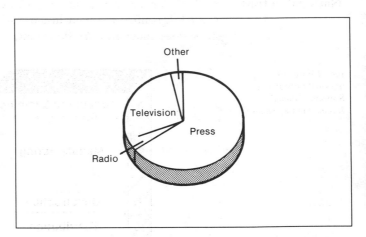

The scale of advertising expenditure in Britain after a period of fairly steady growth, seems to have settled at a level representing a little less than 2 per cent of total consumer expenditure—about the same proportion as is spent on entertainment or vegetables. Most advertising is done by manufacturers and is directed at final consumers, but some is organised by retailers. The press is the most important single medium for advertising, as Fig 23 shows. In fact, revenue from advertisements is a larger source of income for many newspapers than proceeds from sales. Television advertising accounts for only about a quarter of the total, though this might rise after the introduction of breakfast television on commercial channels in 1983.

# 3 | The structure of British industry[1]

This chapter deals with the structure of British industry as it has been shaped by the operation of market forces.[2] The subjects considered are as follows:

- the relative importance of different sectors
- productivity
- regional distribution of industry
- the size of firms
- industrial concentration

**National output**

Fig 24 shows the main groups of goods and services in the UK in 1980. It confirms the conclusion reached in Chapter 1 that the service industries are dominant, accounting for about

*Fig 24* Value of national output 1980
Source: *National Income and Expenditure*

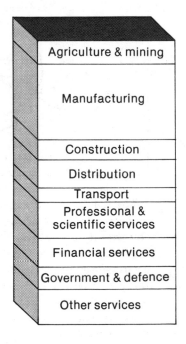

Agriculture & mining

Manufacturing

Construction

Distribution

Transport

Professional & scientific services

Financial services

Government & defence

Other services

---

1 Theoretical analysis relating to the topics discussed in this chapter are to be found mainly in Lipsey Part 4.
2 For a more detailed description of the structure of the chief industries in the UK see *Descriptive Economics*, C Harbury, 6th edition, Pitman, 1981.

two-thirds of total output. Primary production, comprising mainly agriculture and the extractive industries (coal, natural gas and oil), make up a further 8 per cent, while manufacturing and construction together produce the remaining 30 per cent.

Although manufacturing industry has exhibited a long-term decline, it is still important enough to warrant detailed

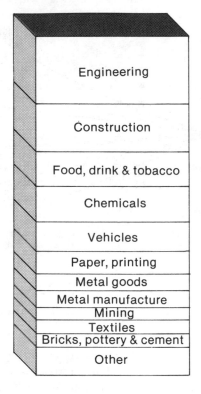

*Fig 25* Manufacturing industry 1979; value of net output
Source: *Census of Production 1979,* Summary Tables, Business Monitor PA 1002, 1982

inspection. Fig 25 distinguishes its various sectors according to the value of net output as reported in the annual censuses of production. This provides a different basis for comparing industries than numbers of employees (used for Fig 10, see page 10). The results, measured either way, are similar, but the latter method is safer because some industries employ comparatively few workers and yet produce a relatively valuable product, and vice versa. The chemical industry, for example, employs about 5 per cent of the manufacturing labour force, while the value of the chemicals it produces is more like 10 per cent of total manufacturing output. The clothing industry, on the other hand, employs over 5 per cent of the labour force in manufacturing industry, while the net value of its output is under 3 per cent of the total.

It should be emphasised that Fig 25 refers only to the pattern of output in one year, 1979. Fig 26 shows changes in the

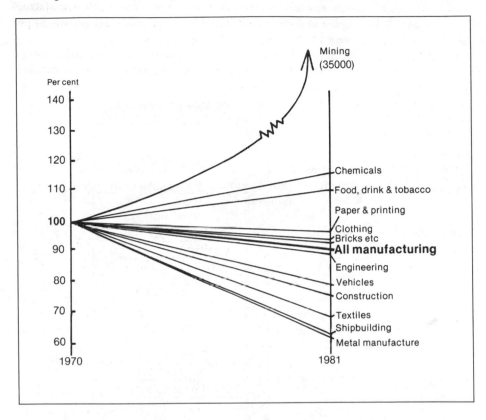

*Fig 26* Industrial production; 1981 output as a percentage of 1970
Sources: *Annual Abstract of Statistics*, and *Monthly Digest of Statistics*

output of the various industrial sectors between 1970 and 1981 (after making allowances for changes in output prices). The period in question was one in which the volume of manufacturing output fell, due mainly to the persistance of the world trade recession, which affected the UK as much as any other country. There were certainly some years when output rose (1970–73 and 1975–79), but over the period manufacturing production in 1981 was about 10 per cent lower than at the start of the 1970s. We can take this average performance of all industries as a benchmark and compare the performance of each sector with it. Three groups may be distinguished— expanding, contracting and stable industries.

*Expanding industries*

Three major industries stand out in this group. The first is mining. Its expansion has been so enormous that it shoots right off the top of the diagram. This is not really surprising in the light of the energy crisis and the North Sea discoveries of oil and gas. The rise in output for the industry as a whole is, of course, an average and conceals an enormous rise in the production of oil and natural gas and a decline in coal. Chemicals is the second industry whose output grew rapidly in the years up to 1981. It has, in fact, been a pacesetter since the end of the Second World War. Finally, there is the food, drink and tobacco industry, the only other industry to produce a larger output in 1981 than 1970. These products are less prone to decline in depressed economic conditions, though it can be seen that the industry's growth was relatively modest.

Fig 26 picks out only very broad industrial categories. However, there are several subgroups of industries which have grown relatively rapidly. Electrical engineering, for example, has enjoyed a fairly long upward trend in spite of the decline in engineering as a whole.

*Contracting industries*

Five industries fall into this category—metal manufacture, shipbuilding, textiles, construction and vehicles. The first of these has been suffering from a worldwide excess supply of steel capacity and keen competition, especially from Japan. Shipbuilding is an industry that has been on the decline almost throughout the present century and would probably be extinct in the UK had it not been for government help. Textiles are in a similar position—Britain held a predominant position in the world in the last century but has suffered from intense competition in the present one, especially from developing countries. The decline in vehicle production is of more recent origin—it was one of the most rapidly expanding industries for about 20 years after the end of the Second World War. Finally, the construction industry is included in this category. This is because building work, both residential and industrial, tends to do relatively poorly during periods of recession.

*Stable industries*

The other main industrial groups may be said to have more or less maintained their relative importance in manufacturing industry between 1970 and 1981. We use the phrase 'more or less' because it must once more be emphasised that the categories with which we are dealing are very broad and conceal subgroups which are either expanding or contracting. For example, it was noted above that the electrical branch of engineering was expanding, whilst mechanical engineering was contracting.

*Industrial productivity*

Expansion in the volume of output can be traced to one of two causes:

- increases in the supply of factors of production
- improvements in their productivity arising from changes in the techniques of production and in factor performance

Increasing productivity has been a major source of rising living standards in most industrial countries for a very long time. This is not surprising since even an apparently modest rate of increase of output per man of 2 per cent per annum leads to a doubling of output every 35 years without any rise in the size of the labour force.

The most common measure of productivity is that obtained by dividing output by the number of workers employed, giving a figure of output per head. However, because of variations in hours worked, output per hour is probably a better measure of labour's productivity in the short-term. The procedure of measuring productivity is fraught with problems, especially when attempting to measure output in the service trades. It is therefore wise to treat estimates of productivity with caution and to regard only broad orders of magnitude as significant.

This warning is relevant when examining Fig 27, which

*Fig 27* Labour productivity in manufacturing 1950–81
Sources: *The British Economy, Key Statistics 1900–70*, London and Cambridge Economic Service, and *Monthly Digest of Statistics*

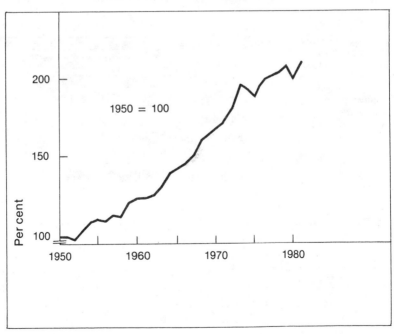

gives an index of labour productivity (1950 = 100). Since it is restricted to productivity in the manufacturing sector, it is probably fairly reliable as far as long-term trends are concerned. It can be seen that output per unit of labour rose fairly steadily over the period between 1950 and 1980. It had approximately doubled after 27 years, implying an average annual rate of growth of just over 2½ per cent.

Productivity increases have varied widely from industry to industry, partly, of course, because of differences in the scope for the application of new technology. Computerisation, for example, is more easily applied to the chemical industry (which has had one of the fastest growth rates) than to the services of solicitors or hairdressers. In spite of certain exceptions, it is broadly true that productivity increases in manufacturing industry have tended to outstrip those in the tertiary (service) sector of the economy.

It is instructive to compare output per unit of labour in the UK with that in other countries. This calls for careful research in order to ensure that all data is on a comparable basis. A recent study has estimated that labour productivity in the USA was just over two and a half times that in the UK. The differential in favour of the US varied quite considerably from industry to industry, as Fig 28 shows, being as high as five- to six-fold in ships and vehicles and less than two-fold in construction. The causes of the higher productivity per man

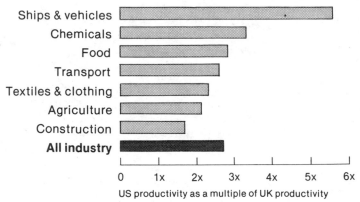

*Fig 28* Comparative labour productivity in the UK and USA 1976–77
Source: *National Institute Economic Review 1982,* A D Smith, Hitchens and Davies

US productivity as a multiple of UK productivity

in the US are complex. They reflect differences in the amount of capital per man, in the scale of output, in plant size, in industrial relations, etc.

The study referred to above also made comparisons between the UK and Germany, where the differential in favour of Germany turned out to be smaller than with the USA, though it was increasing. German output per man was, on average, about half as high again as British. Only in agriculture was productivity significantly greater in the UK. There is an obvious link between productivity and what is called R and D (research and development) which, prima facie, might be expected to lead to technical progress.

The UK currently devotes about 2 per cent of its total output to R and D. This is a little lower than a decade ago, but is not much out of line with expenditure in Germany,

*Fig 29* Research and development expenditure by manufacturing industry 1978 Source: *Annual Abstract of Statistics*

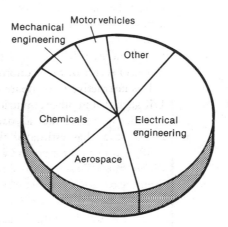

although it is somewhat below that in the USA. The bulk of the work is done by private industry, though about half is financed by the government. Two-thirds of the total is in the field of manufacturing, whose R and D expenditure is displayed in Fig 29. It can be seen that a relatively few industries are responsible for a disproportionate amount of the work, electrical engineering, aerospace and chemicals accounting for nearly three-quarters of the total. R and D tends to be concentrated in large firms which can afford the high costs involved in modern technological research, not to mention the willingness to accept the risks of failure. However, small firms have been responsible for some major innovations.

*Productivity in the short-term*

So far we have discussed long-term trends, but productivity also fluctuates considerably in the short-term. Output per man tends to fall at the beginning of downturns in economic activity as firms hold on to their labour, dismissing the workforce only when the decline in sales is perceived to be lasting. For the opposite reason, productivity typically rises at the start of upturns in output. This pattern is not always strongly exhibited, but it was quite marked in the recession which lasted from 1973 to 1977 (see Fig 27).

# The location of industry

Economic theory tells us that profit-maximising firms tend to locate their businesses where costs are lowest relative to revenues. This basic underlying principle is relevant to the geographical distribution of industry in the UK, although it needs to be applied in the context of considerable government intervention to influence location decisions (see Chapter 5, pages 137–9).

*Fig 30* Regional specialisation in the UK 1981; • signifies that a region has more than the national average percentage of its labour force in a particular sector Sources: *Employment Gazette*, March 1982, and *Regional Trends*

| | London | Rest of South East | East Anglia | South West | West Midlands | East Midlands | Yorkshire Humberside | North West | North | Wales | Scotland | Northern Ireland |
|---|---|---|---|---|---|---|---|---|---|---|---|---|
| **Manufacturing** | | | | | | | | | | | | |
| Food, drink & tobacco | | | | | • | • | | • | • | • | | • |
| Coal, petroleum & chemicals | | | | | | | | • | • | • | • | |
| Metal manufacture | | | | | • | • | • | • | • | | | |
| Engineering | • | | | | • | • | | • | • | | | |
| Textiles, leather & clothing | | | | | | • | • | | | | • | • |
| Other manufacturing | | • | • | • | • | | | • | | | | |
| **All manufacturing** | | | | | • | • | • | • | • | | | |
| **Non-manufacturing** | | | | | | | | | | | | |
| Agriculture, forestry & fishing | | | • | • | | • | | | | • | • | • |
| Mining, quarrying | | | | | | • | • | • | • | • | • | |
| Construction | | | | • | | | | • | • | • | • | • |
| Transport communication | • | • | | | | | | | | | | |
| Distributive trades | • | • | • | • | | | | | | | | |
| Financial, professional misc services | • | • | • | • | | | | | | • | • | • |
| Public administration & defence | • | | | • | | | | | • | • | • | • |
| **All non-manufacturing** | • | • | • | • | | | | | | • | • | • |

We already know something of the regional distribution of the population (see Fig 5, page 5). This gives a first approximation to the location of industry too, since the need to be near both labour supplies and markets for the sale of products are two important determinants of location.

Fig 30 shows the geographical spread of different industries. It should be examined in conjunction with Fig 31, which shows the standard regions used in official statistics. In Fig 30 each area has a column to itself, with spaces for all the main industries. Where a • appears the regional percentage of the total area labour force in that industry is more than that for the country as a whole. Thus, wherever there is a • the region is to some extent specialising in that particular industry. Wherever there is a blank the region is not specialising in that industry although, of course, it may well be producing some of the goods in question.

*The South East*  The South East region employs over a third of the entire British labour force. Half the workers in the region are located in Greater London, which concentrates predominantly

*Fig 31* Standard regions of the UK 1981

on non-manufacturing—hence the specialisation in finance, offices of banks, insurance companies and other financial institutions are in the City. London is the pivot of road and rail networks, it is the chief shopping centre in the country and the site of many government departments.

The rest of the South East is second only to London in the size of its labour force. It is an important producer in engineering and other manufacturing industries and employs more than the national average of its workforce in the distributive trades and financial and professional services.

| East Anglia and the South West | East Anglia and the South West have much in common, despite their geographical separation. They are the foremost agricultural regions in England and Wales, employing some 7 and 3 per cent of their labour forces on the land, respectively. Both regions also specialise in food processing and contain important tourist resorts, which help to account for the fact that they have above average employment in the sector which includes miscellaneous services. The South West is double the size of East Anglia in terms of total employment. Its industrial centre is Bristol, where engineering, including vehicle manufacturing (mainly aerospace) flourishes. |
|---|---|
| The Midlands | The Midlands is divided into East and West regions, the latter being substantially the larger. Both concentrate more on manufacturing than any other region. Both also specialise in metal manufacture. The West Midlands is the more important in the field of engineering, including (road) vehicles, much of the heavy sections of which are in the 'Black Country' around Birmingham and Wolverhampton. The East Midlands industry tends to be lighter and includes more clothing and textiles, and food, drink and tobacco. The region also has a sizeable agricultural sector, as well as taking in the coalfields of Derbyshire and Nottinghamshire. |
| Yorkshire and Humberside | This is a diversified, largely manufacturing region. Its specialisations include food, drink and tobacco, metal manufacture, and clothing and textiles, though there are more workers in engineering than in any of these industries. It is the largest employer, too, in coal mining. |
| The North West | The North West region, encompassing Manchester and Liverpool, is the second largest in Britain. It is also strongly industrial, specialising in all the major industries except metal manufacture. The region's traditional strength, Lancashire textiles, is now overshadowed by other industries including engineering, much of it heavy. |
| Northern England | Centred around Tyneside, the Northern region of England used to be particularly dependent on the heavy industries of coal, iron and steel, shipbuilding and chemicals. A quarter of its labour force is still employed in coal mining, metal manufacture, coal, petroleum and chemical products, and engineering, though the last of these is now more diversified. |

| Wales | Wales is sparsely populated and largely mountainous. However it does have more than the national average percentage of workers in agriculture. It has traditionally been a coal mining area, although only about 3 per cent of the labour force remain in that industry now. These two facts account, to a substantial extent, for Wales appearing in Fig 30 as a region which does not specialise in manufacturing. Welsh specialisation in iron and steel has been on the decline for several years, though there are still more workers in steel than in coal. The range of manufacturing industry has, however, been widening to include engineering, plastics and clothing, etc. |

| Scotland | Scotland is a good deal larger than Wales, but it also is sparsely populated and mountainous. A relatively high proportion of its labour force is in agriculture, and most industry is in the central lowlands, around Glasgow, with textiles in the Paisley area. Coal mining remains important and the Scottish tourist trade helps account for the specialisation in the miscellaneous services category. |

| Northern Ireland | Northern Ireland has the smallest number of employees of any of the regions of the UK—about half a million. Specialisation includes agriculture, food, drink and tobacco, and clothing and textiles. Many attempts have been made at industrial diversification in Northern Ireland, but the region has suffered for many years from both political unrest and the highest rate of unemployment in the UK. |

| Changes in location | We have discussed regional specialisation as it exists in the UK today. For the greater part of this century, however, there has been considerable redeployment of industry over different parts of the country. The decades between the two world wars were outstanding, and witnessed a striking growth in the relative importance of Southern England and the Midlands at the expense of Northern England, Merseyside, South Wales and Scotland. |

Two factors accounted for these changes. In the first place there was a tendency for industrialists to move southwards when erecting new factories because they were attracted by the growing market of Greater London. Moreover, the development of electricity as a source of power released them from the need to be near coalfields. The second explanation is the one that carries more weight. As we saw earlier, not all industries were expanding at the same rate and, in fact, some were declining. Most of the new and expanding industries, such as engineering, vehicles and electrical goods, were those in which the South and the Midlands were specialising, while the staple industries of the 19th century, especially textiles, coal and shipbuilding, largely concentrated in the North of England, Scotland and South Wales, were declining in importance.

The period since the end of the Second World War has seen a continuation of the same broad trends, but it has also seen some different changes in regional prosperity as some of the newer postwar industries, such as vehicles, have in their turn experienced a relative decline.

## Industrial concentration[1]

One of the many outstanding features of industrial development in the past 100 years has been the growth in the size of firms and an increasing concentration of industry in a relatively few large concerns. The days when the majority of goods were produced by a great many small businesses have disappeared. The typical unit in many industries today is the giant corporation. Two of the many reasons for this development are of special importance. First, in many industries costs per unit of output fall as production expands, giving rise to what are known as **economies of large-scale production**. This obviously gives a cost advantage to large firms. The second is the appearance of **market power** for a firm which dominates an industry. Such a firm does not have to accept the market price as given but may be able to fix prices, restrict output and/or stifle innovations which threaten the demand for its product.

## The size of manufacturing establishments

Individual factories and plants are officially known as **establishments** and we start by considering their size distribution. This may, in turn, reflect the relative importance of economies of large-scale production as distinct from a desire for market power.

If there are cost reductions to be realised within a factory one would not expect a firm to spread its output among several plants unless there are other advantages to be had. Hence, if economies of large-scale production are responsible for the concentration of an industry in large firms, they will tend to be associated with large factories too. Large firms which operate several establishments may have grown in size for reasons other than the presence of falling costs of

---

1 The theoretical issues dealt with in the rest of this chapter are examined in Lipsey Chapters 20–23.

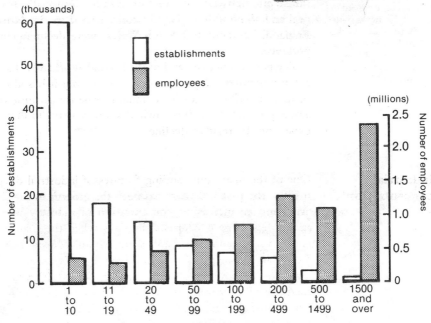

*Fig 32* Size of
manufacturing
establishments 1979
Source: *Census of
Production 1979*,
Summary Tables,
Business Monitor
PA 1002, 1982

production in large plants. In such cases a desire for market power may be the dominant cause.

Although the information on which Fig 32 is based is probably incomplete in its recording of very small establishments, it reveals that they are by far the most numerous. Of the total of about 100 000 manufacturing establishments, over half employ 10 or fewer workers, while about 90 per cent employ under 100.

Nonetheless, large-scale production is dominant in manufacturing. The 2500 establishments employing more than 500 workers each, which represent about 2 per cent of the total, are so large that altogether they employ over half of the entire manufacturing labour force. Furthermore, the 560 largest establishments of all, each of which has more than 1500 workers on its payroll, account for nearly a third of total employment in manufacturing.

Large-scale production is, of course, much more common in some industries than in others. Some idea of this is given in Fig 33 which shows the percentage of total employment in establishments with 1500 or more employees. We find that the prime large-scale industry is vehicle manufacture, where large establishments are responsible for the employment of

*Fig 33* Employment in
large establishments
1979; percentage of
total employment in
establishments with
1500 or more workers
Source: *Census of
Production 1979*,
Summary Tables,
Business Monitor
PA 1002, 1982

about three-quarters of the labour force. In electrical engineering large establishments account for over half of total employment and in metal manufacture and chemicals for over 40 per cent. The figure shows, however, that there are industries, especially in timber and furniture, metal goods and clothing, where large plants are uncommon.

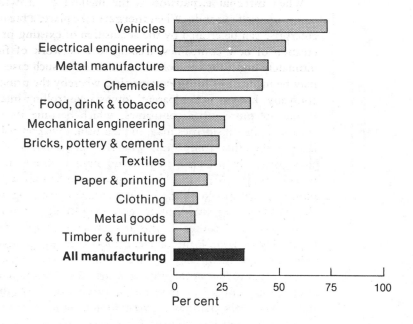

## The size of business enterprises

The concentration of industry in large establishments is, as we have seen, considerable. However, we know that an individual company may own more than one establishment. This is particularly likely to be the case if the firm is a large one. The 100 largest businesses in manufacturing industry in the UK operated 3500 establishments between them in 1979.

The private sector of industry in Britain is not organised in such a way that all establishments are autonomous bodies. In some cases an independent company may own a single establishment, but this is not necessarily the case and we need to look deeper into the links that exist between industrial units in order to identify where control lies and business decisions are taken. We therefore have to distinguish between the following:

- **establishments** (or **plants**)
- **companies** (or **firms**) which may own one or more establishments
- business **enterprises** comprising groups of companies under the overall control of one company

Growth can occur in two ways:

- by internal expansion
- by mergers among firms

When **internal expansion** is the method of growth, a company itself expands. When **mergers** take place, a business enterprise can be created by the acquisition of existing or the creation of new companies, leading to a network of firms ultimately under the control of one of them. In such cases use may be made of **holding companies**, whereby the principal company, known as the 'parent', owns a controlling interest in one or more other companies, which become its subsidiaries. The subsidiaries may, in their turn, own controlling interests in other companies, which are subsidiaries of the subsidiaries. In principle there is no limit to how far the process can go. A pyramid of companies can be built up, all ultimately controlled by the holding company (so long as its shareholdings are sufficient to give controlling interests— as we saw in Chapter 2, this does not necessarily mean ownership of over 50 per cent of the shares (see pages 34–5).

Fig 34 shows, by way of illustration, one such business empire, that of Sears Holdings, built up under the chairmanship of the late Charles Clore. The Sears group is one of the 50 largest companies in Britain, with a sales turnover of nearly £1.5 billion and employing about 60 000 workers. There are nearly 400 companies in the group and control is exercised through 5 pyramidal tiers. There are even larger groups in Britain, such as BP, Shell, ICI, Unilever, Allied Breweries, Rio-Tinto Zinc, General Electric and Marks and Spencer.

Remembering the definition given above of a business enterprise, we can examine the extent to which concentration exists among enterprises of different size in British industry. Fig 35 throws light on this subject. It shows the proportions of total manufacturing output accounted for by *enterprises* of different size; it must not be confused with Fig 32 which relates to *establishments*.

Concentration in large enterprises is very considerable. Nearly 90 000 enterprises were identified in the 1979 census of production, but well over 90 per cent of them were classed as small in that they employed fewer than 100 workers. They were in the main single-establishment independent companies

*Fig 34* Company
structure; the Sears
group 1981

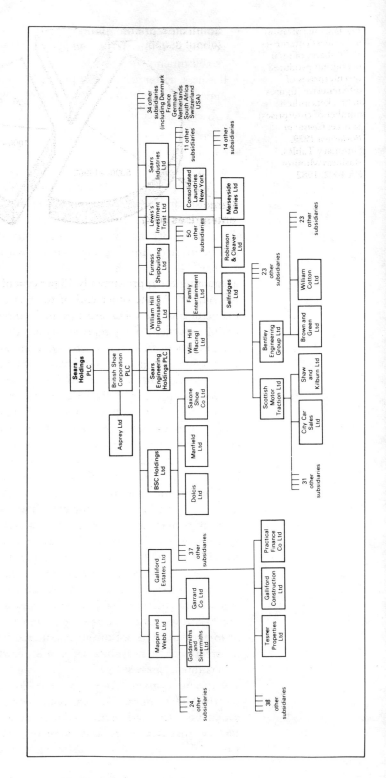

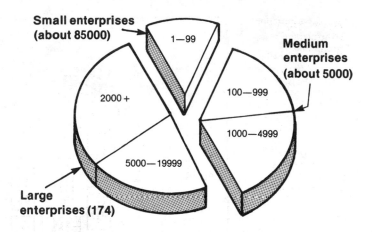

*Fig 35* Concentration in business enterprises 1979; shares of total net output produced by enterprises of different size (figures in brackets indicate number of enterprises) Source: *Census of Production 1979*, Summary Tables, Business Monitor PA 1002, 1982

Small enterprises (about 85000)

1—99

Medium enterprises (about 5000)

2000 +

100—999

1000—4999

5000—19999

Large enterprises (174)

accounting for approximately 15 per cent of total manufacturing output. At the other end of the scale, however, we can distinguish some 174 enterprises, each employing a minimum of 5000 workers. They represented less than 1 per cent of the total number of enterprises, but accounted for almost half of all production in manufacturing. Among them were 34 giants, each with at least 20000 employees and together producing a quarter of the total output.

The degree of concentration in individual industries, of course, varies as much when we take enterprises as our unit as when we take establishments. The measure of concentration in an industry is liable to be influenced by the way in which the industry is defined—the more narrowly the higher the degree of concentration. Fig 36 illustrates some of the differences that exist. It shows, for certain selected industries, the share of the five enterprises in total sales.

The diagram is based on what are known as **concentration ratios** (CRs). They are simply the percentage shares of the largest five enterprises in the total output of each industry group. The very wide range of CRs shown—from 9 to 99 per cent—is just one way of depicting the extent of differences in concentration. Thus, while there are highly concentrated industries, such as tobacco, cement and fertilisers, there are others, such as shop fittings, plastic products and dresses, where the share of the largest five enterprises is much lower. It must be remembered, however, that since Fig 36 is confined to selected industries it can only be used for illustrative purposes. Other industries which are highly concentrated include, for example, man-made fibres, margarine and asbestos.

*Fig 36* Concentration
ratios in selected
industries 1979;
percentage of total net
output by the five
largest enterprises (the
percentage for each
industry is measured
separately, clockwise
from the 12 o'clock
origin)
Source: *Census of
Production 1979,*
Summary Tables,
Business Monitor
PA 1002, 1982

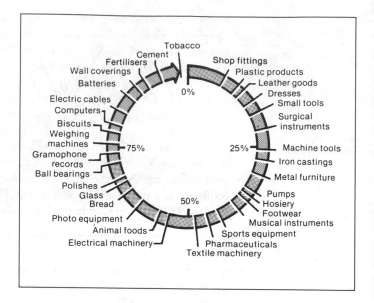

## Diversification

The great importance of large enterprises in British industry, highlighted in Figs 35 and 36, is not open to doubt. However, large size does not necessarily imply the possession of great market power. Market power depends on controlling a large part of one market, eg selling a high percentage of the industry's sales. Large size often arises when a single firm diversifies into a number of markets—indeed, many of the UK's industrial giants are multi-product businesses. The Sears group of companies depicted in Fig 34 page 60, for example, has widely diversified interests including engineering, motor distribution, bookmaking, the gold and silver trade and the ownership of department stores, backing its main line in shoe retailing. Another example is Grand Metropolitan, whose chief interest in hotels is supplemented by others in breweries (Watney, Mann and Truman), milk supply (Express Dairies), bookmakers and entertainment (Mecca).

The extent of diversification among large corporations is not easily quantified. As when measuring concentration itself, the results obtained by using various measures are liable to be sensitive to the way in which industry groups are defined. The narrower the definitions the greater the observed diversification is likely to be. However, a recent study[1] of the spread of interests in a sample of the 200 largest enterprises in manufacturing showed that over half of the total employment of these companies was in the primary industry group, defined in a

1 'Large Firm Diversification in British Manufacturing Industry', M A Utton, *Economic Journal,* Vol 87, No 345, 1977.

broad way. Of course, this is an average figure for the entire sample—certain firms showed an extremely high degree of diversification and others a very low one. In some sectors, too, such as chemicals and textiles, the spread of outside interests was found to be much greater, while in others, such as vehicles and shipbuilding, the amount of diversification was considerably less.

## Changes in concentration

Attention has so far been directed to the extent of concentration in British industry at the end of the 1970s. It is time to look at past trends in the degree of concentration both in the economy as a whole and by sector. Fig 37 shows the share of the largest 100 enterprises in total manufacturing output. The

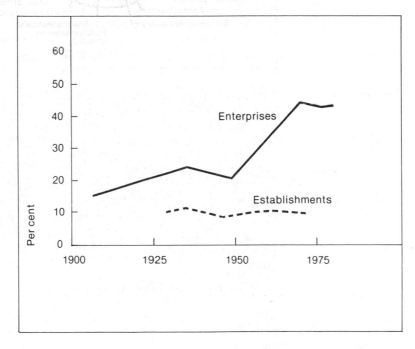

*Fig 37* The growth of concentration in manufacturing industry 1909–79; share of the largest 100 enterprises and largest 100 establishments in total output of manufactures
Source: *The Evolution of Giant Firms in Britain*, S J Prais, Cambridge University Press, 2nd impression, 1981

share of these giants rose from about 15 per cent in the first decade of the century to over 40 per cent at the end of the 1960s, with a particularly sharp rate of increase after the Second World War. Since 1970 the level of overall concentration appears to have more or less stabilised.

It is interesting to compare the rising share of the top 100 *enterprises* with that of the same number of the largest *establishments* (shown for a shorter period of time). The contrast between them could hardly be more marked. At the time when concentration in giant companies was proceeding most rapidly, the share of the largest establishments was virtually constant, at around 10 per cent. This suggests very strongly that whatever the cause of the increase in concentration, it was not substantially due to firms taking advantage of the economies of scale associated with large plants.

Within the trend of increasing overall concentration of industry in relatively few businesses, it is necessary to look at what has been happening in different sectors. This is difficult to measure because of the changes that occur, particularly over long periods of time, in the nature of products offered for sale. However, we can obtain some information by examining the trends in concentration ratios in those industry groups which are most comparable. (The concentration ratio is defined now, much as it was for Fig 36, as the share of total employment accounted for by the five largest enterprises.) The picture here is rather less clear but it can be said that there has been a tendency for concentration to increase in many sectors since the 1950s. This can be illustrated by considering the cases where the concentration ratio exceeded 80 per cent, ie where the largest five enterprises controlled more than four-fifths of total output, and comparing the proportion of such cases to the total at different times. We find that this proportion rose during the period between the mid-1950s and mid-1960s, but the most rapid advance occurred a little later than that. Between 1963 and 1975 the proportion of products where the concentration ratio was at least 80 per cent rose from 34 to 41 per cent of the total. It must be added that concentration did not appear to increase uniformly in all sectors. In some, such as fruit and vegetable products, agricultural and electrical machinery, there was evidence of falling concentration.

## Mergers

It was mentioned earlier that businesses can expand by internal growth or by the acquisition of other companies. While the former method has undoubtedly been an important one, especially in earlier times, growth by merger has been on the increase and is estimated to have been the cause of at least half of the increase in concentration since the late 1950s. Mergers tend to come in waves. They were running at a rate of about 750 per annum from the early 1960s with peaks of more than 1000 in 1972 and 1973. After 1973 there was a decline for a few years until they picked up again around 1977.

Some mergers take place between companies of roughly equal size. In other cases a small firm may be taken over in such a way as to lose its identity virtually completely. From the point of view of concentration of the *control* of industry, however, the most important aspect of amalgamations between companies concerns the nature of the businesses. It is useful to distinguish three types of merger.

1 **Horizontal mergers** are those between firms producing similar products, eg the Dolcis and Manfield shoe chains in the Sears group (see Fig 34 page 60).
2 **Vertical mergers** involve the absorption of suppliers or outlets, eg the acquisition by Dunlop of rubber plantations or the purchase by a brewery of public houses which sell its beer direct to the public.
3 **Conglomerate mergers** lead to a diversification of interests—the Sears group is a good example, since there is little in common between the product lines of some of its companies, eg shoe shops, bookmakers, engineering and property development.

It is not always easy to place a particular merger in the correct category. Some amalgamations may not appear, on the surface, to have elements of either the vertical or horizontal merger about them, but they may conceal less obvious matters, such as disposal of by-products or utilisation of expertise in a related field which might explain such otherwise unlikely combinations as detergents, plastics and ice cream manufacture in the Unilever group.

Horizontal mergers have been the predominant type in post-Second World War Britain, with vertical integration being insignificant. Conglomerate mergers, however, have been becoming increasingly common. They accounted for less than 10 per cent of the total in the 1960s, but had risen to about 30 per cent by 1980.

Horizontal mergers and, to an extent, vertical ones tend to increase the power of a company over its market. Conglomerate mergers, in contrast, often have the aim of diversification in order to reduce risks, by spreading them. They may also increase bargaining power in the financial markets in which a firm raises capital.

Increasing concentration may well be associated with increasing market power. But, in a curious way, it may even heighten competition if giant companies enter each others' markets as a result. There is little doubt, however, that merger activity, especially in the last twenty years, has been an important determinant of increasing concentration. Whether the mergers have paid off is a different matter. Recent studies of the effects of mergers on company profits suggest that there were, on balance, few cases in which the post-merger financial situation was significantly improved.

## Cooperation among firms

The emphasis so far in this section on industrial concentration has been on the power of business enterprises based on common ownership. However there are avenues of cooperation open to separate firms which fall short of the full pooling of sovereignty involved in amalgamation. Some of the most common arrangements among firms take place through a **trade association**. This is a very wide term and includes any body of employers who have agreements with each other. The Confederation of British Industry (CBI) is one such example. It acts as industry's spokesman on economic and labour matters where a national voice is desired.

In individual industries trade associations usually have a more specific role. Their functions vary from industry to

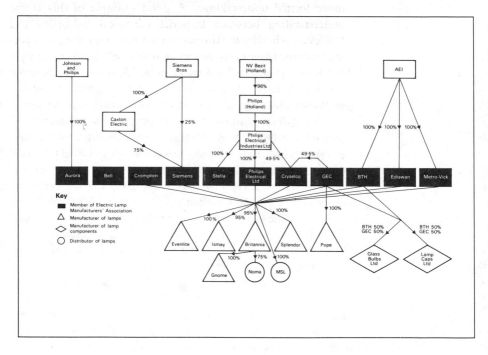

*Fig 38* Links between members of the Electric Lamp Manufacturers' Association 1951 Source: *Report on the Supply of Electric Lamps*, Monopolies Commission, H C Paper 287, 1950–51

industry and include the carrying out of research and publicity. They may also cover activities such as regulating the output or fixing the price of products in the industry and organising the machinery for carrying through policies. Some trade associations have made arrangements for allocating shares of the market to constituent firms on a predetermined basis, involving the setting up of a central sales organisation, often referred to as a **cartel**. Agreements of this kind can have much the same effect as more complete mergers between firms in so far as the restriction of competition is concerned, although they may be less stable. Legislation was passed in the

1950s limiting the operation of such practices by firms acting together, but an example, taken from the early 1950s, is shown in Fig 38. We shall return to this subject when discussing government economic policy in Chapter 5.

There are other devices for inter-firm cooperation, such as that of the **interlocking directorate**. A link between firms is contrived by one or more persons becoming directors of several companies. This practice is common in the area of banking and finance, but is rather less so in manufacturing industry.

Firms also get together for the exchange of information or joint action of one kind or another. They may have unwritten understandings, often called 'gentlemen's agreements', or more formal undertakings. A good example of this is the understanding between Imperial Chemical Industries and Unilever, whereby the former agreed to refrain from competing with the latter in the production of soap. Another example is where a group of local builders decide not to compete for building contracts, but to allocate new orders received by any of them in rotation. A third involves the exchange of 'know how' between companies, extending in some cases to a pooling of patents. Such arrangements are frequently not well publicised and it is consequently extremely difficult to find out what is going on. Governments have to assess the seriousness of these matters, all of which tend to restrict competition to some degree, and then evolve appropriate policies (see Chapter 5).

# 4 | Distribution[1]

Economics is concerned not only with the production of the goods and services which constitute the national 'cake', but also with how the cake is divided up among individuals. In dealing with this latter subject economists refer to the distribution of national income.

**Distribution of income**

The forces of supply and demand operate in the markets for factors of production and in so doing affect the distribution of income, though this is influenced also by government intervention. There are two distributions to be considered:

- distribution according to the size of individuals' incomes
- distribution among factors of production

*Fig 39* Distribution of income before tax 1979–80
Source: *Economic Trends*

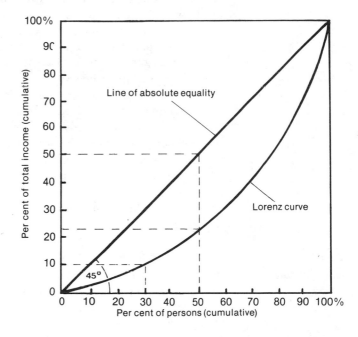

Size distribution

We start by looking at the degree of inequality in income distribution in the UK. Fig 39 presents this information in a

1 The theory of distribution is covered by Lipsey Part 5—see, in particular, Chapters 25 and 26 for general considerations and Chapter 27 for labour income.

convenient, if unusual, way, making use of what is known as a **Lorenz curve**. This shows how much of total income is accounted for by given proportions of persons. The percentages measured on both axes are *cumulative*, so as we move along the horizontal axis we look at the shares of the bottom 1, 2, 3, etc, per cent of the population and then read off their shares on the vertical axis. For example, the bottom 30 per cent of persons received about 10 per cent of total income, the bottom 50 per cent about 23 per cent of income and so on. We can compare the Lorenz curve at any time with the *line of absolute equality*. This is drawn in the diagram as the diagonal going through the origin. It indicates absolute equality because all points along it show that a given percentage of the population receive exactly the same percentage of total income, ie the bottom 1 per cent receive 1 per cent of total income, the bottom 5 per cent receive 5 per cent, etc. Hence the further the Lorenz curve bends away from the diagonal, the greater the degree of inequality.

The simple single line of the Lorenz curve gives a full description of the distribution of income among persons (strictly speaking the data refers not to persons but to 'tax units', whereby the incomes of most husbands and wives are counted as one). It shows, for example, that the top 20 per cent of the population received over 40 per cent of total income while the bottom 20 per cent received only about 5 per cent. Why should this be so?

The answer to this question is complex. The distribution of income shown by the Lorenz curve is partly the result of economic forces, partly caused by the socioeconomic system of the country, and partly because of various kinds of action by the government. We shall consider the last of these in Chapter 6. Here we shall discuss the influence of market forces. They are relevant because a part, at least, of the income of most individuals comes as a reward for their services as factors of production.

**Factor distribution**

Chapter 1 of this book began by explaining that economists usually classify resources, or factors of production, into three main categories—land, labour and capital. Each of these factors receives an income, known respectively as rent, wages and salaries, and interest. There is also a fourth kind of income, called profit, earned by a factor which is sometimes given the name **enterprise**. Of course, a single individual may receive income from more than one source, eg wages from employment, interest on capital lent to industry and rent from land. The factor (or functional) distribution of income

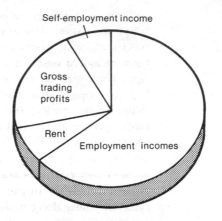

*Fig 40* Factor distribution of income 1981
Source: *National Income and Expenditure*

is shown in Fig 40. It must, however, be understood that the divisions shown in the diagram (derived from published statistics) do not correspond precisely to the concepts used in economic theory, though they come closest in the case of income from employment. Gross trading profits include interest on capital as well as pure profit; self-employment income contains an element of labour income as well as interest and profit; while rent is the return on land and buildings rather than pure economic rent. (**Economic rent** is a payment to any factor of production in excess of its transfer earnings—some data relating to this concept is given in Fig 52, page 90.)

The largest share, about two-thirds of the total in 1980, accrued to labour in the form of wages and salaries. Rent took about a tenth as much as this. The gross trading profits of the private and public sectors are the pool from which dividends and interest are paid. In the diagram, profits are shown before any depreciation allowances are made (see page 29). *All* proportions are shown gross before the deduction of any taxes on income. Self-employment income cannot be regarded as the reward to a single factor of production, as with the first two main categories; it is rather a mixture. Part represents income for work done and part a return on capital invested, either in a business or in education and training to acquire the qualifications without which such professional earnings would not accrue. Self-employment income is about 10 per cent of the total.

*Trends in the shares of factor incomes*

Fig 40 showed the shares of the chief factors of production as they existed in one particular year, 1980. These shares are not always exactly the same. The share of capital tends to be high in years of prosperity, when profits are high. Labour's share falls accordingly in such boom periods and rises, for the opposite reason, when trade is less flourishing. That is not to say that *wages* tend to be high in depressions, only that the *share of employment income* is large. In absolute terms, wages may be high or low.

Apart from short-term fluctuations, some longer-term trends are observable in factor shares. If we look back to the 1870s we can see a fairly stable share of wages alone which persisted until about the middle of the present century. It should be added, however, that the proportion of wage earners was falling at the same time. Taking account of all incomes from employment, the share of wages *and* salaries rose by about 10 per cent over this long period, although towards the end there may have been a slight fall.

The share of self-employment income is of rather less interest, consisting as it does of a mixture of employment and other factor incomes. The long-term trend was downward during the period of growth of joint stock companies. In more recent times self-employment income has accounted for between 8 and 11 per cent of the total of factor incomes. One reason for variations lies in the way in which taxes are levied on people. There have been changes from time to time in the advantages that accrue from being treated for tax purposes as a self-employed person rather than as a wage or salary earner or the owner of a business organised as a joint stock company. Another is the level of unemployment in the country. When it is high, people may seek to set themselves up in small businesses, often assisted by payments made in compensation for being declared redundant.

The income of any factor of production (and hence the share in total income that it is able to command) depends upon the price that is paid for it and the amount that is used. Economic theory tells us that the forces of supply and demand determine the prices of factors of production just as they do those of goods and services, although, as usual, government intervention affects the actual incomes of individuals. The remainder of this chapter will examine the background within which these forces work, with particular attention being paid to the labour market.

**The supply of labour**

The number of persons in the community able and wishing to work depends in the first instance on the size of the total population and its age (and to some extent its sex) distribution.

**Population size**

We saw in Chapter 1 that the population of the UK grew rapidly during the 19th and early 20th centuries, and appears now to have stabilised at a level of just over 55 million.

The size of the population depends on:

- birth rates
- death rates
- the balance of migration movements

The **birth rate** (defined as the number of babies born per 1000 of the population) is determined by the age distribution of the female population and on family size. The number of women of child-bearing age in the population in 1981 is shown in Fig 41; for purposes of comparison the figures for

*Fig 41* Age distribution of the female population 1871 and 1981
Source: *Annual Abstract of Statistics*

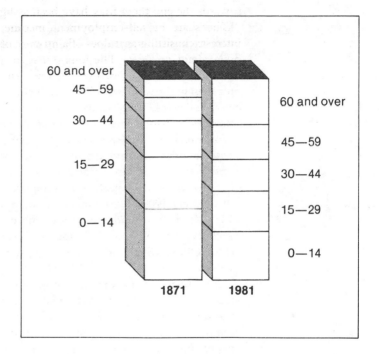

1871 are also given. Not only was the proportion greater during the Victorian period of rapid population growth, but the numbers in the 0–14 age group, coming up later to fertility, were very much higher.

Fig 42 shows that by the interwar years family size had also changed dramatically from that of the 19th century. The contrast between the two periods is startling. Whereas every fourth Victorian family had at least 9 children, only 1 in 40 in the later period had as many. The reasons for this tremendous fall in the size of families are interesting even if they are not all understood. They are clearly associated with increasing

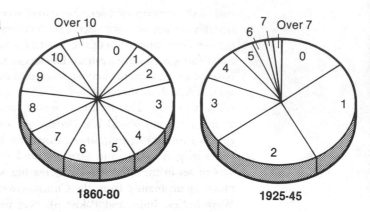

Fig 42 Size of families 1860–80 (England and Wales) and 1925–45 (Great Britain); number of children per family
Source: *Report of the Royal Commission on Population*, Cmnd 7695, 1949, page 26

knowledge and use of contraceptive techniques, which, in turn, reflect other changes—the growth of the middle classes who tend to have fewer children, the emancipation of women, and changing attitudes towards family life and parental responsibility.

These trends have not continued without interruption. In the period immediately following the end of the Second World War the birth rate rose as servicemen returned home to raise families deferred from wartime. Soon, however, the birth rate declined once more. It picked up again in the 1960s but dropped sharply in the following decade to a figure of less than 12 per 1000 of the population compared with 18 in the 1960s (and 28 around the turn of the century). In 1978 the decline in the birth rate was apparently arrested, but no-one really knows whether or not the long-term downward trend will reassert itself.

The second determinant of population size is the **death rate**. This is dependent on the age distribution of the population and has remained fairly constant throughout the present century, reflecting the opposing influences of an aging population and a decline in mortality rates for most age groups, resulting from medical advances and rising living standards. The current situation may be summarised by the fact that a baby born today could expect to live to be almost 70 if he is a boy, or over 75 if she is a girl. By comparison, average life expectancies at the beginning of the century were 49 and 52 respectively.

Finally, **migration** naturally affects the size of the population. Throughout the 19th century migration was an important factor restraining the growth of Britain's population; the range of opportunities, particularly in America, ensured that emigrants greatly outnumbered immigrants. Towards the end of the century immigration into Britain had also assumed sizeable proportions, but in the 60 years after 1871 there was a *net* loss from migration of the order of 4 million. In the 1920s most foreign countries put up barriers to immigrants and the balance of movements between the censuses of 1931 and 1961 was reversed, to become one of a net gain of some half a million people. This figure, however, conceals the fact that after the Second World War Britain reassumed her traditional role as a country of emigration, chiefly to the Commonwealth (especially Australia and Canada), and that this movement was offset in the late 1950s by increasing numbers of immigrants, again mainly from the Commonwealth (especially the West Indies, India and Pakistan). Net immigration around 1960 approached 150 000 per annum. This prompted the government to pass the Commonwealth Immigration Acts, the first in 1962, which gave it power to restrict immigration from the Commonwealth. A sharp fall in the number of immigrants followed, and in the ten years ending in 1980 there was a *net* loss of about a third of a million people through migration.

## Working population

The **working population**, sometimes called the labour force, is not the same as the total population. It comes largely from those in the age group 16–65 and, as we observed in Chapter 1, involves only about half the total population— about 26 million. The occupational distribution is shown in Fig 43 (it is out of date as it is based on data from the latest decennial census of population, relating to 1971).

*Fig 43* Occupations of the working population 1971 Source: *Census of Population 1971*

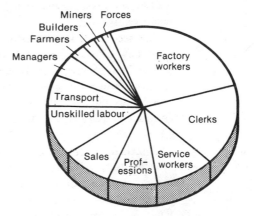

It can be seen that, although the English were once called a nation of shopkeepers, only about a tenth of the working population is engaged in the business of selling (including here commercial travellers, sellers of insurance policies, stocks and shares, etc, as well as actual shopkeepers). Production workers are considerably more numerous—about a quarter of the labour force works in factories. Clerical workers are the next largest single category representing one in seven of the economically active.

There are two other substantial groups, service workers and the professions. The former include firemen, hairdressers, policemen and window cleaners, but the largest single sub-category are hotel and restaurant workers, of whom there are close on a million in Britain. The professions also embrace many skills. They include not only architects, doctors, teachers, etc, but such others as draughtsmen, journalists and nurses. The final categories shown in Fig 43—unskilled labourers, transport workers, managers, farm workers, builders, miners and the armed forces—comprise the remaining third of the working population.

It is interesting to see how this distribution of occupations in the last quarter of the 20th century compares with earlier times, since the occupations of the people are a mirror of the economic state of the country. Without going into detail, two outstanding features may be indicated. First, employment in British agriculture has been decreasing in importance for the past two centuries. Today the proportion of the population working on farms is one of the smallest of any country in the world. Secondly, as agriculture has declined the number of factory workers has risen, until in this century they too began to fall in relative terms whilst the number of ancillary workers crept up. There are now more workers in the combined groups of clerks, service workers and shopkeepers than in the factories.

The size of the labour force in a given population depends on many factors, including conventional views as to the proper age of retirement, the level of pensions, attitudes towards family life and responsibilities, the legal minimum school-leaving age and the tendency for young people to continue education after that.

*Men and women in the labour force*

The **activity rate**, or **participation rate**, (the ratio of the working to the total population expressed as a percentage) for males has tended to fall over the last two or three decades for some of the reasons given in the last paragraph. The rate for females, in contrast, has risen very substantially. In the 30 years after 1950 the rate for married women more than doubled, from 22 to 50 per cent. The reasons for this are complex, but changing social attitudes and the falling birth rate, mentioned earlier, are among the major influences. The

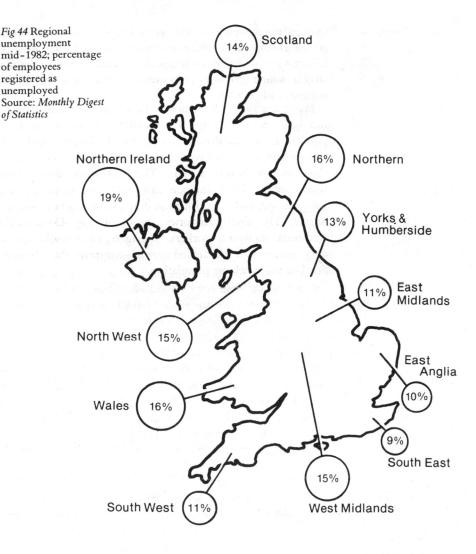

*Fig 44* Regional unemployment mid-1982; percentage of employees registered as unemployed
Source: *Monthly Digest of Statistics*

activity rate for older unmarried women rose too. Perhaps surprisingly, that for younger women (under 25) has fallen, although this probably reflects increases in one-parent families and in women continuing their education after the age of 16.

The overall effect of rising female and falling male participation rates on the sex distribution of the labour force has been substantial. Whereas women comprised less than a third of the total working population in 1950, they made up about two-fifths in 1980. This is the long-term trend. Cyclically, however, the female participation rate fluctuates a good deal more than the male counterpart, rising and falling more with upturns and downturns in economic activity.

**Unemployment**

The size and composition of the working population does not tell us the numbers actually working. The existence of involuntary unemployment means that there may be persons willing to work at going wage rates but who are unable to find jobs.

As pointed out in Chapter 1, the level of unemployment has been rising fairly steadily since the mid-1970s, reaching 14 per cent of the labour force by 1982. We shall deal with the question of the general level of unemployment at some length in the final chapter of this book. However, it is worth noticing here that there has always been a tendency for unemployment rates to vary regionally because of a mismatch between the location of job vacancies and of unemployed seeking work. Fig 44 shows unemployment rates for each of the standard regions of the UK. Those with the lowest levels were the South East, East Anglia and the South West. Those with the highest were Northern and North West England, Scotland, Wales and Northern Ireland. It is no coincidence that most of these areas happen to have relatively heavy concentrations of the labour force in declining industries such as shipbuilding, steel and textiles (see pages 54–5). The unemployment rate in the West Midlands, which is a major producer of cars, illustrates the same point. During the first 20 years after the end of the Second World War the vehicle industry flourished and unemployment rates in the West Midlands were relatively low. In 1982 the car industry was depressed and the region's rate of unemployment was above the national average.

Unemployment rates vary with characteristics other than the region in which workers happen to live. One of some social significance is ethnic origin. As Fig 45 shows, non-whites, especially those of Pakistani and Bangladeshi origin,

*Fig 45* Unemployment rates by ethnic origin 1981
Source: *Employment Gazette*, May 1982

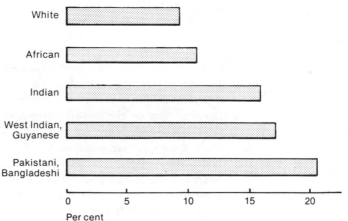

Per cent

have substantially higher unemployment rates, on average, than whites, though some part of the differentials in the diagram are due to the different age structures of the various ethnic groups.

## Wages

Economic theory suggest that the supply and demand for labour affect its price—the **wage rate**. The theory ought to be able to throw light on why wages differ among jobs, industries, characteristics of workers, etc. What differences exist in the UK that need explaining? We consider the following:

- differences among occupations
- differences among industries
- differences by age and sex
- difference among regions

## Occupational differences

To a large extent occupational wage variations may be attributable to the skills needed to perform particular jobs. For example, the head chef at the Savoy Hotel is paid more than the unskilled cleaners and dishwashers there. It is hardly surprising that people with inborn skills and others who take the time and trouble to acquire them should earn higher incomes. How much higher? That is not an easy question to which a general answer can be given because there is no unambiguous way of measuring the relative skills needed for different occupations. A first attempt to throw light on the subject might make use of the distinction, used by official collectors of statistics, between what are called skilled manual and unskilled manual workers. Bypassing the question of how much skill a job requires in order to qualify for inclusion in the skilled category, statistics show that skilled employees earned a little more than 25 per cent more than unskilled workers at the end of the 1970s.

Fig 46 shows the earnings of men in certain occupational groups expressed as percentages of average earnings in 1913 and 1978. The diagram is based on sample data published by a Royal Commission set up to report on the distribution of income and wealth in the 1970s. Too much should not be read into evidence of this kind that extends over so long a period when so many conditions were changing. It serves one very useful purpose, however; that of emphasising that a long-term narrowing of differentials has been taking place. This trend has been the result of changing forces on both the supply and demand sides of the labour market.

One supply side factor is increased labour mobility. The

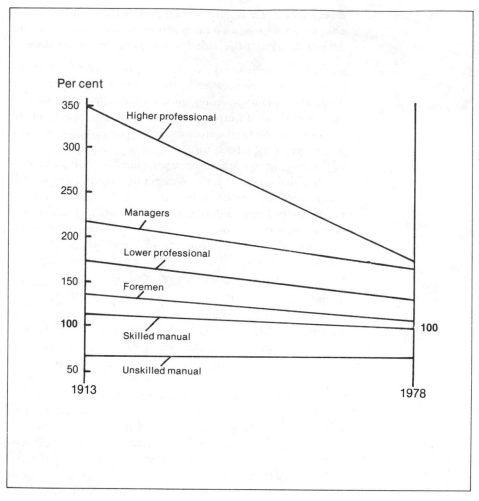

Per cent

350 — Higher professional

300 —

250 —

200 — Managers

Lower professional

150 —

Foremen

100 — 100

50 — Skilled manual

Unskilled manual

1913                                              1978

*Fig 46* Occupational wage differences (males) 1913 and 1978 (earnings for each occupation are shown as a percentage of average earnings) Source: *Report No 8 of the Royal Commission on the Distribution of Income and Wealth*, Comnd 7679, 1979

number of people acquiring qualifications is also greater now than it was near the beginning of the century. Moreover, although it is not visible from the diagram, the evidence suggests that the narrowing of differentials has recently slowed down, if not ceased altogether in some cases. This, too, may be partly due to market forces, but it must also be recognised that differentials built up over many years are not always easily eroded. They acquire a kind of status image that some of those engaged in wage bargaining are reluctant to see altered.

## Industry wage differences

A second source of differences in wages is related to the industry in which people work. Fig 47 shows details of the weekly earnings of workers in a selection of industries in October 1981. The average weekly pay of adult male manual workers at the time was £126. Compared with this, labour in some industries was clocking up at least 20 per cent more, whilst workers in industries at the bottom of the table were receiving at least 20 per cent less.

There are two reasons for the ordering of industries in the diagram. The first relates to the different conditions

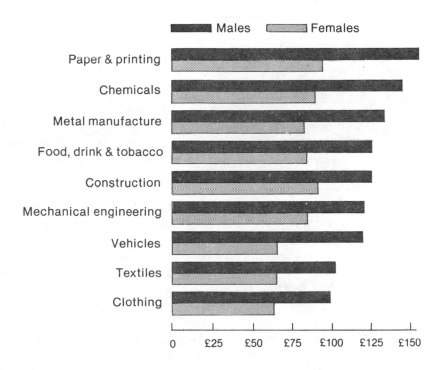

■■■■ Males ▨▨▨▨ Females

| | | | | | | |
|---|---|---|---|---|---|---|
| 0 | £25 | £50 | £75 | £100 | £125 | £150 |

*Fig 47* Average weekly earnings of full-time manual workers on adult rates of pay in selected industries October 1981 Source: *Monthly Digest of Statistics*

prevailing in particular industries at any time, eg differences in the proportion of skilled to unskilled workers and of men to women, in hours worked, in firm and plant size and in the relative strength of trade unions. The second reason concerns industry differentials over time. It must be remembered that businesses expand and contract, and that changing wages may reflect alterations in the underlying conditions of supply and/or demand.

**Age and sex wage differences**

It is commonly believed that people tend to be paid more as they get older. This is certainly true up to a point. The average earnings of male manual workers, aged 18–20, are less than two-thirds of the average for all workers.

What happens later on in life depends very much on the job—and it is dangerous to generalise. However, there is usually a plateau when earnings stop rising, or even fall. This is reached at younger age groups for manual workers than for non-manual, and earlier for women than for men.

As Fig 47 shows, a man is much more likely to earn more than a woman, regardless of the industry in which he works. Average earnings of women in all industries in October 1981 were between a half and two-thirds those of men, and although they differed from industry to industry, the figure is fairly representative. The reasons for this are many and complex and probably reflect an element of discrimination against women, especially before the passing of the Equal Pay Act of 1976 (see Chapter 6). However, the explanation probably lies more in the fact that women are relatively heavily concentrated in low paid occupations and industries than that they receive lower wages or salaries for identical work. Additionally, many women are less job-committed than men, often because of stronger feelings of family responsibility. They tend to spend less (or to have less spent on them by employers) on vocational training, and they are less likely to join a trade union. Women, on average, also work shorter hours than their male counterparts, which keeps down their earnings, especially where they decide to forego hours paid at high overtime rates.

## Regional wage differences

The final source of differences in wages is the region in which one works. Wages tend to be highest, on average, in Greater London. Fig 48 shows the average hourly earnings for manual workers in each region as a percentage of those in the capital. It can be seen that variations are considerable, with several regions having figures less than 90 per cent of those in London. Regional wage differences are, in the main, no more than a reflection of the basic forces with which we have already dealt. Behind the statistics lies the fact that regions differ in the proportions of their labour forces in different industries. We have observed something of the extent of variations in earnings by industry, and these obviously affect the regional statistics. This is only part of the story, however. If we dig deeper we see that regional wage rates may be affected by the state of local labour markets. Employers in relatively prosperous areas, such as London, need to pay higher wages than those in areas such as Northern Ireland which are relatively depressed.

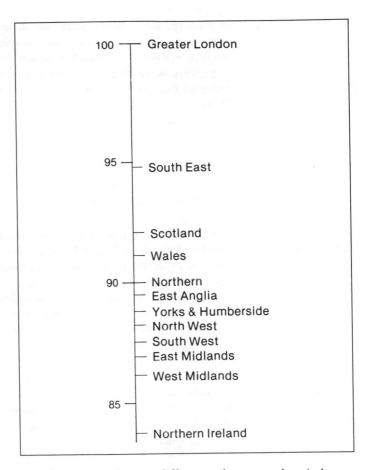

*Fig 48* Regional wage differentials October 1981; average hourly earnings of adult male manual workers for each region shown as a percentage of those in Greater London Source: *Employment Gazette*, March 1982

## Non-pecuniary advantages and disadvantages

The discussion of wage differences has centred entirely on variations in *money* earnings. However, this is not the whole story. An economist once coined the term 'non-pecuniary advantages and disadvantages' of different occupations, in order to emphasise that some people would be happy with relatively low paid jobs if there were compensating (ie non-pecuniary) advantages to go with them. An outdoor job appeals to many people more than one in an office or factory; an interesting one (eg teaching!) more than a dull routine one; a job with long holidays more than one with short; and so on.

These and similar characteristics are difficult, if not impossible, to quantify, but there are other kinds of non-monetary rewards that *are* quantifiable. They are commonly referred to as **fringe benefits** and include such 'extras' as the use of company cars, subsidised lunches, housing, etc. The Royal Commission on the Distribution of Income and Wealth, mentioned earlier, made a special study of this subject in 1978 and found benefits over and above monetary remuneration to run from around a fifth to a third of total pay, on average. It should be added that such fringe benefits may have been particularly high in that year for reasons associated with a government policy of pay restraint (see page 213), but they should not be overlooked at any time when discussing wage differentials.

## Trade unions

Our discussion of the supply of labour and wages has already made passing reference to the trade unions. It is now time to consider them in more detail.

## Historical development

Trade unionism had its origins in the pitifully low standard of living of the average 19th century worker and his family. The explanation of the standard of living throughout the world lay in the small size of the total national output relative to the population. In 1800, even in the wealthiest of countries, an equal division of national income among all families would have left everyone in poverty by our present standards.

Poverty had existed for centuries. It was accentuated, however, by the twin processes of urbanisation and industrialisation. The man who was moderately content working his land usually became restive and discontented when he moved into a grimy, smoky, 19th century city, took employment in a sweatshop or a factory, and settled with his family in a crowded, insanitary slum. (Of course, many moved because they had no choice, having been driven off their land by the enclosure movements. Thus we cannot assume that they made a free choice in the belief that the urban life was preferable to their rural one. Their rural life had been destroyed; the urban life was simply preferable to starvation.) Stories of suffering during the Industrial Revolution could fill many volumes. One example will at least illustrate some of the conditions that lay behind the drive for change and reform.

> In the cotton-spinning work, these creatures (the workers) are kept, fourteen hours in each day, locked up, summer and winter, in a heat of from *eighty to eighty-four degrees*. The rules which they are subject to are such as no negroes (ie slaves) were ever subjected to. . . . The door of the place wherein they work, is *locked, except half an hour*, at tea-time, the work-people are not allowed to send for water to drink, in the hot factory; even *the rain water is locked up*, by the master's order. . . . If any spinner be found with

his *window open*, he is to pay a fine of a shilling! . . . for a large part of the time, there is the abominable and pernicious stink of the *gas* to assist in the murderous effects of the heat. . . . the notorious fact is, that well constituted men are rendered old and past labour at forty years of age, and that children are rendered decrepit and deformed, and thousands upon thousands of them slaughtered by consumption (tuberculosis), before they arrive at the age of sixteen. . . .[1]

Out of these conditions came the full range of radical political movements from revolutionary socialism, which today we call Marxism or communism, to Fabian socialism, which tried to effect change gradually through existing political systems. Out of them also came the union, which was to some extent a club providing protection for unemployed, disabled or retired workers, and to some extent a negotiating agent. For a long time unions were resisted by the full power of both employers and government.

The union organisers perceived that 10 or 100 men acting together had more influence than one man acting alone. The union was the organisation that would provide a basis for confronting the power of employers with the collective power of workers. However it was easier to see the solution than to achieve it. Employers did not accept organisations of workers passively. Agitators who tried to organise other workers were often dismissed and blacklisted; in some cases they were physically assaulted or even killed. In order to realise the ambition of creating some effective power over the labour market, it was necessary to gain control of the supply of labour and to have the financial resources necessary to outlast employers. There was no 'right to organise', and the union usually had to force a hostile employer to negotiate with it. Since early unions did not have large resources, the employer had to be attacked where he was weakest.

All of these considerations explain why it was the unions of the highly skilled and the specialist types of labour that first met with success—it was easier to control the supply of skilled than unskilled workers. Secondly, a union of a small number of highly skilled specialists could attack the employer's weakest spots. Even then unions had their ups and downs. When employment was full and business booming, the cost of being fired for joining a union was not so great. During times

1 *Political Register*, Vol LII, William Cobbett, 20 November 1824, as quoted by E Royston Pike in *Human Documents of the Industrial Revolution in Britain*, Allen & Unwin, 1966, pages 60–1 (parenthetical inserts added).

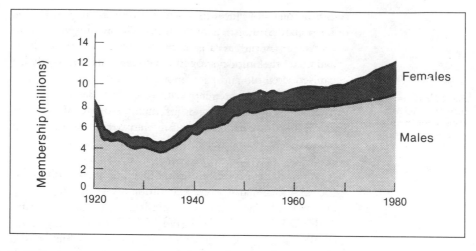

*Fig 49* Trade union membership 1920–80 Source: *Annual Abstract of Statistics*

of depression and unemployment, however, the risks were greater and we can observe cyclical swings in membership with gains in booms and setbacks in slumps—a pattern that persisted into the present century, as can be seen from Fig 49, which charts trade union membership since 1920. There was a substantial drop in the number of unionised workers during the depressed interwar years. More recently, rising unemployment in 1980 was accompanied by a 3 per cent decline in membership in that year.

## Trade union strength

In 1980 trade union membership stood at about 13 million. Since there were about 26 million in the labour force at that time, this represents only about half of the potential membership. The opportunity for continued growth is therefore, in principle, considerable, particularly among women (the number of female workers has risen faster than the number of male workers—see pages 76–7).

Trade union strength varies considerably from industry to industry and from occupation to occupation. It is difficult to be precise about such variations because of the existence of large unions with membership extending over many industries. Fig 50, however, gives a rough idea of the extent of differences among industries, which is noticeably large. The diagram shows some of the traditional strongholds of unionism, such as coal mining and the railways, as well as weak areas, such as agriculture and the distributive trades.

On the face of it, there is little that these areas of trade union strength have in common as far as the product of their respective industries is concerned, and there are often special historical circumstances to account for the growth of unionism. In several industries there are even arrangements between unions and employers which make membership of a union a condition of employment (the **closed shop**). Unionism tends to flourish in large firms and plants where workers spend their working days together and meetings can easily be organised.

An important recent trend that should be mentioned is the growth of so-called 'white collar' unionism over the last 20 years. Office workers have been recruited in substantially larger numbers than previously. This has been of considerable help to the trade union movement in maintaining and even increasing total union membership during a period when the traditional areas of union strength have been declining.

*Fig 50* Trade union membership 1980; trade union members as a percentage of numbers employed in selected industries Source: *Employment Gazette*, February 1982

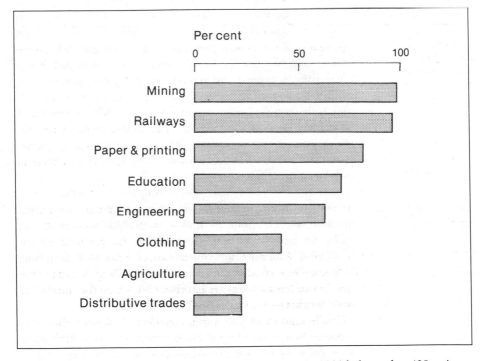

Per cent

Mining
Railways
Paper & printing
Education
Engineering
Clothing
Agriculture
Distributive trades

**Trade union structure**

The 13 million trade unionists in 1980 belonged to 438 unions, most of which were very small. Over half had fewer than 1000 members each, while the 25 largest accounted for about 80 per cent of total membership. In the main, these very large unions have grown over the years as a result of amalgamations. Some unions are organised on an industry basis, such as the National Union of Mineworkers and the Union of Communication Workers. Others, especially the older ones, are organised on a craft basis, like the National Graphical Association. However, the largest unions of all are either general unions covering a wide range of industries and/or occupations, such as the Transport and General Workers' Union with nearly 2 million members, or multi-craft unions like the Amalgamated Union of Engineering Workers.

The central body of the trade union movement is known as the Trades Union Congress (TUC), to which most unions, and all of the large ones, are affiliated. The TUC is often regarded as the representative voice of trade unions, and it negotiates with the government and national employers' associations. However, its formal powers are limited in that individual unions are not obliged to observe decisions taken at its annual conference.

## Collective bargaining

Trade unions are concerned with all aspects of the employment of their members. Their major functions are related to wages, hours of work and unemployment, but extend to general working conditions such as safety, holidays and promotion procedures. In some cases unions also aim to play an influential role in management itself, including seeking representation on boards of directors.

Unions provide some benefits directly for their members, financed out of their subscription income. However, their main role is to engage in collective bargaining with employers. In the inflationary times in which we live, negotiations usually take place at least annually and lead to a series of 'wage rounds' of pay increases. Comparability with workers in similar industries or occupations and the profitability of the business are generally the major issues discussed.

In the majority of cases negotiations are successful, in that the bargaining sessions produce an agreed package, sometimes associated with productivity commitments on the part of unions. Negotiations take place at many levels and can cover a variety of subjects. Wages are usually the central issue, but hours and conditions of work, redundancy, allegations of victimisation of individual workers by management, etc, may also be involved. Government intervention in wage bargaining is discussed in Chapter 9 page 215.

## Disputes

If the parties fail to agree, an industrial dispute follows. At such a time the union may call on its members either to come out on strike or to take other action, such as refusing to work overtime. Employers, on the other side, may decide to close down the business, dismiss staff or implement their offer even when it has not been agreed.

Disputes, of course, involve loss of production and Fig 51 shows the number of days lost as a result of stoppages of work since 1911. The first point to make is that the average number

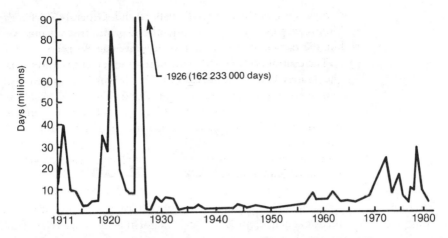

*Fig 51* Industrial disputes 1911–81; number of working days lost as a result of industrial disputes Source: *Monthly Digest of Statistics*

of days lost has been substantially lower in the postwar period than before the 1930s. Secondly, notice the tendency for disputes to involve substantially more disruption in some years since 1970 than in earlier postwar years.

It may be worthwhile adding a general comment on where Britain fits into the international scene. Britain's strike record is often regarded as something of a national disgrace. However, the record is not as dreadful as some people believe. Although statistics on disputes are collected on differing bases in individual countries and are not therefore strictly comparable, it is nevertheless true that many countries have no better records than Britain. These include Canada, Australia and the United States, which are sometimes held up as models. However, strikes tend to come in waves and, when they do come, their effects can be widespread and serious, particularly if they involve wholesale disruption of power and communication services, thereby threatening indirectly both industry and the home.

## Other factors of production

The bulk of this chapter has been devoted to a discussion of one factor of production, labour. This is not unreasonable, partly because incomes from employment take by far the largest proportion of the total, but mainly because of the great importance of labour in the economy as a whole. In a sense, too, some of the material in the preceding sections can be taken as illustrative of productive factors generally.

Although there are special features related to the incomes of other factors of production, especially to rent and profits, it is a little difficult to find much descriptive material that is useful for economic analysis on such matters. Nonetheless, we end this chapter by highlighting some features concerning rent and profits.

Rent[1]

To an economist rent is not just the return received by the factor of production, land; it is a surplus that can accrue to any factor of production which possesses some specific characteristic that others do not. A common example is the so-called **rent of ability** earned by film stars, which greatly exceeds their potential earnings in other occupations. Fig 52 has been

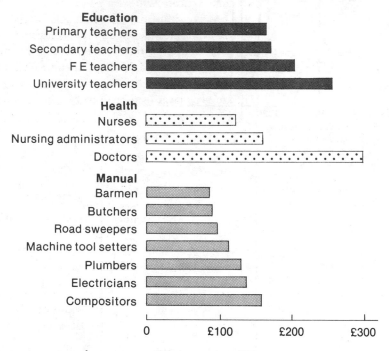

*Fig 52* Average gross weekly earnings in selected occupations April 1981
Source: *New Earnings Survey 1981*, Department of Employment

prepared to try to illustrate the differential nature of the earnings received by individuals with different abilities. The figures must in no way be taken to be precise measurements of the economic rents accruing to different skills. It could be argued, with justification, that at least some of the differentials are part of the returns for the education and training that some people decide to undergo. However, in so far as entry into certain trades and professions included in the diagram may be due to a shortage of talents, or may even be artificially restricted, some part of the earnings differentials are of the nature of economic rent.

Risk[2]

What the man in the street calls **profit** economists call the **return on capital**. As well as an amount that would be earned on a riskless investment, the actual return includes, in

1 The issues discussed in this section are discussed in detail in Lipsey Chapter 20.
2 The issues discussed in this section are considered in some detail in Lipsey Chapter 28.

most cases of equity investment, a substantial risk premium. The riskier the investment in some classes of enterprise, the higher must be the return on those ventures that succeed. The high return on the successful ventures averages out with the losses on the unsuccessful ones, to provide an incentive for people to risk their capital *before* they know whether their particular venture will succeed or not.

Fig 53 gives information on the relative riskiness of investing money in a number of different companies as measured by the yields on their ordinary shares (see Chapter 2 page 30 for a definition of dividend yield). Ten companies are listed in the diagram. They have been specially selected for the purpose. Half are very large 'safe' companies, like Sears Holdings (see

*Fig 53* Dividend yields on selected equities 14 September 1982 Source: *The Times*

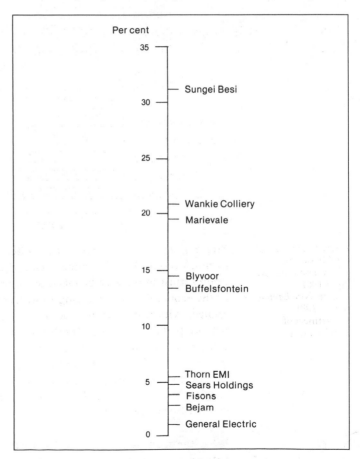

Fig 34 page 60), with a wide spread of commercial interests, or in fairly predictable industries, like Bejam. The other half are deliberately risky investments in mining, where it is something of a gamble whether they will make very large

profits or losses. The average yield on £100 invested in the former group in September 1982 was about a quarter of that in the latter. (Just in case any readers feel the urge to dash off and buy shares in some mining companies, let us warn you that the market assessment of the risk ought to be such as to make a portfolio of investments in the two sectors equally profitable!)

# 5 International trade and development[1]

Very few nations in the modern world are isolated from each other. They engage in trade in goods and services and in financial transactions of many kinds. The total record of international payments and receipts is to be found in the balance of payments of a country, which will be discussed in Chapter 7. For the present, we shall ignore purely financial transactions and concentrate on questions of the international allocation of resources and on patterns of trade.

## The basis of trade

International specialisation is no different in principle from interregional specialisation, which was examined in Chapter 3. We saw how different parts of the UK tend to concentrate on certain lines of economic activity. The reasons for this relate to their natural and acquired endowments of factors of production—the size and quality of their labour forces and their particular skills, the quantity and fertility of the land, the mineral resources below it and the amount of capital equipment that has been accumulated in the past.

In one important respect international variations in factor endowments are of greater significance than are interregional variations—factors of production are much more freely mobile *within* countries than *between* them. The reasons are largely linguistic and political, stemming from the existence of national frontiers which impede factor movement. However, there are also social and psychological barriers reflected in different national life styles, which discourage labour, in particular, from moving in search of the highest paid employment, regardless of where it may be. Moreover, the very existence of national governments and national currencies often leads to state intervention to protect industries from foreign competition.

Most international trade is based upon relative scarcities or abundances of different factors of production, which in turn give rise to relative cost advantages and disadvantages for individual countries when producing particular goods and services. In certain cases the disadvantage may be of an

1 The theory related to the issues discussed in this chapter is covered in Lipsey Part 6. See Chapters 11 and 30 for trade and Chapter 31 for development.

extreme kind, in the sense that a country may be incapable of producing something at all. In the main, however, these differences are due either to the uneven dispersion of minerals over the world or to the existence of regional variations in climate. Canada, for example, is rich in nickel deposits, Spain and Italy in mercury and South Africa in gold, while Britain has virtually none of these metals. Moreover, with her temperate climate Britain cannot grow such tropical and subtropical products as coffee, tea, cotton, rubber or cocoa. The only way in which she can obtain these and similar products is by importing them from abroad in exchange for goods and services which Britain produces for export.

Most trade, however, is between countries who have what is known as a **comparative advantage** in the production of some goods, which they export, and a **comparative disadvantage** in the production of others, which they import. This means that although a country could produce the goods that it imports, the relative costs are such as to encourage specialisation in some goods and importation of others.

**The major nations in international trade**

Before looking at the detailed structure of the trade of the UK we should put the country in perspective by taking note of the major world trading nations. Fig 54 shows the values of total imports and exports of the 10 leading trading nations, which together are responsible for about 60 per cent of all international trade. It is immediately apparent that there are great differences among these leaders. The scene is dominated by the USA, Germany and Japan, which together account for about 30 per cent of world exports.

The UK occupies the fifth or sixth position, depending on whether one is looking at imports or exports. This is a very different picture from that of earlier years, for Britain's importance in world trade has been undergoing a period of long-term decline. This downward trend is of special significance in the case of exports of manufactured goods, where Britain traditionally dominated the field. At the beginning of the present century the UK was responsible for no less than a third of the world total. As Fig 55 shows, however, the last 30 years have witnessed a fairly steady fall in Britain's share. Although the rate of decline tailed off during the 1970s, the UK's share of under 9 per cent in 1981 was an all-time low. In that year the United States, Germany and Japan each had almost double Britain's share, and together accounted for well over half the world total.

The size of a country's exports or imports can be very misleading as a guide to the significance of foreign trade to

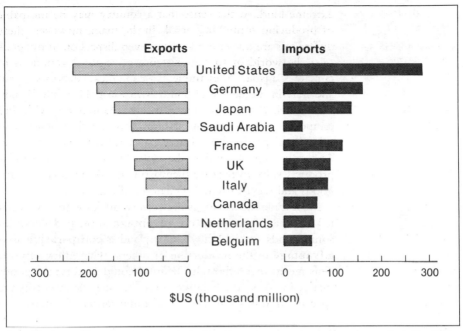

| Exports | | Imports |
| United States | | |
| Germany | | |
| Japan | | |
| Saudi Arabia | | |
| France | | |
| UK | | |
| Italy | | |
| Canada | | |
| Netherlands | | |
| Belguim | | |

300  200  100  0     0  100  200  300

$US (thousand million)

*Fig 54* Major trading nations; values of exports and imports in US dollars 1981
Source: *International Financial Statistics*, International Monetary Fund

*Fig 55* Percentage share in world trade in manufactures 1951–81
Source: *National Institute Economic Review*

that nation. A very large country can have an extensive foreign trade which is nevertheless *proportionately* small in comparison with that of a much less important nation. A useful measure of the importance of foreign trade to a country is the relationship between the value of its imports and its total national income. Fig 56 shows the very wide variations which exist between some representative nations. The USA, for example, which is the world's leading importing country, depends much less on imports than the majority of others. Only about 10 per cent of its total income is spent on imported goods, whilst a relatively small country like

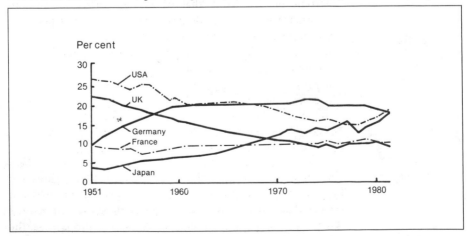

Per cent

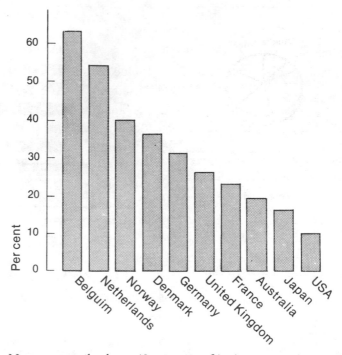

*Fig 56* Imports as a percentage of national income (GDP) for selected countries 1981 Source: *International Financial Statistics*

Norway spends about 40 per cent of its income on imports. Belgium is even more dependent on trade and spends over half of its income on imports. Britain spends about a quarter. Thus, although a decline of, say, 50 per cent in foreign trade in the United States would make a big hole in the total volume of world trade, it would make comparatively little difference to the United States itself. On the other hand, the complete cessation of imports by Norway would have barely a 1 per cent effect on world trade as a whole, but it would disrupt the Norwegian economy very gravely.

**The trade of the UK**

The aggregate importance of trade to the UK has been summarised in Fig 56, ie imports as a percentage of total income. However, the detailed ways in which trade impinges on economic life can only be seen by studying the pattern of trade. We now look at two aspects of the trade of the UK:

- commodity composition
- geographical distribution

Commodity trade

The commodity composition of UK trade in 1980 is shown in Fig 57. It is important to stress that this composition is not typical of earlier periods. Chapter 1 described the major shifts that have taken place in British overseas trade during the

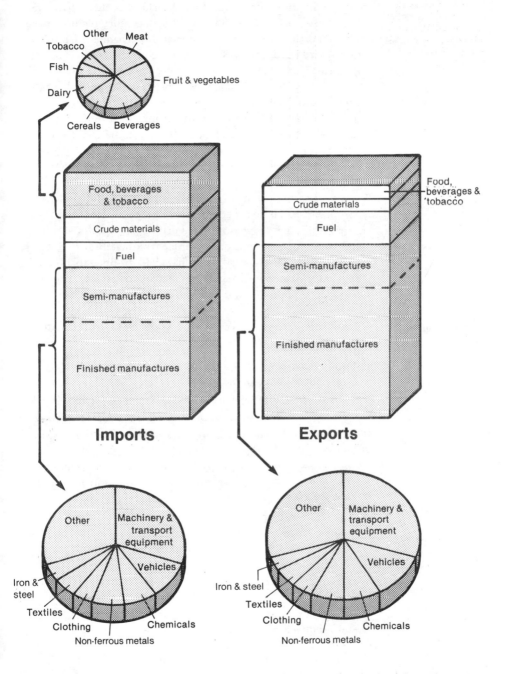

**Imports**

**Exports**

*Fig 57* Commodity trade of the UK 1980 Source: *Annual Abstract of Statistics*

present century—the reader is urged to review these sections, and in particular Figs 11 and 12 pages 12 and 13, at this point.

The pattern of imports today is one where manufactures and semi-manufactures account for about two-thirds of the total, whereas prior to the First World War their share was less than a quarter. The traditional 19th century picture of the UK exporting manufactured goods in exchange for imports of primary products has been eroded over the century, at first gradually and then at an accelerating pace during the last 20 years. British foreign trade now consists predominantly of the exchange of manufactured goods with other countries. The only raw material whose import has increased significantly in recent years has been fuel, although, as can be seen from Fig 57, Britain has become an even more important fuel exporter, largely as a result of the oil discoveries in the North Sea.

Although manufactures remain the solid backbone of Britain's exports, there have been substantial shifts in their composition. These reflect, in part, changes in the structure of British industry itself noted in Chapter 3. Textiles and iron and steel, for example, made up approximately half of total exports in 1913. By 1980 their share had dropped to a mere 5 per cent and their place had been taken by machinery, vehicles, transport equipment and chemicals, as Fig 57 shows.

*Import penetration and export sales ratios*

Two different aspects of commodity trade worthy of attention are:

- the extent to which foreign imports compete with domestically produced goods
- the relative importance of exports to total home production

Fig 58 throws light on both these matters. In the diagram, industries are listed in order of import penetration. The sector with the largest foreign share of the UK market is instrument engineering. Overseas manufacturers also take 30 or more per cent of domestic sales in vehicles, electrical and mechanical engineering, metal manufacture, textiles and clothing.

If we consider the industries with the highest ratio of exports to total sales we find a very considerable overlap with the first group. Of the top six industries in this category no less than five are also in the top manufacturing sectors ranked by import penetration. In the previous section we described British foreign trade as being characterised nowadays by an interchange of manufactures. We see now that this applies as much *within* industry groups as to exports of manufactures as a whole.

Fig 58, it should be added, presents data relating to a recent year, 1980, when imports accounted for about a quarter of domestic sales, and exports a similar percentage of home output. Both these figures show an appreciable increase since the beginning of the 1970s, when the ratios were only 17 and

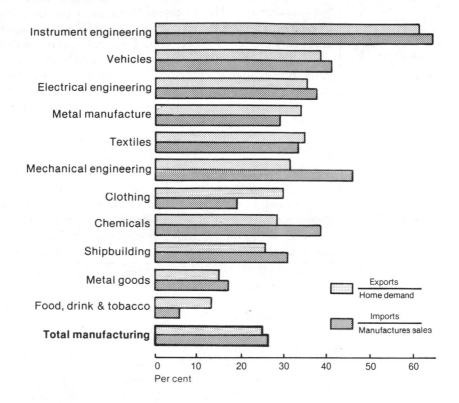

Instrument engineering

Vehicles

Electrical engineering

Metal manufacture

Textiles

Mechanical engineering

Clothing

Chemicals

Shipbuilding

Metal goods

Food, drink & tobacco

**Total manufacturing**

Exports / Home demand

Imports / Manufactures sales

0    10    20    30    40    50    60
Per cent

*Fig 58* UK import penetration and export sales ratios 1980 Source: *Annual Abstract of Statistics*

19 per cent respectively—in virtually every industry the ratios increased, in some cases very substantially, eg import penetration in vehicles rose from 15 to 39 per cent, in others by much less.

## Geographical distribution of UK trade

The geographical composition of UK trade is illustrated by three diagrams; Fig 59 traces the major shifts in percentage distribution by destination of British exports, and Figs 60 and 61 show details of Britain's main markets and suppliers in 1980.

*Europe*

The nations of Europe, taken as a whole, are at once the largest group both as suppliers and as markets for the UK. In 1980 they bought well over half of British exports and provided roughly as high a proportion of the country's imports. This has not always been the situation, however. The importance of Europe as a trading partner has increased substantially and fairly steadily since the Second World War. The growth can be attributed principally to the changed structure of UK trade—the fall in importance of imports of

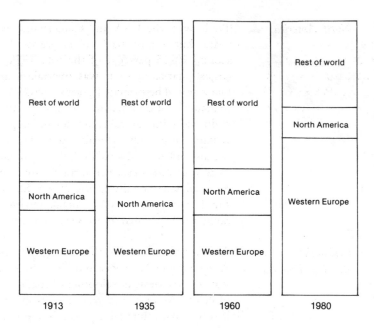

*Fig 59* UK exports; percentage distribution by destination in selected years 1913–80 Sources: *Abstract of British Historical Statistics*, B R Mitchell and P Deane, Cambridge University Press, 1962, and *Annual Abstract of Statistics*

primary products relative to manufactured goods—and to declining trading links between Britain and the Commonwealth, which used to occupy the dominant trading position. The postwar trend towards increasing European trade received a boost in 1973 when the United Kingdom joined the countries of the Common Market in the European Economic Community (EEC—see pages 107–9).

Figs 60 and 61 divide Europe into two parts—members of the EEC, and the rest. The former can be seen to be much the more important of the two; in 1980 it accounted for about 40 per cent of total import and export trade from all sources. The situation may be compared with that of the early 1960s when the same countries took only about half that proportion.

Within the Common Market, Germany is Britain's major market and supplier of imports (mainly machinery and manufactured goods including cars and chemicals). Next in importance are France (which sends Britain manufactures and food) and the Netherlands (dairy produce and other foodstuffs). Ireland is more important as a market for UK exports than as a supplier of imports. The shares of the other EEC member countries can be seen in Figs 60 and 61.

Countries outside the EEC together supplied only about a third of total UK imports from Europe. Of them, only Switzerland, Sweden and Norway were sufficiently important to be shown on the diagram.

*North America*

Trade with the USA and Canada rose in the early postwar years, but is now back to its prewar level, accounting for around 10–15 per cent of the total. The USA was Britain's largest market until it was overtaken in the late 1970s by Germany. The principal goods the USA sends to Britain are machinery and other manufactures, but she is also richly endowed with natural resources and exports some of them to Britain, especially cereals, tobacco, cotton, non-ferrous metals and ores. Canada's links with the United Kingdom were much greater when intra-Commonwealth trade was in its heyday, especially in the 1930s. She is still an important supplier of wood and pulp, metals and ores and foodstuffs, and ranks roughly equal in importance today with, say, Norway.

*Rest of the 'developed' world*

The four nations in this category, Japan, South Africa, Australia and New Zealand, may be said to have reached a state of economic development broadly comparable with that of North America and Western Europe; they are accordingly, if somewhat arbitrarily, placed in the same group. The trade of the four together, however, is only about half that of the United States and Canada. Japan heads the list of Britain's suppliers, with machinery and manufactures, including motor vehicles. Australia, New Zealand and South Africa were of far greater importance in the days of Imperial and Commonwealth preference (see page 106), as was Canada, and remained so for the first postwar decade. Exports to the UK from Australia consist principally of foodstuffs and minerals; from South Africa they are a little more varied and include manufactured goods as well as cereals, metals, fruit and vegetables; from New Zealand they are substantially meat and dairy produce.

*Developing countries*

The final group of countries are the so-called 'developing', or less-developed, countries. There are two main subdivisions within this category—the oil-exporting countries and the rest. The former group sprang into prominence following a quadrupling of the price of crude oil in 1973–74. Since Britain was still a substantial oil importer in 1980 it is no surprise to see the oil-exporting countries accordingly featuring quite large in Figs 60 and 61. For the first few years after the oil price rise Britain's imports from the oil-exporting countries were greater than exports to them. By 1980, however, the position had been reversed, except in the case of Saudi Arabia, Britain's largest supplier.

A host of other developing countries are included in the 'others' section in Figs 60 and 61. Few are of sufficient

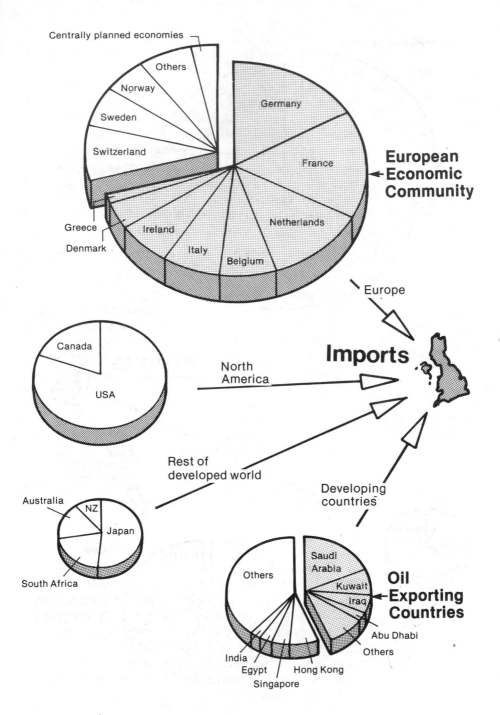

Fig 60 UK imports by
origin 1980
Source: *Annual
Abstract of Statistics*

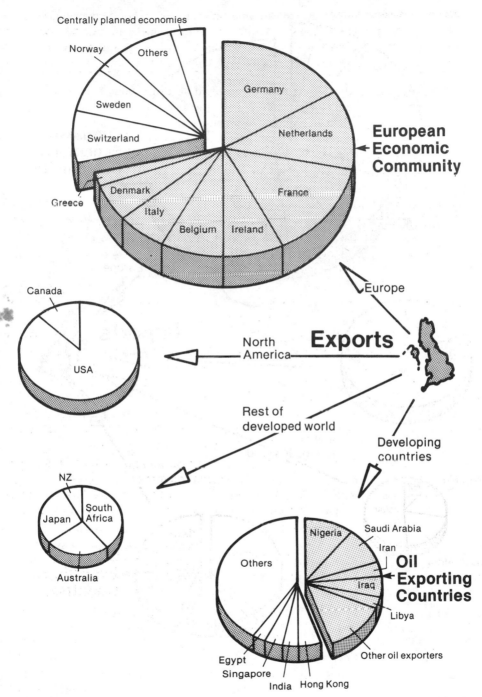

Centrally planned economies
Norway
Others
Germany
Sweden
Netherlands
Switzerland
**European Economic Community** ←
Denmark
Greece
France
Italy
Belgium Ireland

Canada

North America
**Exports**
Europe

USA

Rest of developed world

Developing countries

NZ
South Africa
Japan
Australia

Others
Nigeria
Saudi Arabia
Iran
**Oil Exporting Countries** ←
Iraq
Libya
Other oil exporters
Egypt
Singapore
India   Hong Kong

*Fig 61* UK exports by
destination 1980
Source: *Annual
Abstract of Statistics*

importance to warrant specific mention, but it is worth noting Hong Kong, as a supplier of miscellaneous manufactures, and India and Singapore, with whom trade, quantitatively speaking, is on a par with, say, Finland.

The terms of trade

The trading patterns outlined in the previous sections are the result of many forces. Prime among them are the prices of goods in different countries. Prices are affected by the rate of exchange between currencies, which will be discussed in Chapter 9. We can, however, make a start on this subject by looking at what are known as the **terms of trade**, defined as the price of exports divided by the price of imports.

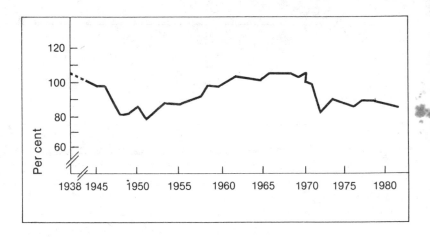

*Fig 62* Terms of trade UK 1938 and 1945–81; quantity of imports obtainable for a fixed quantity of exports (an upward movement corresponds to an improvement in the UK's terms of trade) Sources: *The British Economy, Key Statistics, 1900–70,* London and Cambridge Economic Service, and *Annual Abstract of Statistics*

The movements of the terms of trade since 1938 are plotted in Fig 62. It can be seen that the UK began the postwar period with much higher import prices, relative to those of exports, than in the 1930s. In 1951 there was a short sharp deterioration associated with the shortage of raw materials at the time of the Korean War. The following 20 years saw a gradual improvement in the terms of trade, which greatly helped the trade balance until the violent adverse shock of 1973–74, when the price of oil quadrupled following the action of the OPEC countries and the prices of many other primary products also rose substantially. Between 1972 and 1974 the world price of copper, lead, tin and cotton approximately doubled; that of zinc, rubber and cocoa tripled; and that of sugar went up by a multiple of four. It is true that the prices of goods that Britain exports were also rising at the time, but not nearly so rapidly.

In the last 10 years or so relative prices have moved only slightly, and by 1982 were at about the level achieved just after the oil price shock of 1973–74.

ing nations engage in reciprocal bargaining with each other for tariff and other trade concessions. GATT works slowly— the Tokyo Round took 5 years to complete. With 99 nations participating (only 70 of which were full GATT members, incidentally) this is perhaps not surprising.

The Tokyo negotiations secured pledges for tariff reductions by about one-third over 8 years by the industrial countries. It is, however, difficult to assess their quantitative importance for the volume of world trade for many reasons, not the least being the growth of so-called 'non-tariff barriers', such as the use of arbitrary bases on which to calculate tariffs. An attempt to operate a code for such barriers was begun in Tokyo in 1979.

## The European Economic Community (EEC)

Although the Common Market, or EEC, has been introduced in the context of trade restrictions, it must be appreciated that the creation of the European Community was designed to be a far more comprehensive economic union than a mere free trade area.

The origins of the EEC are to be found in the disruption caused in Europe by the Second World War and in subsequent US (Marshall) aid to the stricken countries, followed by the establishment of the Organisation for Economic Cooperation and Development (OECD).

The first move in the direction of a common market came about with an economic union between Belgium, Luxembourg and the Netherlands (into Benelux) shortly after the end of the war. They then joined France, Germany and Italy in 1952 to form the European Coal and Steel Community, aimed at creating a unified market in these products. Five years later the Six, as they were called, signed the Treaty of Rome establishing the EEC and outlining a programme for the elimination of tariffs between themselves and a unified schedule of import duties for outsiders. There were other aims too, such as a common agricultural policy (see pages 140–1), the free movement of people and capital within the EEC, and the harmonisation of tax rates and structures and even of social policies.

The UK was at first reluctant to join the Common Market, partly on political grounds and partly because of her links with the Commonwealth. Instead, Britain made an agreement with Austria, Denmark, Norway, Portugal, Sweden and Switzerland (and subsequently Finland) to set up the European Free Trade Association (EFTA) in 1960. The aims of EFTA were more modest than those of the EEC. In one particular way they were attractive for Britain. Although tariffs were to be abolished within the Association, a common *external* tariff was not included. This allowed the UK to continue Commonwealth preferences.

Meanwhile, the countries of the Common Market were, in general, enjoying more favourable conditions with regard to living standards, inflation and the balance of payments than the UK. At the same time Britain's trade with the Commonwealth was declining. The UK therefore decided to apply for EEC membership, but the first application was turned down (effectively by the French) in 1962. However the second application, in 1973, was successful. The admission of the UK, Ireland and Denmark thus turned the Six into the Nine and then, with Greece's admission in 1981, into the Ten. Britain's entry was followed by a four year period during which tariffs were gradually lifted, all tariffs between the UK and the other member countries being finally eliminated in 1977, when the common external tariff on goods from non-members was also fully imposed.

The decision to enter Europe was a highly controversial one for the UK, a national referendum even being held in 1974 to determine whether or not to continue membership. Arguments were heard on both sides. Pro-Marketeers stressed three principal potential areas of gain: the advantages of large-scale production; of specialisation under free trade between members of the EEC; and the hope that high rates of economic growth would spill over to Britain. Anti-Marketeers were sceptical about the economies of scale argument. They were more concerned with the common external tariff which discriminates against imports from low cost producers outside the EEC. This was held to apply with force to primary products, including foodstuffs, under the Common Agricultural Policy. Opponents were also sceptical of the belief that high growth rates were *caused* by the EEC and that these growth rates would spill over to Britain. A heavy majority was in favour of continued membership when the referendum was taken.

It is difficult, even with hindsight, to know whether the right decision was taken. On the one hand, food prices are certainly higher than they were before Britain joined the Common Market, and the high growth rates of the first members have not been maintained. Moreover, an aspect which was not, perhaps, fully appreciated in the referendum days subsequently came to light in the shape of a heavy contribution to the Community budget from the UK in the late 1970s. On the other hand, it can be argued that despite these disadvantages, the performance of the British economy would have been much worse if she had remained outside the EEC. No one will ever know for sure which set of arguments is correct. They are exceedingly difficult to test. At least the British experience did not deter others from trying to join the Community; Greece became the tenth country in the EEC in 1981, and Spain and Portugal have outstanding applications for membership.

## Economic development

One outstanding characteristic of the international economy is the inequality of the distribution of income among countries. The world's population is over 4000 million. Over half live in

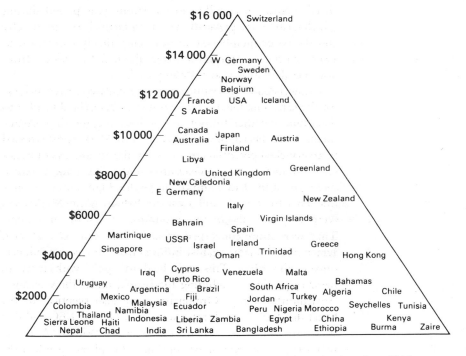

*Fig 64* Average income per head; estimated GNP per capita in US $, selected countries 1980 Source: *1981 World Bank Atlas*, International Bank for Reconstruction and Development

countries where the income per head is less than £200 per year (at 1980 prices), compared with 15 per cent of the population in the richest countries where average per capita income exceeds £5000 per annum.

Fig 64 shows the income per head of the population for nearly 100 countries. It is shaped like a pyramid because there are relatively few countries with high average incomes but many with low ones. It must, however, be treated with great caution for a variety of reasons, some of them technical in nature. Moreover, it is important to emphasise that income per head is not by any means the same thing as 'happiness'.

This is a subject beyond the boundaries of economics and involves consideration of life styles in different countries. It would be foolhardy to offer an opinion that someone in the UK watching a videorecorded colour TV programme was more or less 'happy' than an Indian listening to a local village singer.

Bearing these reservations in mind, we can examine Fig 64. Clearly, some of the differences in income per head are enormous and can hardly be due solely to statistical errors. Countries at the top of the scale enjoy per capita incomes as much as 100 or more times those at the bottom. These are, of course, extreme cases. Grouping countries together gives, perhaps, a clearer picture. If we compare the richest 20 countries in the world with the 20 poorest the difference remains substantial. The former have an average income per head about 50 times that of the latter.

The reasons why some countries have low and others high incomes per head are complex. They relate in part to the natural resources with which nations are endowed. However, per capita incomes are also affected by the size of the populations in different countries. It can hardly be an accident that some of the poorest countries are those with large and rapidly increasing populations. China and India alone have about 40 per cent of the total world population, double that of the whole of Europe and North America.

With the passage of time some countries have lifted themselves out of poverty. However, the overall inequality between rich and poor is increasing rather than diminishing. This is because rates of economic growth tend to be low for the poorest countries, many of which also have rapid population increases to cope with.

The consciences of rich countries have been pricked by the growing gap in living standards between themselves and the poor countries of the 'Third World' and by the large number of nations at the bottom of the scale. However action to help the less developed countries of the world has not been on the massive scale that would be necessary to make a substantial impact on international income inequality. The United Nations Organisation set a target of 0.75 per cent of national income for developed countries to contribute as aid for their poorer neighbours, but few countries have consistently achieved this. The United States has been by far the largest donor, supplying almost half of all aid in recent years, though Saudi Arabia topped the list of donors in 1981. The UK has not fallen as far behind target as some other advanced countries, about half the total British aid being official government financing.

There are a number of international agencies specifically concerned with economic development. They include the World Bank (the International Bank for Reconstruction and Development—IBRD—to give it its full title) which makes loans for economic development and provides expert field service teams to assist with projects. The funds for loans are in the main derived by borrowing in the capital markets of member countries. Accordingly interest is charged to borrowers. Moreover, the charter of the World Bank requires its loans to be guaranteed by governments in borrowing countries. Such guarantees are not always easy to obtain for private businesses. An affiliate but independent organisation, the International Finance Corporation (IFC), was set up in 1956 to help overcome this problem. A second affiliate of the World Bank is the International Development Association (IDA). This was established in 1960 to make 'soft' loans to less developed countries on generous terms, usually without interest charges. The Bank and its affiliates have made loans totalling many billions of dollars since their inception; a substantial sum, though small in comparison with the total of aid from all sources. Only about 20 per cent, moreover, has come from the IDA.

An alternative method of assisting the poorer countries of the world is by 'trade not aid'. The prime international organisation concerned with the promotion of trade is UNCTAD (The United Nations Conference on Trade and Development) established in 1964 under the auspices of the United Nations Organisation. High sounding resolutions have been passed at UNCTAD conferences and a so-called 'north–south dialogue' has attempted to integrate the economies of some Third World countries more closely with those of the developed nations, especially in Europe. One of UNCTAD's policies was the introduction, in 1971, of a general system of preferences (GSP), the object of which is to give the exports of manufactured goods from less developed countries preferential access to markets in developed nations. Success with GSP has, however, been less than the poorer nations had hoped for because of qualifications and limitations placed on it in many advanced countries. UNCTAD did, however, mark up an achievement in 1978 when it was agreed by a number of developed countries, including the UK, that some of the poorest nations should be relieved of at least part of their outstanding debts. GATT is another international organisation which is involved in measures to assist developing countries. Several were included in the Tokyo Round (see page 106) when, for example, tropical products were given priority treatment.

The implications of trade restrictions and economic development discussed in the closing sections of this chapter raise problems for government policy, as we have seen. Chapter 6 will consider the role of the state with regard to resource allocation.

a very large scale, eg to finance wars and, more recently, to pay compensation to industries taken into public ownership. The total outstanding balance is known as the **national debt**. In 1950, after the Second World War and the large nationalisation programme of the Labour government, the debt stood at a figure of about £25 000 million. Compared with the size of the national income, this was an all-time high—approximately 250 per cent. Although by 1982 the total outstanding national debt had risen to more than £100 000 million, this figure was only half the size of the annual national income. Moreover, something like a sixth of the total consisted of government securities held by government departments. The net *change* in public sector debt can be understood as a measure of the government's need to borrow to finance an excess of expenditure over income in any year. It is known as the **public sector borrowing requirement** (**PSBR**).

## International comparisons of tax burdens

The level of taxation as a proportion of national income, as we saw in Chapter 1, has been rising very considerably during the present century. It is of some interest to compare the situation

*Fig 66* Taxes and social security contributions as a percentage of GNP in selected countries 1979 (shaded areas are social security contributions) Source: *Economic Trends*, December 1981

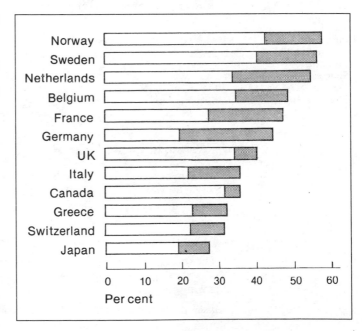

in the United Kingdom with that in other countries. Fig 66 shows that the UK is not, contrary to popular belief, the most heavily taxed nation in the world; Norway, Sweden, the Netherlands, Belgium, France and Western Germany are all ahead of Britain in the 'league table'.

In interpreting Fig 66 it is important to remember that the lengths of the bars in the diagram indicate total taxes *and* social security contributions as proportions of national income. Countries differ greatly as to the relative importance of these components of revenue, as can be seen. Some, such as France, Italy and the Netherlands, derive approximately two-fifths of total government income from social security contributions, while others, including the UK, take less than half this proportion. Countries also vary in their choice of methods used to achieve given objectives, and these can result in the figures being misleading. For example, help can be given to people through the tax system, eg by giving tax deductions for families, or via the expenditure side of the account, eg through a system of family allowances. Lastly, it must be borne in mind that similar overall average tax burdens can conceal quite different tax treatments for particular groups.

## Expenditure

The principal categories of total government expenditure, ie both central and local, are shown in Fig 67. There are several ways of classifying them; the method used here is based on specific programmes, ie for defence, social security, etc.

*Fig 67* Public expenditure 1982–83 (planned)
Source: *Economic Progress Report No 143,* The Treasury, March 1982

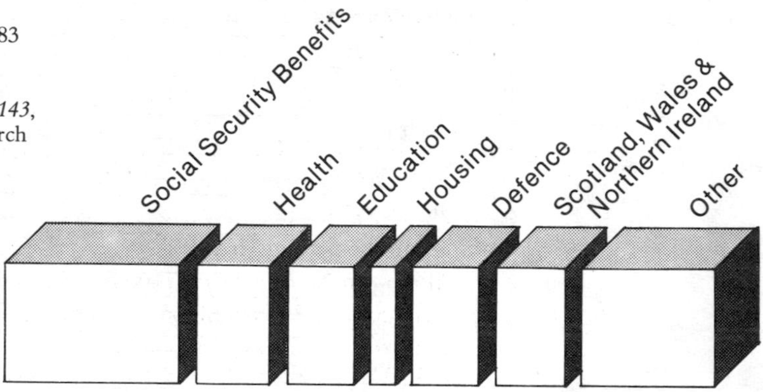

The social services are by far the largest category if the term is used to include health, education, housing and social security benefits provided out of national insurance contributions and taxation. Much of the expenditure on education and housing is paid for by local authorities. Defence is an important category, taking about 12 per cent of the government budget according to plans for 1982–83. The other items of expenditure are of a varied kind. About a tenth of the total is used to provide services in Scotland, Wales and Northern Ireland. The rest is used for such things as law and order, the construction and maintenance of roads, overseas aid, support for industry and agriculture (including both private sector and nationalised industries) and interest on the national debt, which varies both with the amount outstanding and the rate of interest payable on it.

As previously stated, the method used for classifying items of government expenditure for Fig 67 is not the only one possible. We could alternatively distinguish between **current expenditure**, such as retirement pensions and drugs for use in hospitals, and **capital expenditure**, such as the provision of new schools or prisons. The former is concerned with immediate effects on the distribution of income or resources. Capital expenditure, on the other hand, has lasting effects.

A third classification could be based on a distinction between what are known as **transfer payments** as distinct from **exhaustive expenditures**. Exhaustive expenditures are those on goods and services, such as roads and hospitals, where the state decides directly how the money should be spent. In contrast transfer payments, which include personal grants such as pensions and family income supplements, permit individual recipients to allocate the proceeds as they wish. Transfer payments have grown greatly relative to exhaustive expenditures in recent years.

A fourth and final classification could be between goods and services which benefit the community generally as distinct from those that are provided for individuals. The former are referred to as **public goods** and include roads, courts of law and environmental services. The latter comprise all transfers as well as hospital beds specifically for the sick and schools for the young. It has to be admitted, however, that many if not most classes of government expenditure have something of a public nature about them. For example, it is usually claimed that education benefits society generally, as well as the individuals who take personal advantage of it.

**Economic policies in the UK**

We now know enough about the government's budget to look at some of the ways in which it has been employed to pursue certain specific economic policy goals. It must be understood that virtually all the tools of policy have implications for both equity and efficiency. For example, taxation policy designed to redistribute income can affect resource allocation and growth; or competition policy (see pages 133 ff) directed at monopolies almost certainly influences also the distribution of income.

**Income redistribution**

Both sides of the government's budget, as well as rules and regulations, are used to try to bring about a distribution of income which society regards as in some sense fair. Many of these devices do not imply a search for simple equality between everybody, but instead involve questions of equity between the sexes, between different ethnic groups, allowances for varying needs, etc. Moreover, it is usual to accept that a degree of inequality commensurate with the reward of effort is desirable, so that a compromise distribution is sought, even on equity grounds.

The most obvious, though quantitatively not the most important, policy tool is taxation. Certain taxes are designed expressly to bear more heavily on higher income groups than on lower ones. Of outstanding significance in this connection is the progressive income tax. Fig 68 shows the progressiveness of income tax in 1982–83 by expressing the total tax burden as a proportion of total income for different income classes. It is important to emphasise that the diagram shows the situation only for a married couple without children whose entire income comes from the husband's employment

*Fig 68* Income tax for a married couple as a percentage of income 1982–83 (when there is no investment income and the wife is not earning)

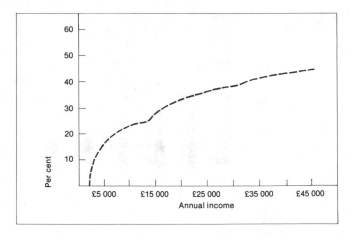

and who enjoy the minimum allowances. A different diagram could be drawn for any individual or family with different circumstances. For example, the tax burden would be higher if a substantial amount of income took the form of dividends on shares. This would make it subject to investment income surcharge. Alternatively, the burden would be lower for a blind person or if the individuals were buying a house on a mortgage, because of the additional tax allowances.

The picture which emerges from Fig 68 is, nevertheless, reasonably representative of the progressiveness of income tax in Britain. It can be seen that the proportion of income paid in tax rises with income. It is zero until all allowances have been used, but rises to a figure of 40 per cent at an income of a little more than £30 000 per annum. The progressiveness is due to the existence of the exemption limit, below which no tax is paid, and to the fact that the marginal rate of tax rises from the basic 30 per cent to 60 per cent on taxable incomes in excess of £27 750 (1982–83).

We should note, however, that the British tax system can involve a rather curious and highly regressive element, in that some individuals with low incomes may find themselves faced with a very steeply rising marginal tax rate. This arises from the fact that certain personal subsidies, such as family income supplement, are income-related. When the income of a person drawing such benefits rises above certain thresholds of eligibility, they may both lose the benefit and find them-selves paying income tax for the first time at the standard rate. The combined effect of withdrawal of benefit and liability to tax can mean that a low paid worker faces a very high effective tax rate on a marginal increase in income, sometimes even exceeding 100 per cent. This situation is sometimes described as the 'poverty trap'.

The general effect of income tax is, however, to reduce the

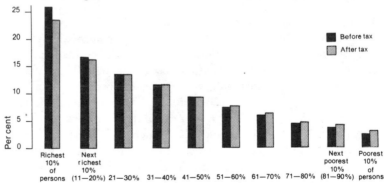

*Fig 69* Distribution of income before and after tax 1978–79 (decile shares)
Source: *Economic Trends*, February 1981

inequality of post-tax income compared with that before tax. Quantitatively, however, this impact is not very great, as can be seen from Fig 69 which shows the shares, pre- and post-tax, of different income groups in total income. (The groups are in ranges of 10 per cent, known as *deciles*, ie the richest 10 per cent of persons, the next richest decile, and so on.) The share of the richest decile declines from 26.1 per cent to 23.4 per cent after tax, while that of the poorest (bottom) decile rises from 2.4 per cent to 2.9 per cent as a result of income tax. If we had used the type of diagram in Fig 39 (see page 69) to show the effect of taxation, the Lorenz curve would have shifted a little towards the diagonal, implying a somewhat greater equality.)

There are two reasons why income tax is not a very powerful redistributive tool. The first is that its progressiveness arises largely from the deductible allowances rather than from rising tax rates. The allowances do not vary with income, though they do mean that the *average* tax paid rises as income rises. The thresholds at which higher rates of tax begin to operate come into play only at relatively high incomes, affecting only about 3 per cent of all taxpayers. In 1982–83 the thresholds were £11 250 taxable income for the 40 per cent rate and £27 750 taxable income for the top 60 per cent rate. Consequently the vast majority of taxpayers pay at the same standard rate of 30 per cent, though, of course, for the very rich the rate is much higher. If you were one of the 1000 or so tax units whose annual income exceeded £100 000 in 1978–79 the proportion of your total income paid in tax would be close to the maximum tax rate of 60 per cent.

The second reason for the relative ineffectiveness of income tax as a redistributive tool is that there are substantial numbers of individuals too poor to be liable to any income tax at all. Their incomes are, by definition, the same both pre- and post-tax.

| | |
|---|---|
| Income redistribution and the government's budget | Even a neutral tax (which is neither progressive nor regressive) can be used to finance spending in a way that involves redistribution. There are a good many items on the expenditure side of the account of the UK government that fall into this category. Benefits are provided both in cash and in kind, both of which have redistributive effects. **Cash benefits** include retirement and other pensions, unemployment and sickness benefits, student maintenance grants, maternity allowances and rent rebates. **Benefits in kind**, for example, are those from state education, the National Health Service and subsidies on housing and rail transport. The chief taxes on expenditure which should be taken into account are VAT, local rates and duties on alcohol, tobacco and fuel oil. |

It should be possible, in principle, to determine the full extent of redistribution brought about by the whole state budget. In practice, however, it is extremely difficult to produce reliable quantitative estimates. This is mainly because there is no sure way of ascertaining precisely how the benefits and burdens of each category in the accounts fall on different individuals and income groups. There are also some benefits, like defence and the police, which can only be allocated on an arbitrary basis. Nevertheless, we can with some confidence make the general point that the expenditure side of the budget is the more important of the two in effecting a more equal distribution of income. While income tax is progressive, if perhaps more mildly so than you may have suspected, the converse is true of certain taxes on expenditure, which tend to be regressive and fall relatively heavily on lower income groups.

**Non-budgetary redistributory tools**

Finally, it is essential to point out that there are many state acts which expressly, or by implication, affect the distribution of income. They include all interventions in the market place, such as price controls, import duties, regulations affecting the regional distribution of industry, etc. We cannot deal with them all here. However two kinds of measure specifically aimed at income redistribution are too important to ignore.

The first set of measures is directed towards the removal of inequalities due to sex or ethnic origin. We saw earlier (see page 82) that women tend to earn between half and two-thirds as much as men in industry. In an attempt to reduce this differential, two Acts of Parliament were passed. One, the Equal Pay Act of 1976, stipulated that men and women doing the same work should receive equal pay for doing so. It was reinforced by the Sex Discrimination Act of 1975 which forbade discrimination in employment between the sexes.

There is little doubt that the first Act did have some equalising effect, in that since it was passed average *hourly* earnings of women have risen from about two-thirds to about three-quarters of those of men. However, the average *weekly* earnings differential fell much less and female unemployment rates rose more rapidly than male rates. The main reasons why women are paid less than men are those pointed out in Chapter 4 page 82. They relate to the concentration of women in certain industries and occupational groups, their lower trade union membership and the fact that they work fewer hours, as well as such matters as job commitment and expenditure on training. These are far harder to legislate away.

Finally we must consider wage settlements as an important determinant of income distribution. We saw in Chapter 4 that in many industries these settlements are the result of collective bargaining between trade unions and employers' organisations. However, the public claims an interest as well as the parties involved, to ensure that negotiations are conducted in a reasonable manner and that the resulting settlements are fair. Government intervention in the field of industrial relations has several aspects. Those directed at the avoidance of strikes are discussed in the final chapter of this book, but we should refer here to bodies known as wages councils which were set up to fix minimum wages in industries where negotiating machinery was regarded as inadequate. There are about 35 wages councils in existence, in industries such as clothing and textiles, and there are similar arrangements for agricultural wages. Review bodies have been formed for assistance in the settlement of pay negotiations, mainly of professional workers and employees in the public sector, eg for members of the armed forces, doctors and dentists and those earning the so-called 'top salaries' (senior civil servants, judges, chairmen of the boards of nationalised industries, etc). For a brief period there was even a standing Commission on Pay Comparability (known as the Clegg Commission, after its chairman). It was set up by a Labour government in 1979 and abolished by a Conservative one in 1980. At the national level governments have from time to time set up pay boards and issued 'guidelines' for wage settlements as part of their anti-inflation policies. Discussion of these is deferred to Chapter 9.

**Trends in the size distribution of income**

Most of the previous discussion has been focused on the current distribution of income. However, we must also consider how it has been changing as a result both of government action and of market forces.

Comparisons of income distribution over longish periods are extremely difficult to make. The subject is, however, an important one and in 1974 the government set up a standing Royal Commission (known as the Diamond Commission, after the name of its chairman) to report on the facts of the situation. The Commission produced eight lengthy and complex reports which are capable of more than one interpretation and are difficult to summarise. However, the Commission did observe a long-term decline in the share of the highest income groups in the period between the late 1940s and the 1970s. Those in the top percentile, ie with incomes which put them in the top 1 per cent of the population, suffered a virtual halving of their share of income, from about 11 per cent to about $5\frac{1}{2}$ per cent of the total. Those in the top 10 per cent (including of course the top 1 per cent) suffered a fall in their share from about a third to a quarter of total income.

If the highest income classes lost, other groups must have gained and it seems clear that the chief beneficiaries were the middle income groups. Within the top half of income earners those lower down the scale gained approximately as much as the top 10 per cent lost, so that the share of the top half of income earners as a whole remained virtually unchanged (at about three-quarters of total income). On balance, the lowest half of the population neither gained nor lost over this long period—both at the beginning and at the end they were receiving about a quarter of total income. Let it be clear that these are long-term changes. In the short-term, from year to year, the experience has at times been different.

It is important to point out that the changing shares described in the preceding paragraphs relate to pre-tax income. Post-tax changes were in general smaller. Moreover, when looking for explanations of the trends we must look at such matters as the determinants of factor shares and of the distribution of earnings (see pages 71–2 and 79–84). Thus, trends in the supply of and demand for labour with different skills and the overall state of the economy, including the general level of unemployment, are likely to be important. We should also recognise the relevance of the social and demographic structure of the population in this connection. In so far as income is related to age and education, for example, changes in the proportion of the population engaged in full-time education or over retirement age will be likely to have an effect on the size distribution of income. Finally, we have to take account of the fact that income is partly derived from the ownership of capital assets which bring in income, and that this, too, is liable to change over time.

*Income distribution and price changes*

One influence on the distribution of income that is not often discussed is that of changes in relative prices. Movements in the *average* level of prices are usually measured by what is called the **Index of Retail Prices (RPI)**, published monthly by the government. This index shows what is happening to the cost of living as represented by the prices of a typical 'basket' of goods and services bought by the average household. In the basket are the goods most commonly consumed, with 'weights' attached to them representing their relative importance in the average household budget.

Movements in the RPI record changes in the cost of living between two dates for an average family. Such a family spends about a fifth of its income on food, about a sixth on housing, a seventh on transport and vehicles, a tenth on services, and a twelfth on each of clothing, alcoholic drink and tobacco, and durable household goods. The average family is, of course, only a statistical artefact. For any individuals or groups the index may not accurately portray *their* cost of living. That will depend on their own expenditure pattern because all prices do not move in line together.

Fig 70 shows price level changes for different commodity groups between 1974 and 1982. During this period the index number for the *average* price level (RPI) was 320 on the base of 1974. However, as can be seen, the price indices for fuel and light and for tobacco were both over 400, while those for clothing and durable household goods were both under 300.

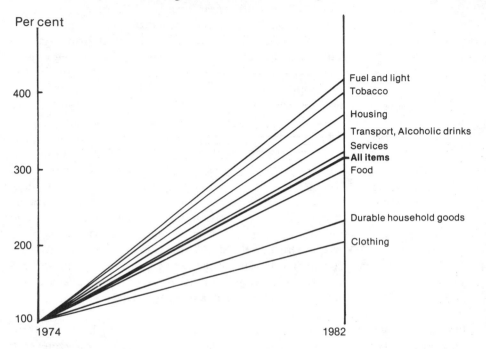

Per cent

400
300
200
100

1974                                        1982

Fuel and light
Tobacco

Housing

Transport, Alcoholic drinks
Services
**All items**
Food

Durable household goods

Clothing

*Fig 70* Index of retail prices; percentage increase of major classes of goods and services in April 1982 compared with 1974 Source: *Monthly Digest of Statistics*

The effect of these wide variations in the rate of inflation for different commodity groups on the distribution of real income depends, of course, on the relative importance of each of these items in household budgets. Fig 71, by way of illustration, shows how households at three different income levels were affected. We can see that the three classes of goods which rose most in price between 1974 and 1982 (fuel and light, tobacco, and housing) were relatively more important in the budget of low income groups than of high ones. At the same time, the two classes of goods which rose least in price during the same period (clothing and durable household goods) were relatively more important in the budget of high income groups.

One should be careful before concluding from the information in Figs 70 and 71 that relative price changes have had an inegalitarian influence. The effect of changing relative prices is a complex matter and the full effect of different weights in the indices must be taken into account. Moreover the evidence of

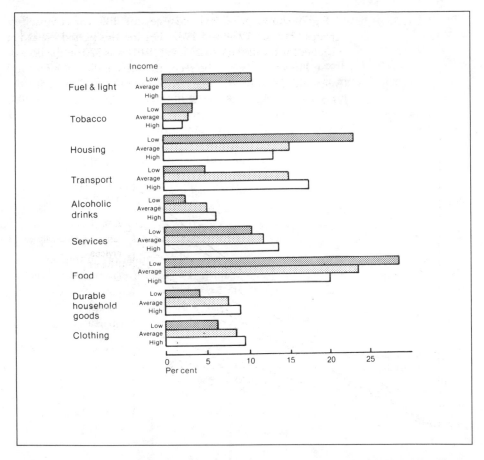

*Fig 71* Household
expenditure at
different income
levels; percentage of
total expenditure on
commodity groups
1980 (high income =
top 20 per cent; low
income = bottom 10
per cent of income
distribution)
Source: *Family
Expenditure Survey
1980*, Department of
Employment, 1982

Fig 70 relates specifically to a precise period (1974–82). Choice
of alternative periods and different base dates can result in
different conclusions—'index-mongering' is a refined sport.

Furthermore, redistribution should not be considered only
from the point of view of different groups of persons distinguished by their income levels. Consumption patterns are
affected by many other considerations, of which family size
and age are perhaps the most important. The government
publishes regular indices of the cost of living for pensioner
households as well as the more general RPI. Over the period
we have been discussing, the pensioner index for 1982 was
321 (on the same base of 1974), while the RPI was 315,
showing a very slight worsening of the purchasing power of
the pound for pensioners compared with the population as a
whole. Between 1977 and 1981, for example, pensioners in
contrast did marginally better than average.

## The distribution of wealth

One explanation of why some people are rich and others poor is that relatively few individuals receive a disproportionately high share of income derived from the ownership of capital. The top 1 per cent of recipients of income receive almost a quarter of the total investment income; for them investment income accounts for a much higher percentage of their total income than it does for the rest of the population. Hence, even if *earned* incomes were evenly distributed, *total* incomes from employment and all other sources would not be equal among individuals because of the distribution of wealth. What then are the facts?

A census of personal wealth has not been taken in modern Britain and it is necessary to rely on estimates of the shares of different groups in the total. This is a particularly difficult exercise and results tend to be highly controversial. It was one of the tasks given to the Royal Commission on the Distribution of Income and Wealth. The Commission admitted that it could make no single unambiguous statement on the ownership of personal property for many reasons, not the least being the difficulty of quantifying the property of the lowest

*Fig 72* Distribution of marketable personal wealth 1980
Source: *Inland Revenue Statistics*

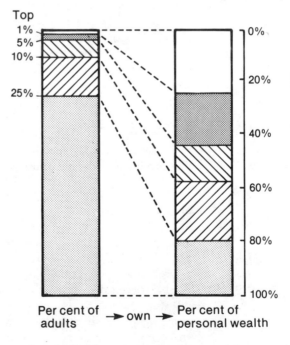

groups of wealth holders. Several estimates of the distribution of personal wealth, based on different assumptions, were therefore presented. Fig 72 uses figures chosen from among them. It should, therefore, be treated with particular caution as far as precise figures are concerned, but it serves to emphasise one undisputed feature; that the degree of inequality in the distribution of personal wealth is substantially greater than that of personal income. For example, whereas the top 10 per cent of *income units* receive roughly a quarter of total income (see above), the share of the top 10 per cent of wealth holders in marketable wealth is about 60 per cent. Even if pension rights are counted as wealth, the percentage is still between 35 and 50 per cent.

The concentration of personal wealth in relatively few hands is no new feature of society. It results from many factors, of which inheritance and the tendency for people to accumulate wealth during their working lives and decumulate it after retirement, are the most important. The distribution is liable to change as the prices of the different assets comprising wealth alter over time. Chief among them are land, houses, shares and other securities, which are held in different proportions by rich and poor. Year to year fluctuations in the distribution of wealth can be very considerable, but one can discern a long-term reduction in the degree of inequality, particularly as measured by a declining share of the top 1 per cent of wealth holders in total wealth during the present century. To the extent that this is partly offset by an increasing share of other wealth holders within the top 20 per cent, it might indicate a spread of wealth within families rather than a more general redistribution.

## Government and economic efficiency

The term efficiency as used in economics has a wider connotation than in everyday speech, where it usually means simply that production is at minimum cost. In economics, efficiency has this meaning too, but it extends also to refer to the allocation of goods and services itself. Cases where there are thought to be too few of some goods and services or too many of others are taken as evidence of inefficient production. They can occur because of the failure of market forces arising from lack of competition, the existence of social costs or benefits differing from private ones, or other failures of the market system.

There are many areas where the state intervenes to try to improve resource allocation—we can only illustrate them here by looking at a few.

## Competition policy

The extent of concentration of industry in large enterprises, both overall and some sectors is, as we saw in Chapter 3 page 56 ff, very considerable. It is clear, too, that the power that stems from the control of a high proportion of an industry's output in a few large businesses can be a matter for public concern. Firms, or groups of firms, which attain such positions are knwn as **monopolies**. Moreover, especially if they can prevent the entry of new firms into the industry, they are able to fix prices and act in other ways that may be damaging to consumers.

Barriers to entry can take many forms. Some are man-made, such as the patenting of products and the deliberate restriction of entry to an industry by large firms or groups of firms acting in collusion. Some are technologically dictated, such as substantial economies of large-scale production that leave room in an industry for only one or a few firms operating at an efficient scale of output.

Government may choose from a range of possible policies to control monopolies. An industry may be nationalised or pricing and investment policies may be regulated. Competition may be encouraged from overseas by lowering barriers to international trade (see pages 106–7). However, a much more general approach towards competition policy has grown up in the UK since the end of the Second World War. It has three main strands, concerned with:

- monopolies
- restrictive practices
- mergers

*Monopolies*

The first step was taken in 1948 with the establishment of the **Monopolies Commission**. The legislation defined a monopoly as existing when a single firm or group of firms controlled at least a third of the supply of a product (subsequently lowered to a quarter). The Monopolies Commission was given broad powers to inquire into industries where a monopoly was suspected, in order to ascertain if this was the case and, if so, whether or not the activities of these businesses operated against the public interest. In the years since it was set up, the Commission has made about 150 reports on industries from electric lamps to cross channel ferries. In the vast majority of cases it found practices to be operating against the public interest, price-fixing and measures to prevent the entry of new firms.

*Restrictive practices*

The second aspect of what has come to be called competition policy is concerned not so much with monopolies as with restrictive practices by *groups* of firms acting together, eg to fix prices. The background to this development was the early work of the Monopolies Commission in uncovering apparently widespread practices which were deemed to be contrary to the public interest. It was felt that the best way of tackling them was by special legislation. The Restrictive Practices Act of 1956 forced firms to register agreements affecting the supply of goods with a Registrar of Restrictive Practices, who could take proceedings against them to a Restrictive Practices Court. The presumption of the law is that all such agreements are contrary to the public interest unless special circumstances can be shown to exist, such as that they provide a substantial net benefit to the consuming public.

About 4500 agreements have been registered, although the vast majority were abandoned voluntarily and only a tiny proportion were contested before the Court, of which about a third were allowed to continue. The majority were found to be against the public interest and declared void, including the famous Cotton Yarn Spinners' Agreement—in spite of the fact that the Court accepted the argument that local unemployment would follow the abandonment of this agreement, it was held that this was not in itself sufficient to offset its detrimental effect of restricting competition.

Another development was the Resale Prices Act of 1964. The Act prohibited agreements, even by individual manufacturers, to fix minimum resale prices of their goods by retailers in advance, unless granted exemption by the Restrictive Practices Court. This piece of legislation was particularly effective. About 500 applications for exemption were made, the vast majority being refused. As a result of the Act the previously widespread practice of fixed prices for goods in all shops virtually disappeared from Britain; by shopping around, one can now usually buy most articles 'at a discount'.

*Mergers*

Subsequent legislation added services as well as goods to the references that could be made to the Monopolies Commission, and a further class of registrable agreement relating to the exchange of information between firms about prices. The next important development, representing the third strand in government policy, focused on mergers. As we saw in Chapter 3 pages 64–5, a merger movement of very considerable proportions began in the 1960s and has been responsible for at least half the increase in industrial concentration since then. Many mergers may even have been stimulated by the effectiveness of the legislation outlawing restrictive practices between firms. The Monopolies and Mergers Act of 1965 was therefore introduced. It gave the Minister (now the Secretary of State for Trade) power to withhold permission for mergers which involved large companies or which would result in or intensify a monopoly. (Large is currently defined as a company with assets of £15 million.) Such mergers could be referred to the Commission, renamed the Monopolies and Mergers Commission (MMC).

The policy on mergers has proved notably less effective than that directed towards restrictive practices, in so far as the number of amalgamations has not substantially diminished, and an increasing proportion have been of the conglomerate type (see page 65). About 2000 have come within the terms of the Act since 1970, but very few have been referred to the MMC. Most of the latter did not pass its scrutiny, while others may have been inhibited by the Act, which should therefore not be regarded as totally ineffective.

*Competition and efficiency*

The major more important recent development in competition policy has been the establishment, in 1973, of a **Director General of Fair Trading** with power to initiate preliminary investigations where 'anti-competitive practices' are suspected. These were broadly defined to include such behaviour as the refusal of a firm to supply another, such as a discount store which might sell its products at 'cut', ie low, prices, and the tying of sales of one product to those of another.

Seen as a whole, British competition policy as it has developed represents a distinctive approach to the problems arising from the existence of monopoly power in the private sector of industry. In contrast to policy in other countries, particularly that in the USA, the underlying philosophy has been one of a case by case assessment whereby, except for certain registrable business practices, monopolies and mergers are recognised as having potential benefits as well as detriments for the public interest. Each case is judged on its merits before an overall assessment is made.

One consequence of this approach is that it tends to work slowly. Other criticisms have been made. The findings of the MMC do not have to stand up to public enquiry as do those of the Restrictive Practices Court. On the other hand, the government of the day has not always accepted the recommendations of the Commission and in most cases reliance has been placed on voluntary assurances from businesses after the publication of reports, rather than on formal orders from the government for implementation.

Finally, it is necessary to mention that Britain's membership of the European Economic Community (EEC) since 1973 (see pages 107–8) has meant that the Community's competition policy is applicable to businesses in Britain. EEC policy is not very different from that of the UK as far as restrictive practices are concerned. The rules, however, apply only where trade between different members of the EEC is involved. These rules came into prominence when it came to light that the price of certain cars in the UK was artificially kept high by refusing to allow right-hand drive vehicles to be produced on the Continent.

Policy measures of the kind described above are not the only means that have been used to try to improve economic efficiency. Others have included special help for small firms, and incentives to encourage 'enterprise'. A rather different approach, difficult to reconcile at times with merger policy, emerged in the 1960s. This was aimed at stimulating increases in company size to realise economies of large-scale production. The **Industrial Reorganisation Corporation** was set up in 1966 and the **National Enterprise Board** 10 years later to try achieve this aim. This strategy was supported by the **National Economic Development Council** (known as Neddy), a body of powerful industrialists, trade unionists and government officials, created in 1962. Nearly two dozen 'little Neddies' were also set up for individual industries.

Distribution of industry policy

As we saw in Chapter 3, industries are not evenly spread over the country but tend to concentrate in particular areas. Heavy dependence on one or more failing industries caused serious local pockets of unemployment in the interwar years and government action was taken to alleviate this problem. The first step was taken in 1934 when certain 'Special Areas' were scheduled as depressed and commissioners were appointed to try to attract new industry to them. Postwar Distribution of Industry Acts reinforced this policy, giving powers to the government. These included building factories for letting in the areas (renamed **Development Areas**) and making loans and grants to encourage individual firms to go there. At the same time a policy of creating **new towns** was started in more prosperous regions.

In a negative way, too, the government's control over factory location was materially strengthened as a result of the Town and Country Planning Act 1947. By this Act new factories required planning permission from the local authority, and larger factories also required the granting of an **industrial development certificate**. the government was therefore able to influence industrial location by granting or withholding these certificates—a powerful weapon.

There have been several Acts of Parliament since 1960

identifying regions in need of special assistance. Categories of need have been identified and given certain names:

- Special Development Areas—small districts with the most serious problems
- Development Areas
- Intermediate Areas, with the least acute problems

Their boundaries are shown in Fig 73. The help available includes capital grants, rent subsidies and, even, favoured treatment on government contracts. In 11 new **enterprise zones**, started in 1980, the incentives also include exemption from development land tax (see page 116) and maximum freedom from government controls. Special mention should also be made of the regional employment premium which operated between 1967 and 1977 and which offered financial aid related to the number of workers on a firm's books. It hit more directly at unemployment than do capital grants, which tend to favour capital- rather than labour-intensive investment.

Regional unemployment rate differentials have tended to fall over the last two decades, though the extent to which this can be attributed to government policy is uncertain. However, the policy of the 1979 Conservative administration is to reduce the scope of specially assisted areas in order to devote relatively more help to those in greatest need.

**Government and agriculture**[1]

In the decades before the outbreak of the Second World War the farming community had, on balance, a fairly difficult time. It is true that every year was not equally bad, but competition from foreign food producers was intense and even the best years were less prosperous in agriculture than in many other industries. By the beginning of the 1930s the situation had become so serious that the government began to adopt a number of piecemeal measures to improve the lot of the farmer.

After the war the major political parties agreed that every effort should be made to prevent agriculture from returning to its depressed state. Over the years a variety of measures were therefore enacted, including grants for land improvement, support for farm amalgamations, sponsorship of agricultural research and the provision of a farm advisory service. However, the principal element of UK agricultural policy, which lasted for a quarter of a century after the end of the war, took the form of subsidies for British farmers. The system

1 Some of the problems that arise in connection with policies designed to assist agriculture are analysed in Lipsey Chapter 10.

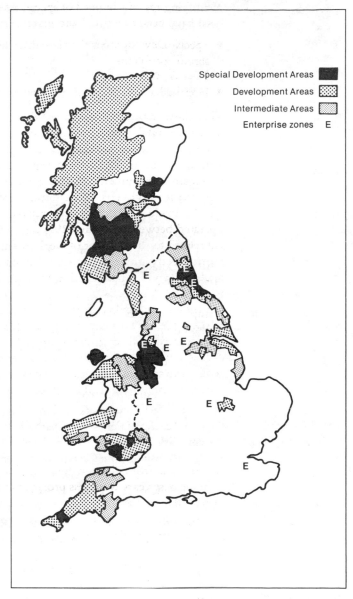

*Fig 73* Location of industry policy 1982; areas entitled to government aid

Special Development Areas

Development Areas

Intermediate Areas

Enterprise zones E

was based on the free import of foodstuffs into Britain while subsidising domestic farmers by means of so-called **deficiency payments**, representing the shortfall in the price they received from the sale of their produce on the open market, and **guaranteed prices** for individual products. These guaranteed prices, as well as standard quantities to which they would apply, were set at annual price reviews after meetings between the government and representatives of British farmers.

| Agriculture and the Common Market | All this changed radically as a result of Britain's entry into the Common Market. The objectives of the EEC policy, including those of stabilising farm incomes at 'reasonable' levels and promoting agricultural efficiency, are broadly similar to those of the UK which it replaced, but the methods of application have certain important basic differences. The most important is that the **common agricultural policy (CAP)** operates through a system of minimum prices which apply in all member states. These prices are maintained both by intervention buying by a Common Market agency and by import levies on products entering the EEC from outside. |

It is beyond the scope of this book to describe the complexities of the CAP, which include grants for farm modernisation and a system of artificial exchange rates used to determine minimum support prices in local currencies—the value of the so-called 'green pound' in the case of the UK. However, it must be made clear that there is tremendous scope for disagreement between member countries on the level of support for individual products and on the means of financing them, not least because of differences in productivity. It is well-known that the levels have sometimes been so high as to generate enormous surpluses of some commodities—'mountains' of butter and sugar and 'lakes' of wine, as they have been called.

One of the most controversial aspects of the CAP is related less to its effect on farmers than to its effect on consumers and the balance of payments. Compared with the previous British system of deficiency payments, based on low-price imports and farm subsidies, the CAP has kept domestic prices above—and in times of recession well above—world prices. This has caused problems for certain countries in the rest of the world which, though low-cost producers, have had to face high import duties on their exports to the EEC, eg New Zealand meat and dairy farmers and West Indian sugar producers. It has also removed a source of cheap food supplies from the UK consumer.

It is no easy task to estimate the increased import bill nor the higher food cost to the British consumer of the CAP, especially as it has not even been constant over the years. The cost of farm support itself has to be borne by someone. In the previous UK system, subsidies came from the general taxpayer. Under the CAP they are derived partly from the proceeds of import levies, with consequent rising food bills, and partly from contributions made to the EEC pool by individual countries. Britain is thought by many commentators to have had to carry a heavy share of this burden at times, and much political bargaining has taken place at a high level on this matter.

**Housing, education and health**

There are several areas where the government intervenes by directly providing goods and services, as well as attempting to influence the private sector of the market. Three important areas where this takes place are housing, education and health.

Housing

Both the supply and the allocation of existing houses are regarded as a target for government social policy. The reason is largely that there is a feeling that a minimum standard of housing should be available for all families, regardless of income, especially where there are children in the household. A relevant distinctive feature of houses is that their cost is high—it is extremely rare that anyone can buy a house outright out of current income. Furthermore, it has often been thought reasonable that those living in rented accommodation should enjoy a certain security of tenure.

State intervention in the housing market occurs through both sides of the government accounts as well as by means of rules and regulations. On the expenditure side of the budget approximately 4 per cent of the total is spent on housing and environmental services such as refuse collection. However, the major item is the direct provision of houses and flats by local authorities. This is largely financed by borrowing and is therefore not included in the 4 per cent. Fig 74 shows the

*Fig 74* Dwellings 1980; stock of houses and flats at end of 1980 and dwellings completed during 1980
Source: *Annual Abstract of Statistics*

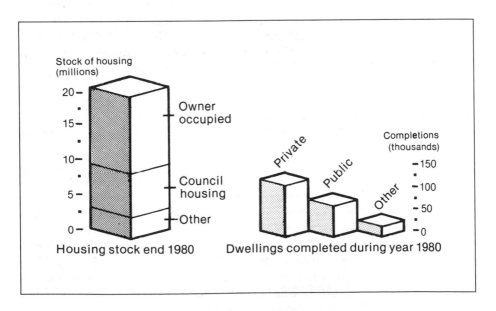

relative importance of council housing, both from the viewpoint of the total stock of dwellings and the numbers completed in a recent year—about a third of all families live in council dwellings. Local authorities allocate these houses to persons on their waiting lists according to criteria decided locally, but they usually take into account such things as family size, current housing conditions, length of residence in the area, etc. Rents charged to council house tenants vary from one authority to another but are almost always below— sometimes well below—those of the free market. Since the Housing Act of 1980 council house tenants of at least 3 years' standing have been given the right to buy the property at a discount related to the length of time they have lived in it. Other tools of housing policy that work through the budget include subsidies paid for the improvement of older dwellings and rent allowances for persons on low incomes.

On the revenue side of the account there is the important provision that mortgage interest payments on loans of up to £25 000, together with other allowances, are deductible from gross income before tax is calculated. This policy is designed to encourage home ownership. Over half of the houses in present day Britain are, in fact, owner-occupied.

The majority of the regulations affecting housing are related to health standards, environmental issues and town planning, but there is one area of special importance to economists—control of rents in the private sector.[1] **Rent control** was introduced as an emergency measure in 1915 during the First World War. Landlords of unfurnished flats and houses at the lower end of the market were prohibited from raising rents above those charged in August 1914 unless improvements had been made (or rates increased). Tenants were also given security from eviction. The measure had been intended as a temporary one but it was in fact continued after the end of the war and has persisted to the present day. As a result, by 1939, in spite of some relaxation of the rules, about a third of all privately rented houses and flats were subject to restrictions.

Since the end of the Second World War there have been several pieces of legislation extending, reducing or varying the scope of rent control. The most important Rent Acts in recent years have been those of 1974 and 1980. The former brought unfurnished tenancies into the network, while the latter introduced the notion of 'shorthold' lettings, reducing the security of tenants against eviction, from one of life to a

1 A detailed analysis of the effects of rent control is given in Lipsey Chapter 10.

shorter period of 1–5 years by agreement. Partly as a result of long-standing rent control legislation, which makes the provision of rented accommodation unattractive for private investors, the supply of private rented accommodation today accounts for only about 12 per cent of the total number of dwellings.

## Education and health

Education and health services have certain similarities which form the basis for state intervention in the market. Expenditure on both can be looked upon as an investment as well as consumption. On the one hand education increases an individual's earning power and job choice, while health services affect a person's ability to work, or at least to work well. On the other hand both education and health are desired for their own sake. They form part of the living standards of present-day society.

The case for government intervention is partly based on the argument that access to a certain minimum standard of health care and education should be available to everyone in the community, regardless of income. In the case of education there is also the fact that decisions about how much to spend on it are not taken by the individual child but by his or her parents. Furthermore, it is widely believed that society, as well as the individual, benefits from having its members healthy and well educated. This is obvious in the case of, say, infectious and contagious diseases, but of wider importance is the beneficial effect on economic growth and, more vaguely perhaps, social cohesion.

The tools of intervention in health and education are both budgetary and via rules and regulations. Health and education each absorb about 12 per cent of total government expenditure, or about half that percentage of national output. There are no provisions for tax deductions in the UK as there are in some other countries, partly because the public sector is so very large (well over 90 per cent of children attend state schools, for example). Most expenditure on education is financed out of general taxation, though there are some user charges, eg for school meals and income-based parental contributions to the maintenance grants of students undergoing higher education. About 90 per cent of the cost of running the **national health service** comes from general taxation, the rest coming from a share in the national insurance fund (see page 120) and from charges for such items as drugs, spectacles and dental treatment.

Regulations are used to maintain standards of quality in both services. In the case of education the rule of compulsion was first introduced in 1876, but the minimum school leaving age has, of course, been raised since then. Compulsory health insurance was brought in by the Lloyd George government in 1912, well before the advent of the national health service (1948). A more recent example of the use of rules is that making the wearing of seat belts obligatory from the beginning of 1983.

**Nationalised industries**

We know from Chapter 1 that the state operates a number of industries which possess some of the characteristics of commercial enterprises. These are the nationalised industries, organised as public corporations and employing about 8 per cent of the labour force. We discussed in general terms the nature of public corporations and the way in which their financial obligations have been set (see pages 39–41). All that remains to be done here is to describe some of the distinctive features of the principal nationalised industries. They fall naturally into three groups:

- fuel and power
- transport and communications
- others

The descriptions that follow relate to the situation existing at the beginning of 1983. It must be remembered, however, that the Conservative government at that time was engaged in transferring some sections of the nationalised industries to private enterprise. This is referred to later.

Fuel and power

*Coal*

The first important industry to be taken into public ownership in the wave of nationalisation that followed the Second World War was coal. Indeed, the transfer in 1947 of the 750 undertakings, employing about three-quarters of a million workers, can be viewed as a major step in the nationalisation of industry.

By the beginning of the 1980s the structure of the coal industry had not materially changed, although its labour force had fallen to less than a quarter of a million. The National Coal Board has charge of all of the coalfields of Britain and has the right to work certain other minerals as well. The distribution of coal, however, is largely in private hands. The members of the Board are appointed by the Secretary of State for Energy, who retains a general power of direction. The Board maintains a centralised form of organisation, but exercises control over its 200 or so collieries by grouping them into 12 areas.

*Electricity*

The importance of the supply of electricity led to some state control as far back as the 19th century. However, the first major Act of nationalisation dates from 1926, when the Central Electricity Board was established to operate a national grid. Electricity generation was added to the public sector 20 years later. Today the industry is run by an Electricity Council, responsible for overall coordination of the work of the Central Electricity Generating Board, and the area boards in charge of local distribution. Altogether the industry employs over 150 000 people.

*Gas*

The supply of gas for domestic and industrial purposes before nationalisation was in the hands of some 1000 private companies and local authorities. The Gas Act of 1948 created a central body, the Gas Council, but the main responsibility for the supply of gas was entrusted from the outset to 12 almost autonomous area gas boards. This situation continued until 1973, when a new Gas Act was passed to increase the amount of central control called for by the changeover from manufactured to natural gas from the North Sea (which now accounts for about 90 per cent of total production). The Act created the British Gas Corporation, which took over the responsibilities of the Gas Council and of the 12 area boards. The workforce in the gas industry is about half the size of that in the electricity industry.

*Oil*

Oilfields were discovered under British waters in the North Sea in 1969 and transformed the UK's energy supplies when they became productive in the late 1970s. Together with the natural gas referred to in the previous section and other energy sources, they made Britain virtually self-sufficient in energy in the 1980s.

Production is largely in the hands of private oil companies operating under licence from the government. The British National Oil Corporation (BNOC) was set up in 1976 to give the state a direct interest in North Sea oil. It is now, however, only a private company in which the state has a large financial interest. Its assets were transferred to Britoil in 1982 and 51 per cent of the shares were sold to the public. By the yardstick of employment the company is of minor significance, with only 2500 workers on its payroll. Its economic importance, however, is considerable as it is actively engaged in exploration and development in the North Sea and has agreements with the oil companies for the purchase of half of their production.

*Nuclear power*

The nuclear power programme in Britain can be traced back to 1956 and the construction of the first nuclear power station at Calder Hall. By 1981, however, nuclear energy still only supplied less than 5 per cent of the country's energy needs.

Britain has 15 nuclear power stations, the majority of which are operated by the electricity authorities. The remainder are run by the research oriented UK Atomic Energy Authority (1954) or its more commercial subsidiary, British Nuclear Fuels Ltd, which also provides nuclear fuel services, including some to overseas countries.

*Transport*

Most forms of inland transport, the second important industry to be nationalised after 1945, had already been subject to public control for a long time. The railways had always had to comply with a variety of state regulations and had even been run by the government for the duration of both World Wars. The traffic problems of London also led, as early as 1933, to the creation of the largest public corporation established before 1939—the London Passenger Transport Board—in order to provide a 'properly coordinated' system of transport in the capital.

The transport industry that was nationalised by the Act of 1947, however, was by far the most complicated that had ever been transferred to a public corporation, and employed close on 900000 workers. Disagreement between the principal political parties at the time was, moreover, strong and both the organisation of the industry and the sections of it remaining in the public field have since been subject to more than one radical change.

The 1947 Act set up a highly centralised structure with a single Transport Commission responsible for all public road and rail services, including those in London. Six years later the road haulage industry was largely denationalised by the then Conservative government and, in 1962, the Transport Commission was replaced by separate autonomous authorities. A later change was the establishment by the Labour administration in 1968 of a new National Freight Corporation and the National Bus Company. The latter was subjected to increased competition as a result of the 1980 Transport Act, which removed restrictions on private passenger road services, while the former was denationalised in 1981 when it was sold to its employees.

*Civil airlines*

The British Overseas Airways Corporation (BOAC) and British European Airways (BEA) were the last of the prewar and the first of the postwar public corporations. Since 1971 they have been embodied in a single corporation, British Airways (BA).

The government entered the field of civil aviation in order to develop a national service in circumstances which inevitably involve important political issues and impinge on international relations. The nationalised airlines were given a statutory monopoly position in Britain until 1961, after which time they had to face increasing competition, from independent airlines, such as British Caledonian and the now defunct Laker Airways. The government also set up the Civil Aviation Authority, an independent body, responsible for the regulation of the industry. It oversees charges, routes, safety, etc, and issues licences to approved operators.

Other nationalised industries

The most important of the other nationalised industries, as measured by the size of their labour forces, are steel, the Post Office and British Telecom.

Steel

The last of the industries transferred to public ownership by the first postwar Labour government was steel, and without doubt it was the most controversial of the nationalisation measures. Delays were caused by the Conservative majority in the House of Lords, and the Iron and Steel Corporation of Britain did not come into being until 1951. The new corporation was, however, to have a short life. By 1953 the succeeding Conservative government had brought in a second Steel Act to denationalise the industry, and by the time a new Labour government, committed to renationalisation, had been elected in 1964 all but one company had been sold back to private owners. The 1967 Iron and Steel Act then transferred the assets of 13 major steel companies to a new British Steel Corporation (BSC).

At the time of the second nationalisation BSC employed around a quarter of a million workers and produced about 90 per cent of the UK's crude steel output. This share has dropped since then to nearer 80 per cent. The industry has also been trying to reduce capacity in the light of falling world demand and intensified international competition. Employment had fallen accordingly to below 100 000 by 1982.

Postal and telephone services

The Post Office, run directly as a government department, had a monopoly of postal and telephone services until it was turned into a public corporation in 1969. In 1981, however, the two services were separated and British Telecom was created, the largest employer of labour of any of the nationalised industries.

Brief mention must also be made of two other nationalised industries—British Aerospace, which engages in aircraft production, and British Shipbuilders, set up in 1977 to acquire the assets of certain failing private shipbuilding firms on whom employment in regions such as Clydeside depended quite heavily.

The government has also bought up the shares in other important companies to prevent their closure, chief among them being Rolls Royce and British Leyland. They are not run by public corporations in the strict sense, neither were they taken over for any specific economic reason other than as rescue operations (sometimes described as saving 'lame ducks').

## Privatisation

Privatisation is a word that has crept into our language in order to describe the policies of the Conservative government which took office in 1979. A variety of measures aimed at increasing competition in the public sector are included under this term (see pages 41–2). Some include the sale of parts or all of specific public corporations to private buyers; for example, 52 per cent of the shares in British Aerospace were sold in 1981 and proposals have been announced for sales of shares in British Airways, British Telecom and Rolls Royce. Whether these proposals are proceeded with depends in the main on whether the industries concerned are sufficiently profitable to attract purchasers.

## Profitability of the nationalised industries

Economists often use the yardstick of profit to measure an industry's efficiency. However, this approach is not always helpful for nationalised industries for two basic reasons. In the first place, they may be asked to fulfil social obligations which may not be profitable. For example, they may be expected to prevent unemployment in an area, eg on Clydeside; they may have to provide transport for people living in isolated parts of the country; they may need to maintain national prestige, eg airways; they may be told to keep their prices low as part of an anti-inflation policy, eg gas. Even in such cases, however, profit calculations, correctly interpreted, can be useful. When other goals are being pursued, the size of the losses that must be covered from other sources gives some measure of the cost of achieving these objectives.

In the second place some nationalised industries possess a degree of monopoly power which might allow them to make large profits without necessarily reflecting great efficiency. One should, therefore, be cautious about judging the efficiency of nationalised industries according to whether they make profits or losses. Having said this, however, we might perhaps venture the general observation that telecommunications have been quite profitable in recent years, while the railways and steel have made substantial losses.

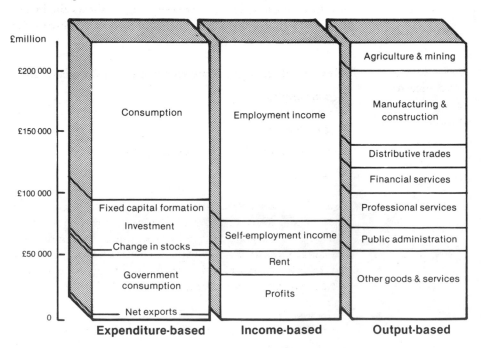

*Fig 75* Gross domestic
product 1981
Source: *National
Income and Expenditure*

# 7 National income and the balance of payments

In this chapter we pass from a consideration of the allocation of resources between industries and sectors to look at the economy as a whole and, in particular, at the sum total of all outputs—what is known generally as the national income.

**National income**[1]

The national income is a measure of all goods and services produced in the economy during some period of time (usually a year) and valued in money terms. It can be estimated in any one of three ways by summing:

- incomes
- outputs
- expenditures

In principle all three of these methods will give the same answer. This is because the value of output produced is equal to the value of expenditure needed to purchase it and to the income claims generated by its production (because all value produced must belong to someone). Fig 75 shows the breakdown of national income estimated in each of the three ways listed above.

**Expenditure-based measure of national income**

There are three major components of national expenditure:

- consumption
- investment
- government

and a fourth of relatively small magnitude:

- net exports

*Consumption*

Private consumption expenditure is the largest category. It is also a fairly stable one. As can be seen from Fig 76, most consumer expenditure is on regular needs for food, fuel, clothing and household goods, and therefore does not fluctuate greatly. Moreover, the *proportion* of personal income which is spent on consumption can be relied on to be quite stable.

1 National income accounts are discussed in some detail in Lipsey Chapter 34.

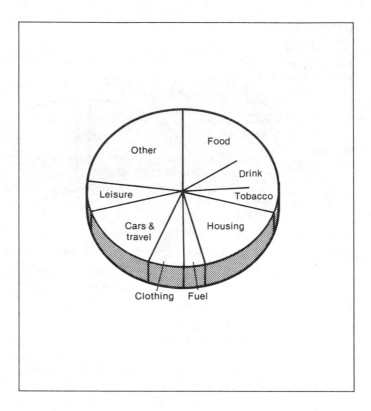

*Investment*

The second component of national expenditure, investment,
is the most volatile. Investment is of two kinds:

- **fixed capital formation**, in plant, machinery, equipment
  and housing

- **changes in stocks of goods** at different stages in the
  production process

Fig 77 shows the composition of fixed capital formation in
1981. It can be seen that between two-thirds and three-
quarters of the total is invested in the private sector, the
remainder in the public sector. All the items, with the
exception of dwellings, raise the productive potential of the
economy and, given favourable circumstances, can lead to
economic growth. Excluding dwellings, **gross fixed investment** has averaged about 16–18 per cent of gross domestic
expenditure over the last 10 to 15 years. Private sector
investment is certainly less stable than private consumption,

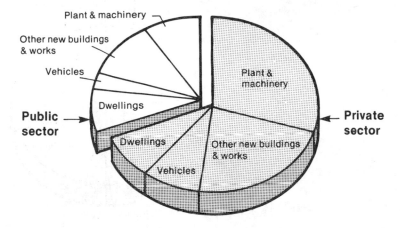

*Fig* 77 Gross domestic
fixed capital formation
1981
Source: *National
Income and Expenditure*

but *total* investment has tended to fluctuate less because of the behaviour of government capital spending which has, on the whole, expanded when private investment was contracting and vice versa.

The volatility of investment expenditure, however, derives not from fixed capital formation but from its other component, that of changes in stocks (or inventories) of goods and materials held by businesses. They are considered in economics as part of investment and play a key role in economic theory. Although the size of stocks is to a certain extent decided upon by firms, it is also liable to change *involuntarily* as a result of unexpected alterations in levels of sales. Fig 78 shows the annual movements in the changes in stocks between the start and end of each year between 1971 and 1981, confirming their great volatility.

*Government and
exports*

The other categories of national expenditure are government and (net) exports. The former constituted the subject of Chapter 6, where some of the determinants of government expenditure were discussed. Somewhat surprisingly, perhaps, it fluctuates remarkably little in the short-term mainly because much of it is the result of long-term commitments which are procedurally difficult to alter.

Finally, net purchases of goods by foreigners (exports net of imports) are a part of national expenditure. They are discussed in the second part of this chapter.

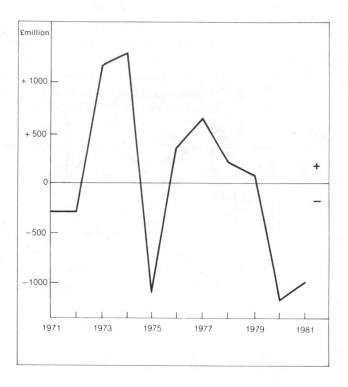

*Fig 78* Change in value of stocks (at 1975 prices) 1971–81 Source: *National Income and Expenditure*

**Income-based measure of national income**

The second column in Fig 75 on page 150 shows the main categories of national *income*. They were discussed in Chapter 4 when we were looking at the distribution of income among factors of production (see pages 70–2 and Fig 76). Only two matters need further attention. In the first place, it needs to be emphasised that the only incomes included are *factor* incomes, ie incomes earned by supplying factor services for current production. As we know from Chapter 6 on government policy, some individuals receive incomes from the state, eg retirement pensions, unemployment benefits, etc. These are *transfer* incomes. They are paid by taxing some people and then using the proceeds to pay state benefits. Since we are interested in measuring the income derived from contributions to production by factors of production we do *not* wish to include these transfer payments.

For some purposes we want to know how much people have to spend. This is called **disposable income**. To calculate it we take total factor and transfer incomes to persons and deduct income taxes and national insurance contributions. One of the key variables in national income analysis is savings, which is closely related to **personal disposable income**. Personal savings do not appear in Fig 75 because they are, by definition, income *not spent* on consumption. They can, however, be estimated and Fig 79 shows the course of personal savings expressed as a percentage of personal disposable income between 1971 and 1981.

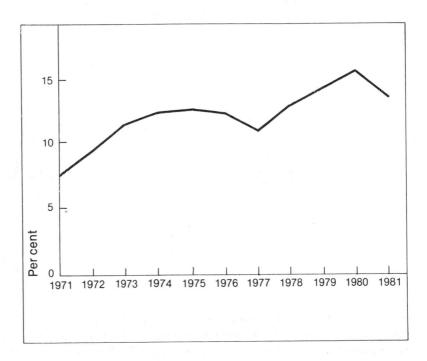

*Fig 79* Savings as a percentage of personal disposable income 1971–81
Source: *National Income and Expenditure*

It can be seen that there has been a very considerable rise in the proportion of personal income saved over these years, virtually doubling from 7½ to 15½ per cent between 1971 and 1980, though there was a slight fall back in 1981. No one knows for certain why this rise has taken place. One partial explanation is that accelerating inflation eroded the purchasing power of accumulated savings, leading people to save more to replace their lost value. Rising unemployment and uncertainty about the future level of prices may have had a similar effect. There is also the fact that some saving is contractual, eg mortgage repayments on house purchase loans, which tends to rise automatically with inflation.

Output-based measure of national income

This measure of national output was encountered in Chapter 3 which described the structure of British industry (see page 45 and Fig 24). There is, however, one aspect that requires explanation here. The value of the output of each of the main sectors in the economy is known as a **net output**, or **value added**. Since we want to know the value of final output, we must not count the total value of sales every time a good changes hands. If we added together the gross sales revenues of all businesses this would involve a considerable amount of **double counting**, as the outputs of some firms are the inputs of others. Hence, when calculating national output, we deduct the purchases of inputs by firms from other businesses from the gross output in order to arrive at the proper figure for added value. An illustration of the method of calculation used in the vehicle industry is shown below.

### Method of calculating value added

|  | £ million | £ million |
|---|---|---|
| Revenue from sales |  | 15 067 |
| *Add* Increase in stocks of |  |  |
| finished products |  | 674 |
| Gross value of output |  | 15 741 |
| *Less:* |  |  |
| Purchases of inputs | 8 835 |  |
| Increase in stocks of |  |  |
| materials, stores, |  |  |
| fuel, etc | 282 | 9 117 |
| Net output (value added) |  | 6 624 |

Source: Census of Production *Business Monitor*, PA 1002

**The national accounts**

In a complex economy like the UK, where there is a large government sector and many international transactions, the national income is estimated annually and published in the national accounts—the so-called 'Blue Book' of *National Income and Expenditure*.

There are several standard forms in which the accounts may be used in economic analysis. The relationship between them in shown in Fig 80.

**Foreign trade**

The top row in Fig 80 shows total *domestic* expenditure, broken down in the manner to which we have become accustomed, ie into consumption, investment and government sectors. To allow for the inclusion of all expenditures it is necessary to add expenditure on British exports by non-

*Fig 80* National
income and product
1981; relationship
between major
definitions
Source: *National
Income and Expenditure*

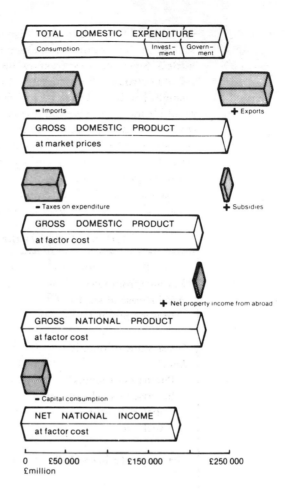

*Fig 80* National income and product 1981; relationship between major definitions

residents and subtract that on imports from the rest of the
world. This gives the **gross domestic product (GDP)**.

*Taxes and subsidies
on expenditure*

It will be noticed that the wording in the bar in the second
row of Fig 80 is: **GDP at market prices**. These, however,
reflect taxes on expenditure, eg on tobacco, and subsidies, eg
on housing. To convert GDP at market prices to that at factor
cost, such taxes (net of subsidies) have to be deducted **to yield
GDP at factor cost**.

*Property income
from abroad*

The national income of the residents of the UK must take
account of receipts (net) of income derived from the ownership of property overseas. This is added to the GDP to yield
**gross national product (GNP)** in the fourth row of Fig 80.

*Capital
consumption*

All measures of national income or output dealt with so far
have been termed *gross*. This is because they are calculated

before any allowance has been made for the depreciation that takes place in the value of the national capital as a result of age and market forces. Very roughly, 10 per cent of the national income is needed to make good such depreciation. When this is deducted from GNP it gives the **net national product** (or **national income**) in the final row of Fig 80.

The reliability of national income statistics

Figures of national income in official statistics appear to have a high degree of numerical precision. However, one should not be misled by their apparent accuracy. It is no simple task to estimate all the elements needed to compute the national income. Of course, some of the data are more reliable than others—unfortunately not always those most important for economic analysis. The level of personal savings, revised annually, is a good example. Consider, for example, the official figure for total personal savings in 1971, as published in the 'Blue Book' (1982 edition)—£2873 million. However, 8 years previously, in the 1974 edition of the same book, the figure given for personal savings in 1971 was £3438 million, which is some 20 per cent higher than the (presumably most accurate) recent estimate—a considerable difference!

When the national income is estimated from each of the three methods the answer should, as we have seen, be the same. An indication of the minimum errors involved is shown by the differences in the figures arising out of each method. To reconcile them the Blue Book gives a 'residual error' which must be included to make the income data add up to the same total as the expenditure data. Since 1971 the discrepancy has been as high as 2 per cent and as low as $\frac{1}{2}$ per cent of GDP.

Errors of 1 to 2 per cent are bothersome when calculating totals, but they are extremely serious when calculating annual growth rates, which are usually based on changes in GDP of no more than 3 to 4 per cent per year, ie the error in the estimated GDP is typically about a half of the growth rate being measured. For this reason, although trends in the growth rate over several years can be significant, not too much should be read into changes in the measured growth rate from one year to the next. Figure 81 illustrates this point by showing annual growth rates calculated using each of the three methods. To take the worst of the years covered by the official statistics, the GDP appears to have risen in 1975–76 by nearly 4 per cent using income data, as against a mere $1\frac{1}{2}$ per cent on an expenditure basis.

Living standards

We now know national income to be a measure of the goods and services produced in a country. It would not be unreason-

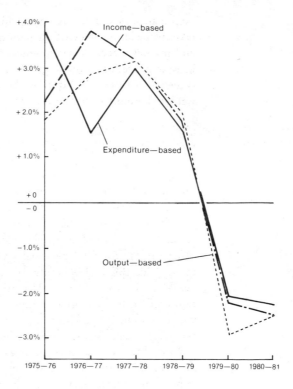

*Fig 81* Estimated year to year changes in gross domestic product 1975–76 to 1980–81
Source: *National Income and Expenditure*

able to imagine that it is, therefore, a good indicator of the standard of living there. If we divide the national income, or product, by the number of people living in a country we obtain a figure of income per head of the population, and it is true that this is fairly closely related to living standards. However, they are *not* the same thing.

The national income does not measure *everything* that contributes to living standards. There are many differences between the two concepts and we can do no more than mention some of the most important here. Nearly all arise from the fact that the only goods and services that are included in the national income total are those that are bought and sold in the market place or provided by the state (in which case, incidentally, they are mostly valued at cost). Things that are excluded therefore include the beauty of the environment, the pleasures of a good climate and all the cultural legacies inherited from the past. A different type of exclusion is the leisure that is enjoyed. In so far as people in a country decide to produce no more goods and services but to spend more time at home or on holiday, for example, their living standards may be considered to have risen while the national income remains unchanged.

We must also consider various exclusions that are simply due to the nature of economic organisation in the country. Some services, for example, are performed without any money transactions taking place, while others, which may be equally important, go unrecorded. Principal among the former are the services of housewives, as distinct from those of paid housekeepers, the do-it-yourself jobs undertaken by men and women rather than paying for the work to be done, and illegal unrecorded transactions, eg in drugs and work done 'for cash only' by individuals who wish to evade paying tax, in what has come to be called the 'black economy'. These cash-only transactions have become increasingly common in recent years. No one knows precisely how much all these would add up to if they could be counted, valued and added into the national income as conventionally defined. Estimates of the size of the black economy put it at around 5 per cent of the total GDP, but this is not a firm figure, of course.

A further, final, exclusion which is relevant to comparisons of national income over time is the inability of the statistics to make full allowance for changes in the *quality* of products. A switch from black and white to colour television, for example, is widely regarded as raising the quality of satisfaction derived from watching TV, but it is not automatically catered for in the national accounts. Moreover, as the price of colour television sets has come down (reaping economies of large-scale production) this component of output has not really fallen in one sense, although as conventionally measured it has.

The only conclusion that can be drawn is that there are substantial differences between the measured national income and what goes to make up the standard of living of the population. We must therefore treat the statistics with caution, especially if there are grounds for believing that there have been any significant changes in the circumstances affecting either.

One last consideration deserves comment. The matters mentioned so far tend to suggest that living standards may be higher than would be indicated by the size of the national income. There are, however, some reasons why the opposite may be true. The most important is the existence of what have rather unfortunately been called economic 'bads' (the use of the word 'bads' is analogous to that of the word 'goods'— both imply value judgments on the part of society). These are things like pollution and spoliation of the environment that have sometimes been observed to accompany rapid economic growth. They can lower the standard of living even though the national income appears to be rising.

The previous section concerned the living standards of a country taken as a unit. We discussed the meaning of *average* national per capita income. Such a figure, however, can be extremely misleading since income is not evenly divided among all the population. Some people are better off than others. We began to deal with the question of the distribution of income in Chapter 4 and returned to it in our consideration of government policy to change it (see pages 123–8). We now consider one aspect not covered so far—poverty.

Poverty is a concept that can have many meanings. We can set standards for drawing a poverty line, below which an individual would have insufficient means for survival (a 'starvation line'); other lines could be drawn where he or she would be deprived of access to conditions of life commonly regarded as necessary for a minimum standard of living (a 'subsistence line'). Such a subsistence level must to an extent be arbitrary. Once one gets away from the basic essentials for continued existence it is very much a matter of opinion where one sets a benchmark to separate the 'poor' from the rest of the population.

As conventionally conceived, therefore, poverty is a *relative* concept, which changes over time with the average standard of living of the rest of the population. This leaves room for debate about how far below the average the poverty line should be drawn. One guideline often employed by workers in the field is the minimum income needed to qualify for social security relief, known as supplementary benefit, from the state. Such a standard is no less arbitrary than others, but it has a number of substantial advantages. It can be examined in detail; it changes from time to time; and it is adjusted to allow for individual needs, eg the number of dependents in the family.

On the basis of the supplementary benefit scale, recent estimates of the numbers in poverty in the UK are about 6 million people, or 4 million families, *before* the receipt of benefit, reducing to 2 million people, or $1\frac{1}{4}$ million families, *after* benefit is taken into account. These figures represent approximately 10 to 15 per cent of the total population before benefit, and 4 to 5 per cent after benefit. (It is important to note that the data by themselves do not quantify the size of the poverty problem since they do not take account of how far below the benchmark the poor are living, nor the extent to which there is a hard core of permanently poor rather than a changing number of people in temporarily reduced circumstances.) The main reason for poverty remaining after payment of social security benefits is that some people, mainly pensioners who are entitled to claim, do not do so.

While there may be differences of opinion as to *how* many people should be counted as 'poor', there is less room for argument about *who* they are. Poverty is associated with age (especially with being old, but also with being very young and with workers over 50), with being unemployed, with being female, with being sick or disabled, with having little education or ability, and with family size (single-parent families in particular). Poverty also varies regionally, the South West, East Anglia and Scotland having the highest proportions of poor. What is not fully understood is whether the underlying causes of poverty are to be found mainly in individual personal characteristics or in the structure of jobs. There is a good deal of evidence of the existence of a **dual labour market** in countries like the UK—a primary market, where pay and employment prospects are good, a secondary market with high unemployment and low pay—and little movement between them, with many of the poor trapped in the secondary market.

## Real and money[1] national income

GDP measures the total *money* value of final goods produced during a year. Thus it has a price and a quantity component; a particular change in GDP can be caused by many different combinations of price and quantity changes. A 10 per cent rise in GDP might, for example, have been caused by a 10 per cent rise in prices, all quantities remaining unchanged; by a 10 per cent rise in quantities, all prices remaining unchanged; or by any appropriate changes in both prices and quantities. For some purposes the money value of national income is just the measure required. This is not always the case, however. Sometimes we wish to know what is happening to the actual quantity of output, in which case we need to separate changes in the GDP caused by variations in market prices from changes caused by variations in the quantities of output.

To estimate the physical change in GDP, output is valued in **constant prices**. Each year the total quantities of output are determined. Instead of being valued at current prices, however, they are valued at a set of prices that ruled at some time in the past, called the **base year**. When current GDP is valued in constant 1960 prices, for example, we measure what the total value of output would have been if prices had not changed since 1960. The change in the GDP valued at constant prices is a measure of the pure quantity change. Thus, if GDP at constant prices is 30 per cent higher than

1 American terminology, using the term 'nominal' for 'money' income, appears to be creeping into use in Britain.

1960, this means that physical output has increased by 30 per cent since 1960 in the sense that price changes have not been allowed to affect these figures.

Fig 82 shows the experience of money and real national income between 1960 and 1981 and it can easily be seen how far apart the two series have moved. Money income in 1981

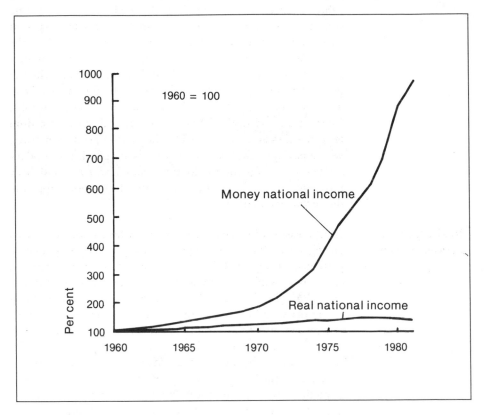

*Fig 82* Gross domestic product 1960–81 Source: *National Income and Expenditure*

was almost ten times its level 20 years earlier, but real income, allowing for the rise in the general level of prices, was only up by about 50 per cent. (This, of course, is the result of inflation, which is considered in detail in Chapter 9 pages 197–9.) One should add, perhaps, that the population of the UK grew by about 6 per cent over the period, so that real income *per head* rose by rather less than 50 per cent.

## The balance of payments[1]

The influence of transactions between resident and non-residents of the UK on the calculation of the national income has been described earlier in this chapter. There is, however, a

1 This section is complementary to the discussion in Lipsey Chapter 37.

separate account involving such flows of expenditure. It is known as the **balance of payments**, and is a record of all payments and receipts between residents and non–residents over a period of time, usually a year.

**Current and capital transactions**

The balance of payments is usually divided into three sections:

- the current account
- the capital account
- official financing

The **current account** records all payments and receipts involving purchases and sales of goods and services. The **capital account** lists transactions related to the movement of capital. **Official financing** refers to the transactions made by the Bank of England (see pages 188–91) on behalf of the government. Taken together the three sections must always balance out. Since the balance of payments is an accounting concept, this is true, by definition.

*Fig 83* Current account balance of payments 1971–81
Source: *Annual Abstract of Statistics*

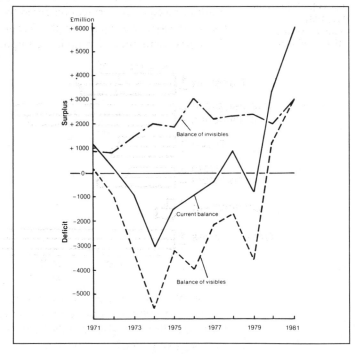

**The current account**

Two sets of items are contained in the current account:

- transactions involving goods, called **visible trade**
- transactions involving services, known as **invisibles**

Fig 83 shows the history of the current account balance of payments since 1971. The UK has traditionally recorded a surplus of receipts over payments on its current account as far back as the early 19th century, if not earlier. This has usually been due to invisible earnings which have, in the past, been more than enough to offset the deficit on trade in goods. Apart from one or two years, the latter hardly ever showed a credit balance. The balance of visible trade went through a particularly adverse period in the 1960s and, although invisible transactions continued to show a surplus, the gap between the visibles and the invisibles narrowed. This was partly because British exports did not keep pace with expanding world trade, and partly because imports were maintained at a relatively high level. More recently the balance of visible trade has improved substantially, partly, though not primarily, as a result of North Sea oil—oil exports exceeded oil imports for the first time in 1980.

In view of the importance of invisible transactions, it is worthwhile looking at the main categories in more detail, as in Fig 84. On the top lines are the invisible exports (+). They result in receipts for services rendered to foreigners in exactly the same way as do exports of physical goods. The lower lines show payments made for invisible imports (−).

*Fig 84* Invisible trade UK 1981
Source: *Annual Abstract of Statistics*

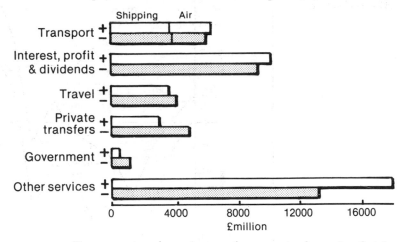

Transport is a large item and covers, in the main, freight charges for shipping. Traditionally this used to be a substantial net credit for the UK but the decline in Britain's merchant fleet relative to those of other countries has caused this credit to disappear, though there is still a small surplus on the civil aviation account. Interest, profit and dividends result from past investments by British and foreign investors. The credit balance tends to fluctuate quite a lot—1981 was a particularly good year. Foreign travel payments and receipts cover spending by tourists and travelling businessmen. It has shown a net credit in the last few years, largely reflecting an upward trend among foreigners for holidays in Britain. The item called private transfers consists mainly of personal transactions, involving gifts and the transfer of assets by migrants. These fluctuate from year to year, but are usually a net outflow for Britain. The major source of drain among invisibles is government expenditure, much of which is military, but also includes diplomatic expenses and grants made to developing countries in the form of aid.

The one category of invisibles which traditionally shows a substantial credit balance for the UK is that labelled 'other services'. It covers several important items, including receipts by the City of London for banking, insurance and other financial services and royalties.

An important feature of the current balance record displayed in Fig 83 is its great volatility. This is almost entirely due to swings in the balance of visible trade, sometimes reaching crisis proportions, outstandingly so in 1974. The experience of that year is almost entirely attributable to the quadrupling of the price of oil by the major oil-exporting countries belonging to the group known as OPEC. Other occasions on which the current account has been particularly unfavourable have tended to be associated with boom conditions. These lead to rising incomes and imports and at the same time provide less incentive to export since the home market is buoyant. In so far as booms are worldwide, which they often are, they also have an effect similar to the oil price rise of 1973–74, ie they push up the price of raw material imports.

|  |  |
|---|---|
| The capital account | The capital account records movements of capital funds between residents and non-residents, lending to and borrowing from the rest of the world, both on short and long terms. |

Foreign investment can take one of two main forms:

- **direct investment** in overseas subsidiaries of home owned companies
- **portfolio investment**, involving merely the purchase of foreign securities or shares in foreign owned companies

These transactions appear in the capital account of the balance of payments, but it is exceedingly difficult to know, especially with portfolio investment, which are really long term. Once a person or a company has bought shares in a foreign company they may be held indefinitely, perhaps resulting in the acquisition of a controlling interest. Alternatively, they may be sold the week after they are bought. Moreover, a great deal of

*Table 2* Balance of payments of the UK 1979–81 (£ million)[1]
Source: *Annual Abstract of Statistics*

|  | 1979 | 1980 | 1981 |
|---|---|---|---|
| *Current account* | | | |
| Visibles: | | | |
|   Exports | 40 678 | 47 389 | 51 100 |
|   Imports | 44 136 | 46 211 | 48 087 |
| Balance | −3 458 | +1 178 | +3 013 |
| Invisibles: | | | |
|   Credits | 23 694 | 25 764 | 29 338 |
|   Debits | 21 099 | 23 736 | 26 315 |
| Balance | +2 595 | +2 028 | +3 023 |
| Current balance | −863 | +3 206 | +6 036 |
| *Investment and other capital transactions*[2] | | | |
| Overseas investment in the UK: | | | |
|   Public sector | +902 | +589 | +188 |
|   Private sector | +3 405 | +4 676 | +2 743 |
| UK investment overseas: | | | |
|   Private | −6 555 | −8 039 | −11 171 |
|   Long-term government | −401 | −91 | −335 |
| Trade credit | −779 | −1 176 | −935 |
| Foreign currency lending by UK banks | +1 623 | +2 024 | +1 404 |
| Exchange reserves | +756 | +1 262 | +113 |
| Other external borrowing or lending | +3 242 | −917 | −206 |
| Other transactions | −68 | −222 | +90 |
| Total investment and capital transactions | +2 125 | −1 894 | −8 109 |
| *Official financing* | | | |
| Net transactions with overseas monetary authorities | −596 | −140 | −145 |
| Foreign currency borrowing (net) | −250 | −941 | −1 587 |
| Official reserves (drawings on +, additions to −) | −1 059 | −291 | +2 419 |
| Total official financing | −1 905 | −1 372 | +687 |

Notes
1 The balance of payments does not balance exactly because of errors in certain reported totals.
2 Assets increased/liabilities decreased −
  Assets decreased/liabilities increased +

international investment in the modern age is done by corporations known as **multinationals**. Companies such as General Motors (USA), Shell (Netherlands/UK), IBM (USA) and BP (UK) own subsidiaries throughout the world—BP has subsidiary companies in well over 50 countries. The multinationals switch funds among their subsidiaries in different countries, and the accounting practices they employ sometimes make it difficult to identify all the international investment that takes place.

The fact that we cannot distinguish all long- from short-term investment does not mean, of course, that we are completely ignorant about what is going on. Some short-term capital movements, such as the purchase of Treasury bills and the running up of sterling bank accounts by non-residents, can be identified, though the early estimates of these and several other items in the official balance of payments are liable to be substantially revised in later years when more information is available.

Before studying the figures in Table 2 on capital transactions for the three years 1979–81, bear in mind that the statistics on the balance of payments are rather less reliable than those for the national income (see page 158). You will see, too, that several categories of capital movement appear to be very volatile. This is not simply a statistical artifact. Capital movements do fluctuate in the real world. They are greatly influenced by the level of confidence of investors, as well as by interest rate differentials, which depend in turn on government policies in individual countries (see pages 209–10).

Private long-term capital outflows exceeded inflows by considerable amounts in the three years 1979–81, as can be seen from Table 2. This, however, is a new trend. In the previous 10 years or so, outflows and inflows more or less balanced, as Fig 85 shows. The remarkable rise in UK investment overseas since 1979 is due mainly to the decision

*Fig 85* Private investment outflows and inflows 1971–81 Source: *Annual Abstract of Statistics*

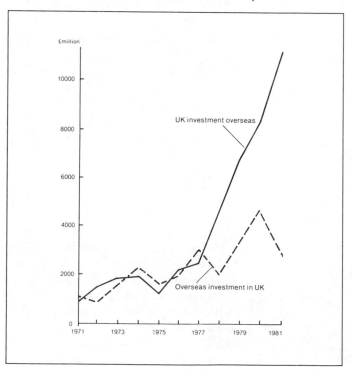

by the government to abolish all controls on capital movements by UK residents, which had existed for half a century. Total overseas assets owned by British residents at the beginning of the 1980s stood at about £85 000 million, compared with total liabilities of about £70 000 million.

The other items in the balance of payments consist of transactions by the UK government; short-term borrowing and lending in the banking sector; trade credit (revenues earned but not yet received); and changes in the official reserves of gold, foreign currencies and borrowing rights with the International Monetary Fund (IMF) (see pages 223–4).

Official financing

Finally it is necessary to refer to the set of items described as 'official financing'. These are transactions involving the Bank of England acting on behalf of the government (see pages 188–91). There are three ways in which the Bank's activities enter the account:

- by adding to or drawing on its reserves of gold and foreign currencies
- by altering the amount that it borrows from the International Monetary Fund
- by borrowing from or lending to monetary authorities overseas

In the three years shown in Table 2 Britain was on balance, increasing her credit position or reducing her debits with both the IMF and foreign banking authorities, and both adding to and drawing on her reserves. These years must not be regarded as typical, if indeed any are. Official financing is not something which can be regarded as having a 'normal' pattern, but involves responses to the needs and opportunities of the time.

# 8 Money and banking[1]

Aside from a brief reference in Chapter 1 to money, this book has been written as if the 'filthy lucre', as the New Testament called it, did not exist. A visitor from space, reading the previous chapters might well think that money, per se, was of insufficient importance to merit much attention. He would, of course, be wrong. Although we have concentrated almost exclusively on the *real* side of the economy—on the supply of real resources, goods and services—we have valued them always in money terms. Indeed, in Chapter 7 on the national income we used money values to add together production of various kinds, this being the only economically relevant way to add such diverse things as aerospace equipment, bread, cinema tickets and dwellings.

**Money**

Money, however, has more functions than merely to act as a **unit of account**—it is also a **medium of exchange** and a **store of value**. Its existence is of immense help in lubricating the complex economic system of a country like the UK, although it can cause major problems too—outstandingly, that of inflation if the supply of money grows too rapidly.

Forms of money

In primitive societies man has employed a variety of objects to perform the functions of money, from seashells and cattle to cigarettes in prisoner of war camps. Although we do not use such primitive forms of money today, there are more types of money in current use than we might at first imagine.

*Coins*

The kind of money most commonly used to make small payments is coins. Gold and silver used to circulate in Britain before the First World War. Today coins are made of bronze or of alloys of copper and nickel. They are manufactured by the Royal Mint and are only legally acceptable up to certain amounts, known as **legal tender**. The term legal tender means the money must be accepted if you offer it to someone in payment of a debt. Coins below 50 pence are legal tender up to £5.

1 Related chapters in Lipsey are as follows: Chapter 38 deals with the general nature of money and the banking system; Chapter 39 deals with monetary theory; and Chapter 44 deals with the activities of a central bank.

For somewhat larger payments, where coins would be unsuitable, debts may be settled in notes. Bank notes, or paper money as it is sometimes called, have an interesting origin. In the 17th century the most general form of money was the gold coin. Rather than keep a large quantity of gold at home, people naturally used to take it for safe keeping to local goldsmiths, who were early bankers. In return for the gold the goldsmith issued a receipt, on which it was stated that he promised to pay on demand to the holder of the receipt the amount of gold mentioned. Following upon this, the custom grew for individuals to accept such receipts, or notes, in payment for debts, since with the signature of a reputable goldsmith, and later a banker, they were 'as good as gold'.

Today, bank notes are the principal form of currency, although it is no longer open to any banker or goldsmith to issue them. In England and Wales this right is now exclusively reserved for the Bank of England. Bank notes, however, still retain their original form. If you look at a £10 note you will still find printed there a statement, which no longer has any real meaning (since gold is no longer obtainable on demand in exchange for notes), but which is signed by the Chief Cashier on behalf of the Bank of England and reads 'I promise to pay the bearer on demand the sum of ten pounds'. Bank notes are legal tender up to any amount without limit.

The money used to settle most small debts consists of either notes or coin. Before we consider the most common means of making large payments, we should mention that there are a large number of alternative mechanisms, such as the use of credit cards, IOUs, promissory notes, etc. The Post Office also operates a National Giro for the transfer of money through post offices, but all these mechanisms are unimportant relative to the use of **banks**.

Bank deposits

By far the most important means of settling debts in modern Britain is carried out with the assistance of banks, and usually involves the drawing of cheques. Cheques originated at roughly the same time as bank notes. After depositing gold in a local bank or with a goldsmith it became common for a person to write a letter to his banker instructing him to pay a sum of money to a person he would name. He would then give the letter to the person to whom he owed money. The latter would then dispatch it to his banker who would arrange to collect the cash for him. Quite soon this form of settling debts became so important that it was unnecessary to write a special letter every time one wanted to make a payment, as the banks themselves began to print letter forms, known as cheques. These need only the insertion of the amount, the date, the name of the payee and the signature of the person making the payment. Today banks issue books containing such cheques to their customers, although there are other means of transferring money in bank accounts.

The advantages of making payments through banks are simplicity and safety, especially when the sum involved is large. All businesses use banks, as do many private individuals. The importance of bank deposits in comparison with the volume of notes and coin in circulation is shown in Fig 86.

It must be understood that Fig 86 is a simplification of the stock of money in existence. There is no single statistic that

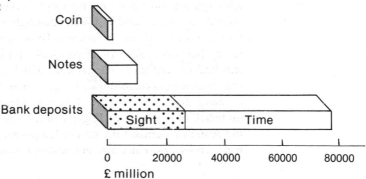

*Fig 86* Sterling money stock 21 April 1982 Source: *Financial Statistics*

can be regarded as *the* measure of the supply of money. Several are available, based on different definitions and all have their uses. However, there are three main sources of complication.

*Sight and time deposits*

As Fig 86 shows, there are two kinds of bank deposits:

- **sight deposits**, kept in current accounts
- **time deposits**, kept in deposit accounts

Sight deposits are withdrawable on demand and without notice, merely by presenting a cheque. They generally do not earn any interest—in fact customers may even be called upon to pay a charge to cover the office work involved in running the account.

Most businesses do not need to keep all their money on current account, so they put some of it in a deposit account. Here it earns interest, but seven days' notice is legally required for its withdrawal. In practice, however, banks seldom object if customers make transfers of reasonable amounts from deposit to current account for immediate payment. For this reason time deposits may be considered, for some purposes, as part of the money stock.

*Non-sterling deposits*

Fig 86 includes only bank deposits held in sterling. However, businesses and individuals may choose to hold some of their cash balances in foreign currencies, either to make purchases overseas or to convert them into sterling when circumstances are favourable.

In mid-1982 foreign currency bank deposits in the UK amounted to about £11 500 million—a sum similar to that circulating in notes and coin. The proportion of total money assets held in foreign currencies varies widely, however. It was high in mid-1982—about 12 per cent—but it has been as low as 2 per cent in the early 1970s.

*Deposits of non-banking financial institutions*

As we shall shortly see, banks are only one of a range of financial institutions performing overlapping functions. Others include building societies and insurance companies (see pages 184–6). In so far as people choose to keep credit accounts with building societies, for example, rather than with banks, their deposits can be drawn on to settle debts. These deposits are therefore included for some purposes in the calculation of the total money supply. The total deposits of building societies are in fact very substantial—of the order of two-thirds of those of the banks. They are regarded by many people, however, as long-term investments, and only a small proportion of them are used to settle current transactions.

Alternative definitions of the money supply

Economic theorists like to define an abstraction called money that is clearly distinct from all other financial assets. In the real world, however, there is a whole spectrum of assets which have some or all of the characteristics of money. Thus there is no clear and obvious dividing line between what is and is not money. As a result there are alternative definitions and measurements of 'the' money supply.

If we concentrate on money as a medium of exchange the definition is clear—notes and coins and chequable, ie sight, deposits, which together are called **M1**. However, if we consider money as a store of value, there is a range of alternative assets that can act as a store of value but that can be turned into a medium of exchange at a moment's notice and at a fixed rate of one for one. For example, you cannot pay your bills with a time deposit but in practice you can easily transfer it into a sight deposit on a pound-for-pound basis. This makes a time deposit almost as good as money.

Depending on where we draw the line among assets used as stores of value that are easily transferable into a medium of exchange, there are many possible definitions of 'the' money supply. Three of the most common in use in the UK are:

- **M1**
- **Sterling M3**
- **M3**

In addition to these widely used and relatively straightforward measures of the money supply there are three other measures, the first narrower and the other two broader:

- high-powered money
- $PSL_1$ and $PSL_2$ (private sector liquidity 1 and 2)

*M1*

This comprises notes and coin plus the sterling sight deposits of the private sector.

*Sterling M3*

This is M1 plus sterling time deposits of the private sector plus sterling sight and time deposits of the public sector.

*M3*

This is sterling M3 plus UK residents' deposits in other currencies.

*High-powered money*

This is the deposit liabilities of the Bank of England (excluding special deposits—see pages 189–90) plus notes and coin.

*$PSL_1$*

This includes notes and coin, time and sight deposits of the private sector plus what are known as 'other money-market instruments', of which the largest are deposits with local authorities and certificates of tax deposit.

*$PSL_2$*

This is the broadest measure of all and includes deposits with building societies, National Savings and Trustee Savings Banks, in addition to the those items listed under $PSL_1$.

*Domestic credit expansion*

Finally there is **domestic credit expansion (DCE)**. This is a measure of *changes* in the money supply (adjusted for international transactions), and must not be confused with the above definitions which quantify the money stock itself. (DCE consists of changes in the following: notes and coin, bank lending to the public and private sectors, and external financing of the public sector.)

*Fig 87* Alternative
measures of the
money supply
21 April 1982
Source: *Financial
Statistics*

The six measures of the money supply referred to above are set out in Fig 87. They can be useful in examining the operation of the government's monetary policy, to be explained in the next chapter. It is more important to have an idea of their relative magnitudes than to remember precisely how each measure is defined. All are stated at their current

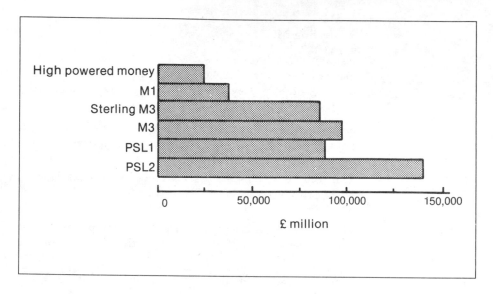

values but changes in the money supply can be adjusted to allow for inflation, thus yielding the *real* money supply (in a fashion similar to that used to derive real income from money income—see pages 163–4).

**The banking
system**

The importance of banks has already been mentioned in connection with the supply of money. Now we must examine them in more detail. This can best be done under two headings:

- **commercial banks**, the most important of which are known as clearing banks
- **the Bank of England**

The clearing
banks

For well over 100 years the principal type of banking institution for the conduct of everyday business has been a commercial enterprise, formed as a joint stock company. However, this has not always been the case; previously the joint stock form of organisation had been prohibited to banks, leaving the business in the hands of a multitude of small private partnerships and the Bank of England, the latter being founded by Royal Charter (see page 188). It took a year of financial crisis in 1825 to bring about a change in the law.

Bank mergers in the 19th century, during the First World War and in the 1970s brought the number of banks down to the present level. Four large banks—Barclays, Lloyds, Midland and the National Westminster (NatWest)—now account for well over 90 per cent of the total business of the London clearing banks (see below).

*Bank clearing*

Earlier we stated that the major commercial banks in Britain are known as clearing banks. Here is why.

Every time someone draws a cheque in favour of another person it is necessary to transfer a sum of money. If the people have accounts at the same bank it is a simple matter; the bank makes entries in the two customers' accounts, debiting one and crediting another. If they have accounts at different banks, however, this procedure is not possible. One solution would be for the bank of the person making the payment to transfer cash to the other bank, which is what happened in the past. However, the bank clerks who used to travel around the City of London transferring sums of cash soon realised that their work would be minimised if they all met to sort out the payments that were due, particularly as it often happened that a clerk from bank A was collecting from bank B, while his counterpart from bank B was collecting from bank A. Obviously if the sums involved were identical there was no need for either clerk to be collecting at all. Even if the amounts were not equal the smaller could be offset against the larger and the clerk from the latter bank could collect the difference, thus halving the work.

The essential requirement for the successful working of this system of offsetting claims against one another, known as **clearing**, was that the clerks should meet. In the 18th century they organised this themselves, but there is now a bankers' clearing house in the City where computerised data on the transfer of sums between different bank accounts is reconciled and the subsequent differences between the banks settled.

*Assets and liabilities of the clearing banks*

Commercial banks are in business to make a profit. They are essentially borrowing and lending institutions, ie they borrow from one set of people and lend to others at a profit. How is it possible for a bank to 'lend other people's money' which it is supposed to be keeping in safe custody? What happens if the people who have deposited their money in the bank demand payment and the banks are unable to satisfy them?

The answers to these questions cannot be provided in full here. However, they depend on a fact which the earliest goldsmith-bankers did not take long to grasp, namely that it is extremely rare for any significant fraction of their customers (let alone all of them) to demand money *at the same time*. The banker therefore needs to hold only enough cash to meet the needs of those that do make demands.

The banker can keep his cash reserve low by holding also some financial assets which are, so to speak, 'near money' in the sense of being speedily and easily exchangeable into cash. So protected, the banker can make loans which earn interest. The best proportions of cash and **liquid assets** (as money and near-money assets are called) to deposits have evolved in the light of experience. Traditionally a figure of about 8 per cent was preferred. In modern times, however, the freedom of the banks to decide how to allocate their assets in different forms is subject to some control by the government, acting through the Bank of England. We shall consider these matters in Chapter 9.

Fig 88 shows the two sides of the business of the London clearing banks, as depicted by their balance sheet accounts of assets and liabilities.

*Liabilities*

The liabilities, which we have already mentioned, consist almost wholly of current and deposit accounts standing to the credit of their customers. The difference between them has been explained earlier (see page 173).

There are two sets of liabilities included in the 'other' category of Fig 88. One consists of liabilities to the banks' shareholders, while the other is **certificates of deposit**. These are notes (receipts) issued by the banks and which are in circulation in the money market; they have to be paid when presented by a holder at the maturity date.

*Assets*

The asset side of the balance sheet of the clearing banks may best be examined using the concepts of profitability and **liquidity**, the latter referring to the speed and ease with which an asset may be turned into cash.

*Notes and coin* held in the vaults are the banks' first line of reserve—they are perfectly liquid and earn no return at all.

*Accounts at the Bank of England* are the credit balances of the clearing banks at the Bank of England which, among other things, acts as the 'bankers' bank'. The deposits kept

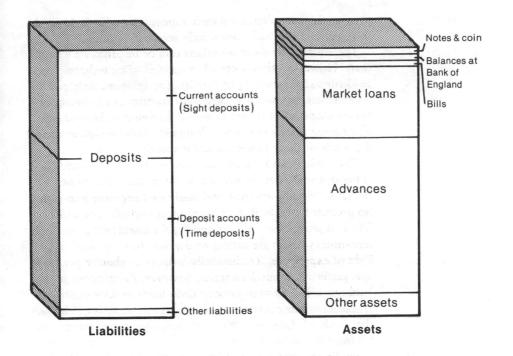

**Liabilities**       **Assets**

Labels in figure:
- Current accounts (Sight deposits)
- Deposits
- Deposit accounts (Time deposits)
- Other liabilities
- Notes & coin
- Balances at Bank of England
- Bills
- Market loans
- Advances
- Other assets

*Fig 88* London clearing banks' liabilities and assets 21 April 1982 Source: *Bank of England Quarterly Bulletin*

there by the clearing banks are of two basic kinds. The first are the balances which the banks freely decide to hold at the Bank of England for their own convenience. The second are balances which the banks are required to hold there by the government, as decided by the Bank of England itself. The latter are also of two types:

- special deposits
- cash ratio deposits

**Special deposits** are non-interest bearing frozen assets called for and released at the direction of the Bank of England. **Cash ratio deposits** are also in a sense frozen assets, although they do earn interest. They are the result of undertakings by the banks to hold a small percentage of their liabilities in their Bank of England accounts (the percentage in mid-1982 was less than 1 per cent of so-called 'eligible liabilities'—mainly sterling deposits). These are related to monetary policy, to be discussed in Chapter 9.

**Bills of exchange** and **Treasury bills** are fairly liquid assets; they are, in effect, short-term loans with an average duration of about 6 weeks. Bills of exchange come into existence as a result of an individual or institution needing cash for a short period. Suppose, for example, an exporter of goods needs finance to cover the time between the merchandise leaving his factory and arriving overseas, at which point a foreign importer will pay for them. The exporter can draw up a bill of exchange to cover the expected revenue. The importer then formally accepts the obligation to pay the sum involved in, say, 3 months time, thereby enabling the drawer to sell (or **discount**) the bill in the City and receive cash immediately. The price of the bill depends on the **discount rate** which determines the rate of interest paid on the bill. If it is eg 12 per cent per annum, a 3-month £100 bill will yield £97. (The discount rate is almost, but not quite, the rate of interest. Thus a £100 3-month bill sold for £97 carries a 3 per cent quarterly discount rate, although the borrower pays £3 interest and gets £97 which implies an interest rate of 3/97 per cent, ie 3.09 per cent.)

**Treasury bills** are similar to bills of exchange; they are promises by the government to pay sums of money in the future. The Treasury issues them from week to week to finance current government expenditure (see discount houses pages 182–3).

**Market loans** are assets with a high degree of liquidity comprising short-term loans to city financial institutions. They include **money at call and short notice**, lent at relatively low rates of interest, and other lending to the money market.

**Investments** are longer-term securities, mainly issued by the government. The liquidity of the banks' portfolio of securities depends on how long the securities have to run to maturity. Those which are almost due for redemption are highly liquid, whilst those with longer periods of time to run are less so. Securities can, of course, be sold at any time at the prevailing market price, but this varies from day to day as market interest rates vary, the liquidity of the securities being related to the certainty of the sum realisable on sale as well as to their mere marketability.

**Advances** to customers are the largest group of assets held by the banks. They are both the least liquid assets and the most profitable. Such advances may be made on **overdraft**, with permission for borrowers to overdraw their accounts up to stated limits, or on straightforward loans. The overdraft system is particularly convenient for borrowers whose needs fluctuate, as interest is paid only on the amount actually borrowed. Sometimes the banks require **collateral** security, eg businesses may be required to deposit share certificates, but loans are often made to businesses on the strength of trade prospects. The rates of interest charged vary from time to time with the riskiness of the project for which the loan is to be used and with the credit standing of the borrower. Banks publish **base lending rates**, and actual interest rates charged to borrowers are usually linked to these. The distribution of advances among the main classes of borrowers is shown in Fig 89.

*Fig 89* Advances of the London clearing banks; amounts outstanding 21 April 1982 Source: *Financial Statistics*

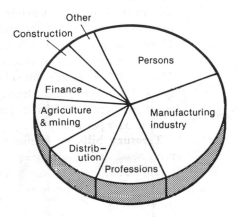

The other assets of the banks are a miscellaneous category and include bank premises and equipment. We must, however, mention that the classification used for Fig 88 and the accompanying text neglects certain formal distinctions between what are known as **eligible assets** and **liabilities**. These are part of the mechanism of monetary policy and will be explained in Chapter 9 (see pages 208–9).

We conclude this section on the clearing banks with a general comment. All the ways in which banks choose to use their resources (except only holding cash) involve the sacrifice of ready money for some asset which will bring in a larger sum at a future date. As a general principle it may be said that the longer the wait and the greater the risk, the more profitable the loan should be. To sacrifice all for the chance of large profits, however, could soon lead to the collapse of a bank, and it is the maintenance of a portfolio which shows a nice balance between profitability and liquidity which is the art of banking.

## Non-banking financial institutions

The London clearing banks form the major part of what is known as the UK monetary sector, although there are other clearing banks in Scotland and Northern Ireland. There is also a great variety of other financial institutions which perform some functions similar to the clearing banks. For example, the building societies play a role in the supply of money (see page 174) as their deposits are regarded as very liquid assets. There are also many other fringe and **secondary banks**, including several hundred overseas banks, accepting, discount and finance houses, merchant banks, trustee savings banks and the National Girobank. The monetary sector as a whole is

*Fig 90* UK monetary sector April 1982
Source: *Financial Statistics*

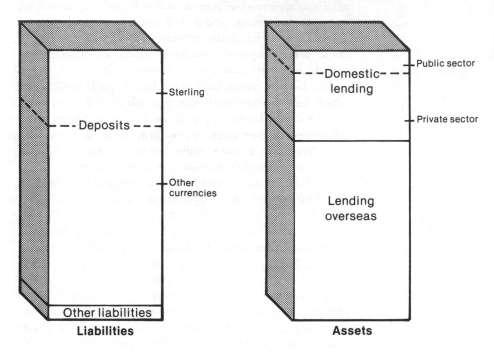

Liabilities                  Assets

particularly important in financing overseas transactions, as can be seen from Fig 90.

We now turn our attention to the specialised activities of certain major types of non-banking financial institutions which are part of the monetary sector.

Discount houses    As their name implies, these institutions are involved in discounting bills of exchange and Treasury bills (see above). When they do so, either for the government or for a private trader, they must, of course, have a supply of cash, which they finance by short-term borrowing from the banks, who lend at relatively low rates of interest. The discount houses are able to make a profit by charging a rate for discounting slightly above the rate which they have to pay for this accommodation.

Although the bills which they discount usually become due for payment only after anything from two to six months, and the money which they borrow is repayable at shorter notice, the discount houses are not usually left short of funds since it generally happens that when one bank is calling in its loans another is offering more to the discount market. Even if this is not the case the discount houses can always turn to the Bank of England which, as we shall see, acts as a **lender of last resort**. As they may have to borrow from the Bank at relatively high rates of interest, they will probably show a loss on such transactions, which they naturally try to avoid. The frequency with which the discount houses are forced 'into the Bank' depends upon the general financial state of the country and the monetary policy of the government.

The discount houses hold a considerable number of the bills which they discount until maturity, but they also rediscount some with the banks which, as we have seen, like to keep a proportion of their assets in this form. In fairly recent times they have also become quite important dealers in other government securities as these approach maturity.

Twelve London discount houses are members of the **London Discount Market Association**. Their freedom of action is limited by controls similar to those on banks. Since 1981, for instance, they must hold minimum percentages of their assets on deposit at the Bank of England (see page 209).

| Accepting houses | The willingness of discount houses to discount bills of exchange must depend on their estimate of the risk that when a bill is presented for payment it may not be met. Consequently, unless they have reliable information about the creditworthiness of the acceptor of a bill they will, in all probability, refuse to discount it. For an exporter in the 19th century, perhaps selling to a small firm in South America, this risk could have been a serious matter, had it not been for the existence of accepting houses. These financial institutions, including such names as Rothschild, Baring, Hambros and Lazard, and sometimes known as '**merchant bankers**', grew up to meet this need. By establishing agents in the major trading centres of the world they were able to check on the financial standing of most traders. They were therefore willing, in return for a commission, to guarantee that an appropriate bill would be paid on maturity, which they signified by adding their name to the original acceptor's or by accepting the bill themselves. The British exporter had no trouble discounting such a bill in the market for, thus guaranteed, the discount houses knew that, if need be, the Bank of England would always advance them money on the strength of such 'eligible paper'. |

Today, merchant banks still perform this traditional function, although British and overseas deposit banks also offer a similar service. The government also runs an Export Credits Guarantee Department (ECGD) which provides insurance against risk of default by importers. Merchant banks have also diversified. They indulge in a certain amount of ordinary deposit banking business and make a speciality of offering an advisory service with regard to investment management, raising new capital, and mergers and takeover bids.

Finance houses
The provision of funds for hire purchase and credit sales comes from several sources, including clearing and merchant banks. There are also a number of specialised finance houses, or 'industrial bankers' as they are occasionally called, operating in Britain. Just over 40 belong to the Finance Houses Association and account for about 80 per cent of total business. The total outstanding balance of instalment credit at the end of 1981 was approximately £10 000 million.

The main business of finance houses is in retail trade, but leasing of cars and equipment by businesses has become popular in recent years, partly as a result of tax concessions. Like other financial intermediaries, these institutions borrow in order to lend and they obtain some finance from depositors. For this reason they have, rather like building societies, taken on some of the characteristics of banks.

Building societies
In terms of sheer size the largest category of non-banking financial institutions is building societies. Their total accumulated funds at the end of 1981 amounted to about £60 000 million, their deposits even exceeding the sterling deposits of the London clearing banks.

Building societies have a history going back to the 18th century, when many were founded by small groups of people to finance the building of their own homes. Today there are about 250 building societies, although the number has been decreasing as the smaller societies have been absorbed by the larger ones. Over half the business is in the hands of half a dozen societies, of which the Halifax and the Abbey National are the largest. The banks have, in recent years, started to compete vigorously in supplying loans for house purchases.

The prime function of building societies is not the building of houses but the lending of money to borrowers for house purchase—this accounts for about 80 per cent of the societies' funds. The remainder is held in short- and longer-term securities. The method of borrowing money from a building society is known as obtaining a **mortgage**. An individual wanting to buy a house obtains a loan by surrendering to the society the title to the property and paying interest on the loan at a rate varying with conditions in the market. For suitable houses in first class condition societies are, in normal times, prepared to lend about 90 per cent of the value of the house. The borrower then has to find the balance elsewhere and to pay off the mortgage over a period of 15 to 20 years, or even longer.

Building societies obtain the money they lend by borrowing from the general public at a lower rate of interest than that charged when they lend, and in this they are assisted by a concession which makes them liable to income tax at a reduced rate. Money is lent to borrowers either on deposit or in return for shares in the society. The distinction between these two is close to that between the two types of deposit of the clearing banks, ie sight and time deposits. Withdrawal of funds in the form of shares may require formal notice but shareholders, like deposit account-holders at the commercial banks, can normally make withdrawals much more quickly. Indeed, as mentioned earlier, people have come to treat accounts with building societies as highly liquid assets, with the effect that the societies have themselves taken on some of the characteristics of commercial banks and are, like them, subject to government controls.

Insurance companies

The business of insurance companies is to take over from individuals specific risks in return for a payment known as a **premium**. They can do this because, although the risk is uncertain for an individual, it is not so for a company which specialises in risks of a particular type. A businessman can have no idea whether his factory will be damaged by fire next year, nor can a motorist know whether he will meet with an accident. However, an insurance company, dealing with thousands of similar risks, is in a different position as the law of averages works well with large numbers.

On the basis of claims experience and detailed statistical analyses, insurers are able to assess risks, the essential principle of insurance being the pooling of risks and their proper classification into groups. For example, the premium payable to insure family cars used for social and domestic purposes is very different from that to insure high performance cars for youthful drivers.

There are several types of insurance to be distinguished. Marine insurance covers ships and cargoes for maritime perils. (Much of this insurance is done through the institution known as Lloyd's, where the risks involved with single vessels are spread among a number of **underwriters**.) Fire insurance covers material loss to buildings and contents from fire and kindred perils. Accident insurance means what it says, the principal class being cover for motor vehicles.

By far the most important single category of insurance from the viewpoint of sources of finance is **life assurance**. This differs from the other types in an important respect. Whereas in the case of fire or accident there is uncertainty as to whether an incident *will* take place, in the case of life assurance there is no doubt as to whether a person will die. The uncertainty is *when* the unfortunate event will take place. Life assurance enables individuals to provide for their relatives on their death or to provide for their own retirement. The life assurance companies have data on the risk of death for various classes of individual. For example, they know that the risk varies with age and premiums rise accordingly—the older a person is when he or she takes out a life assurance policy, the higher the rate of premium.

The great importance of insurance funds arises from the fact

*Fig 91* Assets of insurance companies 1981
Source: *Financial Statistics*

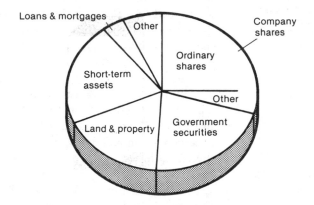

that they are accumulated over long periods and are invested in ways which allow for claims to be met and profits to be earned. The Life Offices have the largest sums to invest but the total accumulated funds of all insurance companies stood at over £70,000 million at the end of 1981. The relative importance of the different classes of asset held is shown in Fig 91. Government securities used to be the largest category, but almost 30 per cent of the total is now in the form of shares in joint stock companies. The bulk of these are ordinary shares and they give a significant role to insurance companies in the ownership of British industry (see page 35).

**Pension funds**  Employers in the public sector and many privately owned companies provide their employees with pensions on retirement, as do some trade unions. In certain pension schemes employees make contributions as well as employers. Pension (or superannuation) funds accumulate from the contributions made during the working life of employees and they are used to earn interest and dividends by the purchase of securities and shares in British companies. Pension funds may be self-administered or handled by insurance companies or banks.

Total funds increased very substantially during the 1960s and 1970s, and by the end of 1981 amounted to about £60 000 million—almost as large as the insurance funds. Moreover, nearly half of the assets of such funds consist of ordinary shares in joint stock companies. The managers of pension funds therefore play a role similar to that of their counterparts in insurance companies in the ownership of British industry.

*Fig 92* UK financial institutions 1981; increased funds accrued in selected institutions Source: *Financial Statistics*

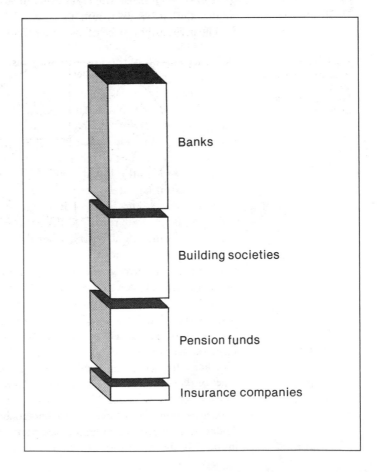

Banks

Building societies

Pension funds

Insurance companies

## The monetary sector as a whole

In previous sections we have considered the nature of most major UK financial institutions—banks, discount houses, building societies, etc. Inevitably the list is incomplete. There is no space to describe each and every financial intermediary, though they may, like the National and Trustee Savings Banks and the National Girobank, be important in their own ways.

Fig 92 tries to put some of the main institutions in perspective by showing their relative sizes in terms of *new* funds accumulated during 1981. The diagram shows the aggregate importance of each set of institutions. We explained earlier the specialised and semi-specialised nature of some of them and it follows that overall size does not necessarily indicate importance in particular markets. Used with care, however, Fig 92 does indicate relative orders of magnitude.

## The Bank of England

We have left until last a single major financial institution that stands apart from the rest—the Bank of England. Whilst all the important institutions mentioned so far are privately owned commercial bodies, the Bank of England is not. It is the **central bank** of the UK—a nationalised industry operated on behalf of the government.

The history of the Bank of England goes back to 1694 when it was founded by Royal Charter. Originally a private concern owned by its shareholders, its great importance led to nationalisation in 1946, when the shares were taken over by the government. A few relics of ordinary banking business remain, but today the Bank is on an entirely different footing from the commercial banks, over which it exercises a profound influence. The Bank of England controls the currency and acts as banker both to the government and to the commercial banks. It also plays a key role in the government's monetary policy. Its activities are discussed below under the headings of the two main departments into which it was divided by the Bank Charter Act of 1844.

## The Issue Department

The Bank of England has a monopoly of the note issue in England and Wales, though certain banks in Scotland and Northern Ireland have limited issuing rights. The balance sheet of the Bank's Issue Department shown on page 189 lists its assets and liabilities.

At one time the Bank's notes had to be backed by gold. Today, they are covered by government and other securities in the **fiduciary issue** (from the Latin *fiducia* meaning trust).

| Liabilities | | Assets | |
|---|---|---|---|
| Notes in circulation | 10 623 | Government securities | 2 527 |
| Notes in Banking Dept | 27 | Other securities | 8 123 |
| | 10 650 | | 10 650 |

## The Banking Department

The more important, as well as the more interesting, of the Bank of England's activities concern the Banking Department. It is here that the Bank functions as the government's bank and the bankers' bank.

The chief classes of assets and liabilities of the Banking

*Fig 93* Bank of England (Banking Department) liabilities and assets 21 April 1982
Source: *Financial Statistics*

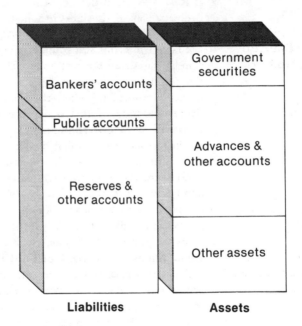

**Liabilities**        **Assets**

Department of the Bank of England are shown in Fig 93, which bears a similarity to Fig 88 on page 179 which displayed the balance sheet of the London clearing banks on the same date. This is more apparent than real because of the totally different functions of these institutions.

## Liabilities

**Bankers' accounts** relate to the Bank of England's function as the bankers' bank. They are the credits standing on deposit in favour of the clearing banks and discount houses, ie credits to them but liabilities to the Bank of England. They consist of two types of deposit. **Operational deposits** are working balances held mainly for settling debts among the London clearing banks. **Non-operational**, non-interest bearing **deposits** have been required since August 1981 to fulfil the cash reserve requirement that the banks (and the discount houses) must hold against their liabilities. Included in this category would also be the special deposits referred to earlier (see page 179), although it so happened that none needed to be held on the date in question.

**Public accounts** relate to the Bank's function as banker to the government. It is under the title of public accounts that the government banks its money. The size of the public accounts reflects the current state of official finances—the flow of tax receipts and public expenditure—though the government tries to keep a low balance here to avoid unnecessary costs.

**Reserves and other accounts** include the small amount of ordinary banking business in which the Bank of England still engages. The private customers are overseas banks and other City institutions, the total also covering liabilities to overseas central banks.

*Assets*

The assets side of the Bank's activities shows a marked difference from that resulting from the search for profitable lending of the commercial banks. There are three principal groups of assets.

**Government securities** (including Treasury bills) are not purchased by the Bank of England for the interest they carry, nor for liquidity purposes, as is the case with the commercial banks. The Bank of England engages in the purchase and sale of securities in order to influence the liquidity of the commercial banks, as will be explained in Chapter 9.

**Advances and other accounts** include those made to its ordinary customers. However, the most significant advances are those made to banks, discount houses and other financial institutions. As has been stated earlier (see page 183), the Bank of England operates as a 'lender of last resort' and is always prepared to make advances to such institutions if they are temporarily in need of cash. It does this by discounting bills of exchange and Treasury bills, although in doing so it may charge a rate of interest which is penal, ie in excess of the current market rate. Such loans are regarded by borrowers as temporary expedients, to be avoided if at all possible.

**Other assets** include premises and equipment and notes and coin. The latter are not a safety reserve to fall back on, as are the commercial banks' cash holdings, for the Bank of England can always have more notes printed if it is short of cash. These assets are, rather, the carry-over of the note issue from the Issue Department, and are available for release at any time as required.

The ways in which the Bank of England operates in the course of implementing the government's monetary policy will be examined in Chapter 9.

# 9 Growth and stabilisation policy[1]

Chapter 6 dealt with government policies in pursuit of two objectives related to the allocation of resources—efficiency and equity. These goals were described as microeconomic, in contrast to **macroeconomic** targets. This chapter now considers government policy aimed at such macroeconomic objectives as the promotion of growth and the stabilisation of the economy as a whole.

## Fluctuations in output and employment

The value of real output has grown in Britain at an average rate of about 2 per cent per annum since the beginning of the present century. If you look closely at year to year changes, rather than at long-term trends, you will find that economic activity proceeds on an irregular path, with forward sprints interrupted by pauses and even relapses. These short-term fluctuations are commonly known as the **trade cycle**, or **business cycle**.

Trade cycles are characterised by four fairly distinct phases:

- a **boom** period, when output and employment expand
- a **crisis**, or upper turning point
- **recession**, when output stagnates (or **depression**, when it declines substantially)
- **recovery**, the lower turning point, marking the return towards boom conditions

Trade cycles can be observed well back into the 19th century, when their duration was reasonably regular, lasting 8 to 10 years, and there were no prolonged periods of boom or slump (see Fig 94). The experience in the present century, however, has been rather different. The period between the two World Wars was one of lengthy depression lasting for the greater part of 20 years. It culminated in the Great Depression of the 1930s, which was unparalleled in its severity and was international in that very few countries escaped it.

During the Second World War unemployment fell to an extremely low level. For the first 25 years following the war unemployment still fluctuated, but the fluctuations were over a much narrower range than in any comparable period, as Fig 94 shows. Even with all possible allowances for changes in the definitions of the unemployment statistics, that period was

1 This chapter deals with material discussed in Lipsey Chapters 42–47.

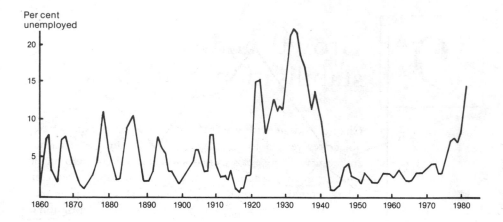

Per cent unemployed

*Fig 94* Percentage unemployment 1860–1982 (figures for 1860–1926 relate to the unionised labour force; subsequent figures relate to the total registered working population) Sources: *Abstract of British Historical Statistics*, B R Mitchell and P Deane, Cambridge University Press, 1962, *Annual Abstract of Statistics*, and *Monthly Digest of Statistics*

one where the average level of unemployment was exceptionally low.

In the early 1970s the pattern changed yet again. Fig 95 shows that an upswing was in progress at the start of the decade. Then, in 1974, the UK and the rest of the world slipped into recession which bottomed out in 1975. The following recovery was short-lived, however, and by 1980 the economy had entered a new recession, the worst since the 1930s, which was still continuing at the time of writing (1983).

The most recent period, charted in Fig 95, was different in another extremely important respect from previous experience. In the typical cycle of earlier years the tendency was for inflation to be associated only with booms, while slumps were periods of relatively stable, or even falling, prices. After 1971, however, the price level rose substantially every year. The lowest inflation rate was 8½ per cent and the highest 24 per cent (1974–75), while the average rate was over 12 per cent per annum. Moreover, the rate of increase in the general level of prices, as noted above, no longer followed its traditional pattern of falling off during recessions. For the first time high unemployment and high rates of inflation existed simultaneously, giving rise to a new phenomenon which has come to be called **stagflation**.

## The goals of macroeconomic policy

Three primary goals of macroeconomic policy can be identified as:

- a high rate of economic growth
- a relatively stable price level
- a low and stable level of unemployment

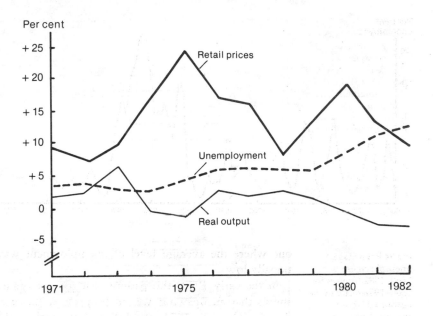

Per cent

+25 ····· Retail prices

+20

+15

+10

+5 ····· Unemployment

0 ····· Real output

-5

1971          1975          1980    1982

*Fig 95* Fluctuations in
output, prices and
unemployment since
1971; percentage
unemployment and
year to year changes in
prices and output (per
cent)
Source: *Annual
Abstract of Statistics*,
and *Monthly Digest of
Statistics*

In addition, a fourth goal related to the balance of payments
and the exchange rate may be distinguished. It is, however,
secondary in nature in the sense that there is no immediate or
lasting advantage to a country from having a favourable
balance of payments position per se. An unsatisfactory
balance of payments position may, however, inhibit attain-
ment of one or more of the other three primary goals.

Each of the primary goals will be discussed in turn, and the
balance of payments afterwards. It may be useful, however,
to start by contrasting the British position over the last decade
with that of other industrialised countries. Fig 96 does this. It
shows comparative rates of growth of output, inflation and
unemployment, and puts the UK experience into an international perspective. The three parts of the diagram are effectively 'league tables', in which the UK is shown up in a
distinctly unfavourable light. We shall refer back to Fig 96
later.

## Economic growth

There is no need to elaborate on the reasons why economic
growth is a desirable objective of policy—it is the major cause
of rising living standards. Moreover, as we explained earlier
(see page 15), even quite small differences in growth rates can
lead to large differences in income per head because of the
power of compound interest. This is exactly what has hap-

*Fig 96*
Comparative rates of
growth, inflation and
unemployment in
selected countries
Sources: *a World Bank
Atlas*, International
Bank for
Reconstruction and
Development; *b* and *c*
*National Institute
Economic Review*

*a* Comparative
growth rate; average
annual rates of
growth of output

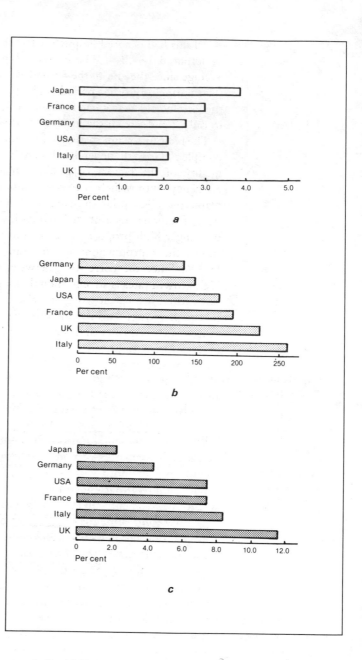

*b* Comparative
inflation rate;
consumer prices in
1981 as a percentage
of 1975

*c* Comparative
unemployment
rate; percentage of
labour force
unemployed 1981

pened. In 1960 UK income per capita was well above the
average of all EEC countries. However, the UK's subsequent
growth rate lagged behind all of them with the result that by
1980 income per head in Britain was only about two-thirds
that of France, less than 60 per cent that of Germany and only
20 per cent above that of Italy, a country which 20 years
previously had a per capita income of only half the UK's.

**196** *Introduction to the UK economy*

All this had occured despite the fact that the rate of growth of output in the UK had been almost 2½ per cent per annum on average since the end of the Second World War, a higher rate than during any other period in the present century—before the First World War it had been about 1 per cent and had risen to only 2 per cent in the interwar period.

The reasons for international differences in growth rates are complex. Growth depends ultimately on the quantity and quality of the factors of production available and on the efficiency with which they are combined. Observers often blame the UK's poor showing on its relatively low proportion of national income devoted to investment (and correspondingly high proportion devoted to consumption). Fig 97 shows these proportions for the same six countries as in Fig 96. Since the correlation between high investment and high growth rates is strong, though not perfect, it is clear that other forces are also at work. It is also important to remember that high growth is only one of several policy goals. When others, such as quality of life and reduction of pollution, come into conflict with the goal of high growth, some compromise has to be sought.

*Fig 97* Comparative investment ratios in selected countries (Investment/GNP, 1970–80 average) Source: *International Financial Statistics*

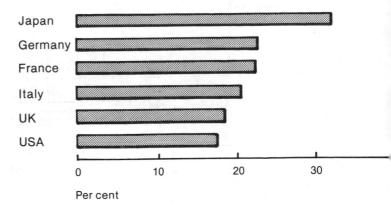

*Price stability*

The second macroeconomic goal is that of stability of the general level of prices. This target must be distinguished from the stability of all prices, which is not possible, let alone desirable. Changes in *relative* prices are important signals of changing costs or demand and they can activate the appropriate changes in the allocation of resources.

The price stability which is the aim of macroeconomic policy is stability in the *general* level of prices, ie the prevention or moderation of inflation. Fig 98 shows changes in the prices of the basic items—food, clothing and fuel—in a worker's budget in southern England between 1275 and 1959, calculated some time ago by Professor Henry Phelps Brown.

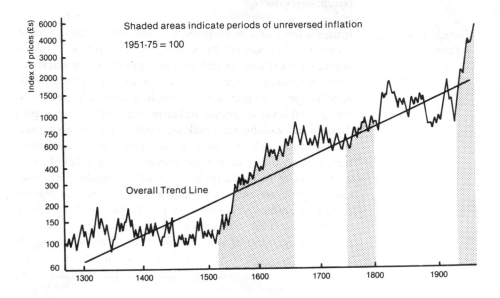

*Fig 98* Price index of consumables in southern England 1275–1970 (the cost of living index has been used to extend the series beyond 1959; shaded areas indicate periods of unreversed inflation)
Source: *Lloyds Bank Review*, October 1960

The trend line shows that the average change in prices over the whole period was about 0.5 per cent per year. The data also show that our current inflationary era is not unique. Although there have always been substantial short-term year to year ups and downs, 800 years of price level history is divided between periods of a stable price level, on average, and periods when the trend in the level has been sharply rising. The overall long-term trend, though, has been upwards, and only in the 19th century was there any appreciable period of a slightly falling trend in prices.

Experience in more recent years is better known. In the 1950s the price level rose relatively moderately, by about 3 to 5 per cent per annum. In the 1960s the inflation rate rose a little, prices being about 50 per cent higher by the end of the decade. The 1970s then witnessed a significant upsurge in the rate of inflation, especially after the oil price rise of 1973–74 (see page 104), though certainly not just because of it. So-called double digit inflation, ie 10 per cent per annum or more, first occurred in 1974, and the rate subsequently accelerated, reaching 24 per cent the following year. Over the decade of the 1970s prices rose on average by 250 per cent. Inflation continued into the 1980s, though the rate had fallen back to the single digit level by 1982. Over the whole period 1960–82 the level of prices was on average about 6 times higher at the end than at the beginning of the period. A pound in 1982 was worth only about 17 pence in terms of its 1960 purchasing power.

*The effects of inflation*

Inflation has many consequences. It distorts the allocation of resources, for example by making 'investment' in 'collect-ables', eg works of art and postage stamps, more attractive than investment in 'real' productive activities, as individuals seek 'hedges' for their savings which at least keep pace with the general level of prices. Inflation, especially at an unpredictable and variable rate, makes it difficult for businesses and private individuals to plan with confidence for the future and it may affect the balance of payments (see pages 218 ff).

However, one of the main effects of inflation is redistributive. It penalises those whose incomes are fixed in money terms, eg holders of annuities, while favouring those whose incomes rise faster than the rate of inflation itself. Chapter 4 showed something of the way in which different groups of workers manage to increase their relative earnings (see pages 79 ff), and it is important to recognise that the relative strength of trade unions in various occupations and industries may have been influential in combating the effects of inflation on their members.

*Full employment*

There is no need to elaborate on why a high level of employment is regarded as a desirable target. Unemployment causes economic waste and human suffering, especially if it is heavy and prolonged. The experience of the interwar years, when unemployment never fell below 10 per cent per annum, and exceeded 20 per cent in the Great Depression, was dramatic. During the Second World War the two main political parties in the then coalition government made a statement accepting 'as one of their primary aims and responsibilities the maintenance of a high and stable level of employment after the war'[1], a policy accepted also by succeeding postwar governments and continued to the present day, though other, at times conflicting, objectives have interfered with its achievement.

The extent of unemployment in Britain has been charted in

1 *Employment Policy*, Cmd 6527, 1944.

Figs 94 and 95, as well as in Fig 44 page 77, which noted the regional variations. The statistical basis for these diagrams must be understood before one can draw conclusions from them. The numbers counted as unemployed were those persons who decided to register as such and who were also 'capable of and available for work'. It is known that there are some forces causing the figure to overstate and other forces causing it to understate the true numbers of those who would accept work at the going wage rate if such work were available. The *under*statement arises from the fact that some persons may not actually register at Job Centres. The most important category here is married women who, especially in times of recession, do not bother to register, and either stay at home until the job market picks up or seek employment through such channels as newspaper advertisements or private agencies. People over retirement age and others who are ineligible (or believe themselves to be ineligible) for social security benefits are also unlikely to register. The *over*estimation of the numbers recorded as unemployed results mainly from individuals registering for benefits who are unable or unwilling to work, or who are working in the black economy (see page 160).

A change in the method of measuring unemployment was introduced in October 1982. The new basis substituted benefit claimants for registered unemployed persons available for work. Its use resulted in an immediate drop of nearly a quarter of a million in the numbers officially jobless. Although disabled unemployed are counted for the first time, the main difference between the new and the old bases relates to those (mainly married women) who do not claim benefit on losing their jobs because they are not entitled to it. The probable effect of the change has been to increase the number of hidden unemployed, but neither series of statistics (nor any other) is as completely accurate or easy to interpret.

Estimation of the amount of so-called **hidden unemployment** resulting from the matters described in the previous paragraphs is not an easy matter. Several attempts have been made, but there is no agreement on the precise amount that exists. All that can be said with certainty is that the relative reliability of the official estimates varies considerably with underlying conditions of the economy and that comparisons of unemployment rates over time and among countries must be treated with caution.

Statistics of the numbers unemployed expressed as a percentage of the labour force can, if taken by themselves, be misleading for two additional reasons:

- they ignore the length of time that the unemployed are out of work
- they need to be considered in the light of jobs available

*The duration of unemployment*

The duration of unemployment affects the stock of workers in the total at any given time. It is important because a major reason for rising unemployment percentages in recent years has been that the out of work have stayed in the job queue longer.

There are several ways to measure unemployment duration. Two of the most important involve asking: *a* the currently unemployed, and *b* those finding new jobs, how long they have been out of work. The former measures *uncompleted*, and the latter *completed*, spells of unemployment. The former also tends to be biased downwards and is used in Fig 99 which shows, therefore, the distribution of uncompleted spells of unemployment in 1972 when the rate was 3.8 per cent, and in 1982 (July) when it was 13.4 per cent. It can be seen that the percentage out of work for longer periods was substantially greater in 1982, especially among females.

*Fig 99* Duration of unemployment 1972 and 1982 (July); number of weeks out of work
Source: *Monthly Digest of Statistics*

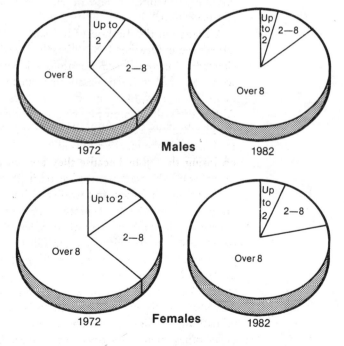

*Job vacancies (U–V ratio)*

Comparisons of the number of unemployed with the number of job vacancies is shown in Fig 100[1]. The relationship

1 For discussion of theoretical issues concerning inflation and unemployment see Lipsey Chapters 46 and 47.

Fig 100
Unemployment and
job vacancies; number
of registered
unemployed and
number of unfilled
vacancies
Sources: *Annual
Abstract of Statistics* and
*Monthly Digest of
Statistics*

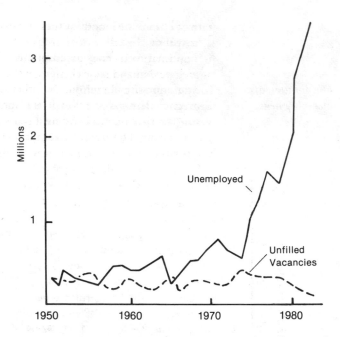

between these two variables is sometimes referred to as the
**U–V ratio**. When the number of unemployed is equal to the
number of vacancies (U = V), as it was approximately in the
1950s and 1960s, there is a job available of some kind for every
person looking for one. In the aggregate, the demand for
labour is then equal to its supply, so that unemployment is not
due to deficient aggregate demand. When U = V the unemployed can be regarded either as **frictionally unemployed**
(those moving between jobs) or **structurally unemployed**,
or both. Structural unemployment is caused by a mismatch
between the skill and regional components of labour demand
and supply, eg a vacancy existing for a plasterer in Perth when
there is an unemployed carpenter in Cardiff. A boom is
associated with V being greater than U, ie there is an excess
demand for labour compared with the supply of people
seeking jobs. In contrast, a slump is associated with U being
greater than V, ie there are more people seeking jobs than
there are jobs available.

*The Phillips curve*     In 1958 Professor A W Phillips, then of the London School of
Economics, published a paper showing a relationship between
unemployment and the rate of change of money wages in the UK
over the preceding century. This paper became famous and the
relationship subsequently came to be known as the **Phillips curve**.
     The curve itself showed no more than a statistical associa-
tion—that between percentage unemployment rates and the

rate of change of money wages. It was interpreted, however, as revealing the effect of aggregate demand on inflation. This is legitimate on two assumptions. First, that changes in aggregate demand *cause* changes in the level of unemployment in the opposite direction. In other words, the higher the aggregate demand the lower the unemployment (and vice versa), so that unemployment becomes a measure of aggregate demand. The second assumption is that wage costs are an important element of final prices, so that as wage costs go up

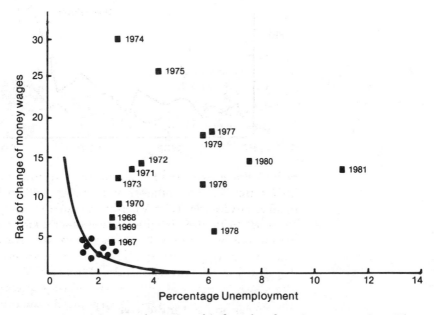

*Fig 101* The relationship between wage inflation and unemployment 1862–1981; (the curve is fitted to the data 1862–1957; the unlabelled dots cover the period 1958–66; the labelled squares cover the period (1967–81) Sources: 'The relation between Unemployment and the Rate of Change of Money Wage Rates in the UK 1861–1957', A W Phillips, *Economica*, 1958, *Annual Abstract of Statistics*, and *Monthly Digest of Statistics*

(give or take quite a bit for other forces) so must prices. Thus the Phillips curve provided an explanation of the influence of aggregate demand on inflation, through its influence on wage costs.

Fig 101 shows this relation. The original curve that Phillips fitted to the data for the period up to 1957 is drawn, together with a series of points for subsequent years. The latter are marked with their years, except for 1958–66, for which the closeness of the cluster of points makes their individual identification both difficult and unnecessary. It is clear, however, that the observations for the decade after Phillips wrote his article suggest a fairly constant relationship between unemployment and money wage increases.

This relation was shattered at the end of the 1960s by the money wage explosion when, for no obvious reason, wages rose faster and faster. Clearly the stable Phillips curve relationship that had lasted for a century had broken down.

By 1974, with unemployment not significantly different from the 1967 level, wage inflation had jumped from 4 per cent to nearly 30 per cent! The observations over that period are consistent with a major upward shift in the Phillips curve. Since that time the observations suggest that the pressure of aggregate demand, as measured by unemployment, still affects money wages but at a much higher level. The data for 1974 to 1981 trace out a fairly clear but different Phillips curve showing that the rate of increase of money wages is less the higher is the rate of unemployment, but at a much higher average level of wage increases than existed in the earlier period.

## The tools of macroeconomic policy

The effectiveness of government policy directed at the goals of growth, price stability and full employment depends upon a number of factors.

1 The *ranking* of the goals, especially in so far as there are **trade-offs** between them.
2 An understanding of the causes of unsatisfactory behaviour in the economy.
3 The availability of up to date information upon which policy can be based.
4 The tools (or **instruments**) used in pursuit of the goals. Three sets of tools can be distinguished:

- **fiscal policy**
- **monetary policy**
- other policies (**incomes policies, labour market intervention** and **indicative planning**)

We shall deal with each of these tools in turn, having regard to the policy objectives already discussed. However, it must be remembered that there may be balance of payments implications involved in each. For a country such as the UK, with a large foreign sector to its economy, these can be, and have been, at times, extremely important. Balance of payments policy will be discussed at the end of the chapter.

### Fiscal policy[1]

Fiscal (or budgetary) policy refers to attempts by the government to influence the level of total spending by varying the public sector component inversely with that of other sectors, in order to stabilise the total and so even out fluctuations in economic activity. Since such policies act through the level of aggregate demand they are often referred to as **demand management**.

1 The theory and practice of fiscal policy are analysed in Lipsey Chapter 43.

Fiscal policy can be used in a variety of ways. In the first place, taxes and subsidies can be varied to discourage spending on consumption and/or investment in times of excessive boom and, conversely, to encourage such spending when the level of economic activity is low. The government can make changes in the budget and, for speed and flexibility, it also has the power to vary tax rates on customs and excise duties by up to 10 per cent in either direction without the prior approval of Parliament. This provision is known as the **regulator**. It has not often been used in recent years, but can be invoked when required.

The second means of influencing total spending relates not to the private sector but to the government itself. There is no very good reason why the state has to balance its own budget, ie raising in taxation exactly the same amount as it spends. In times of boom it can run a budget surplus, while in periods of recession or depression it can run a budget deficit. Deficits tend to stimulate the economy because the government is putting more into it by way of spending than it is taking out in taxes. Surpluses tend to depress the economy (which might be a good thing if there is an overly strong boom) because they do the reverse. The extent to which the government and the nationalised industries borrow to finance an excess of expenditure over receipts is known as the public sector borrowing requirement (PSBR).

There is a third method by which the state can affect total spending. It is particularly relevant in periods when the government is trying to reduce total demand. At times it is easier for the central government to issue instructions for the reduction of public spending than actually to reduce it, simply because programmes for spending are in many cases long term and difficult to cut. **Cash limits** were introduced in 1976 for particular categories of expenditure by government departments, local authorities and the nationalised industries, putting limits on the amount that they can spend in a year. This method relates to the PSBR.

The overall impact of the government's fiscal policy is sometimes referred to as its **fiscal stance**. In Britain this has often been assumed to be adequately measured by changes in the PSBR. This is not so, however, because changes in the PSBR are partly the result of alterations in the level of activity in the economy itself, as well as of changes in the government's fiscal stance. Fiscal policy is affected by the relationship between government expenditure and tax rates. Changes in either alter the PSBR, but so does a change in the level of economic activity. A slump tends to lower tax revenues, because incomes fall, and to raise expenditure, especially on welfare payments. The combination of the two can raise the PSBR with no change in the government's fiscal stance. (To get round this problem economists often calculate a **high employment budget balance**, which is an estimate of what the PSBR would be on the assumption of current tax and expenditure policies and a high level of employment.)

*Fine tuning*

Fiscal policy developed from the ideas of John Maynard Keynes in the late 1930s and enjoyed widespread support among economists for more than three decades, during which time it was widely practised by governments in the UK and in many other countries.

Fiscal policy attempts to influence the economy through controlling the level of total demand for all goods and services. The ideal objective is to stabilise aggregate demand at a level just sufficient to produce full employment, without causing excess demand to build up inflationary pressures from the demand side. Since private sector expenditure is constantly changing, this type of stabilising fiscal policy requires that the government's fiscal stance be continually adjusted in an offsetting manner. Such a policy involves so-called **fine tuning** and many governments attempted it in the 1950s and 1960s. Experience over these decades suggests that fiscal fine tuning often worked to destabilise rather than to stabilise aggregate demand. Why was this so?

One reason why fiscal policy is difficult in practice is that the available data on which it must be based may be unreliable and out of date. We saw something of the reliability of some national income data in Chapter 7 page 158. If the government alters its fiscal stance this will affect the economy's behaviour over the coming months. To adjust its stance in a stabilising way the government must know what private expenditure will be over the forthcoming months, not what it was over past months. Thus what the government really needs is information on *ex ante* or planned expenditures, whereas, apart from surveys by the Confederation of British Industry on investment intentions, almost all such information is of the *ex post* realised kind.

*Cyclical indicators*

It is vital for successful economic forecasting that *advance* signs of changes in any of the major components of economic activity should be available. This is because it is much more difficult to identify cyclical *turning points* than to project steady trends, whether upwards or downwards.

A great deal of research has been carried out to establish

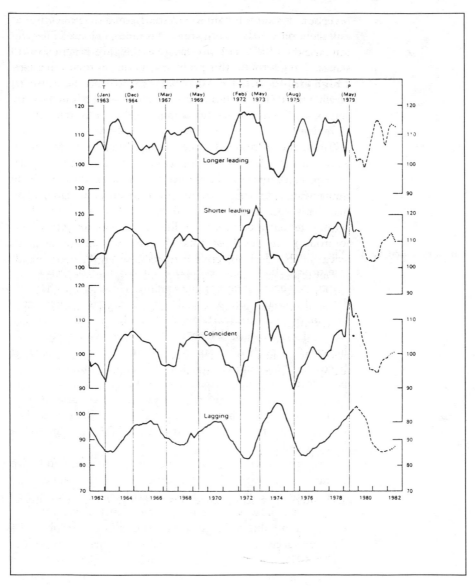

| | T | P | T | P | T | P | T | P |
|---|---|---|---|---|---|---|---|---|
| | (Jan) 1963 | (Dec) 1964 | (Mar) 1967 | (May) 1969 | (Feb) 1972 | (May) 1973 | (Aug) 1975 | (May) 1979 |

Longer leading

Shorter leading

Coincident

Lagging

*Fig 102* Cyclical indicators 1962–82; composite indices of indicator groups; (lines are liable to revision because in incomplete sets of component indicators) Source: *Economic Progress Report No. 149*, September 1982

reliable **leading indicators** of cyclical activity for this purpose, ie statistical series which lead rather than lag behind movements in the general level of economic activity. Some of them, eg the rate of interest on 3-month bills of exchange and the number of dwellings started, have an average lead of a year or more, while others, such as HP credit extended and new car registrations, have a lead of only a few months. None is entirely reliable and the government uses composite index numbers of 'shorter' and 'longer' leading indicators, whose behaviour during the period 1962–82 is charted in Fig 102.

↓      ↗

*Inflation*
*Not responsive to demand restriction*

*Fiscal Policy can deal with unemployment*

A further reason for the downgrading of fiscal policy is that inflation, one of the most pressing problems of the 1970s and early 1980s, does not appear to be highly responsive to demand restriction. Unemployment, in contrast, does respond to changes in total demand, so fiscal policy *is* a way of dealing with it. Inflation seems to be heavily influenced by supply side forces in the labour market, eg trade union bargaining postures and the social security system. Since inflation therefore responds only sluggishly to conditions of deficient aggregate demand, fiscal policy has been less to the fore in recent years. No matter how effective it may be in influencing aggregate demand, it is ineffective in dealing with problems that are not caused by too much or too little aggregate demand.

## Monetary policy[1]

The second set of instruments available to a government for controlling the level of economic activity are grouped under the general heading of monetary policy. This is operated by the Bank of England (see pages 188–91). It seeks to influence the amount of lending undertaken by the clearing banks and other financial institutions, which itself depends both on the willingness of the banks, etc, to lend and their customers to borrow. These supply and demand aspects roughly correspond to the two main techniques available to the Bank. The first involves what are called **open market operations**, which bring about changes in the liquidity of the banks. The second, acting through **interest rates**, is directed more to the amount of borrowing.

The technicalities of monetary policy are complex and have changed substantially over the years. No attempt can be made here to offer a comprehensive description of all of them. There have, however, been two landmarks in recent years which are notable for signifying changes in the emphasis of different facets of monetary control techniques. They occurred in 1971 and 1981 when the Bank of England published two important papers, entitled *Competition and Credit Control* and *Monetary Control—Provisions*, respectively.

## Bank liquidity

*Competition and Credit Control* concentrated on the liquidity of the banks in a wide sense. A new concept was introduced—that of so-called **eligible reserve assets.** Certain of the banks' assets were declared to be reserve assets and the banks were required to hold a minimum of $12\frac{1}{2}$ per cent of their total sterling liabilities in one or other of them. The assets included were credit balances at the Bank of England (other than special

1 The theory and practice of monetary policy are discussed in Lipsey Chapter 44.

deposits—see page 179, money at call and short notice, Treasury bills, a proportion of commercial bills of exchange and British government securities with less than 12 months to run to maturity.

The reserve asset system weakened the control of the Bank of England over credit creation by the commercial banks. This was because many of the reserve assets were also held by the non-banking private sector; thus the commercial banks could always replenish their reserves by buying some of the required assets from other private-sector sources. Indeed, the introduction of the system was accompanied by an unparalleled increase in the UK money supply.

The reserve asset system operated for nearly 10 years until 1981, when *Monetary Control—Provisions* shifted the emphasis of the techniques of monetary policy towards the control of the growth of money and credit created by the banking system. There was some move towards a **cash base** system, in that banks and discount houses were required to hold a small percentage of their **eligible liabilities** in a non-operational account at the Bank of England. There seems little evidence at the time of writing, however, that the Bank will seek to control the system in the traditional textbook fashion that is used in many other countries, ie that of varying the cash base that is available to the banking sector.

The 1981 provisions are not limited to the clearing banks, but apply to a range of financial institutions described as a new **monetary sector**. This range is considerably wider than the previous **banking sector** and covers the clearing banks, other '**licenced deposit takers**', including most acceptance houses, as well as non-clearing banks and trustee savings banks, all of whom are subject to similar controls. The clearing and certain other banks are also bound by the revised 'rules' to hold minimum percentages of their eligible deposits with members of the London Discount Market Association (see page 183) and as call money with institutions in the London money market. The latter provisions are designed to broaden the market for bills in which the Bank of England engages in open market operations. (Eligible liabilities are defined slightly differently for the clearing banks and for the other financial institutions. For the former they are sterling deposits, other than those arising from loans for more than two years.)

*Interest rate policy*    The arrangements summarised in the previous section relate to the way in which the Bank exercises control over the money supply. Control over lending through interest rates was demoted by the 1981 paper. Traditionally the Bank had the power to change interest rates directly and thereby influence the demand for borrowing. This power arose from the Bank's function as 'lender of last resort'. In times of cash shortage, for example, the Bank could charge a rate of interest above the market rate, and this higher interest rate would then filter through to the rest of the financial system. Indeed, for over 200 years the weekly announcement of **bank rate**, the rate of interest at which the Bank of England was prepared to rediscount eligible bills of exchange (such as Treasury bills), was watched closely by financial institutions all over the world. After 1972 the bank rate became known as **minimum lending rate** (**MLR**), but any changes announced by the Bank were still regarded as evidence of whether the government wanted to see interest rates rise or fall generally. In 1981, however, this use of MLR was abandoned, though it could be restored in special circumstances. This emphasised the relative importance newly attached to control of the supply of money rather than demand for it. The Bank continues to provide funds to the discount houses when they are in need, but does not publicise the rate at which it is prepared to do so, though this may often be inferred from its activities.

*Other techniques of monetary policy*

Other techniques of monetary policy have been used from time to time. Ceilings have been placed on bank advances, and informal requests to banks to restrict lending have been employed. A system was also in use between 1973 and 1980 whereby the banks were set target rates of growth for their deposits and were penalised if they overshot them (the so-called **supplementary deposit scheme**, otherwise known as the 'corset').

Finally we should mention the introduction in 1960 of **special deposits** (see page 179). These are 'frozen' deposits of the clearing banks held at the Bank of England. They can be called up or reissued as and when the Bank wishes to raise or lower pressure on the banks' liquidity, although they have not been used since July 1980.

Fiscal versus monetary policy

Monetary policy in the UK was generally regarded as subordinate to fiscal policy until the mid- to late 1970s. Restrictions on the effectiveness of fiscal policy in dealing with stagflation, however, raised monetary policy to prominence and it found favour with the school of thought known as monetarism, then gathering strength under the leadership of Professor Milton Friedman of Chicago.

At this time inflation was accelerating into double figures, with the result that politicians were beginning to think more of inflation than of unemployment as the major enemy. People were also attracted by the idea of monetary policy being easier to implement than fiscal policy. The latter had been shown to involve *active* decision-taking while the former was alleged to involve the more *passive* setting of targets for the growth of the money supply. This is the controversy between supporters of **discretionary** versus **automatic** stabilisation policies. (It is not of course true that fiscal policy is wholly discretionary and monetary policy automatic—there may be elements of both in each.)

At about the same time a shift was occurring in the policy horizon of stabilisation targets. Short-term fine tuning was fairly widely discredited around the world and the new Conservative government of Mrs Thatcher, elected in 1979, adopted a policy that chose to ignore very short-term fluctuations and to focus its attention instead on what it described as the **medium-term economic strategy**.

Assessment of the effectiveness of monetary policy is as hard to make as is that of fiscal policy. Since both sets of policies have been in use throughout most of the postwar period it is difficult to untangle their separate contributions to the course of events. The distinguished economist Professor Brian Tew expressed what to us seems a reasonable conclusion[1].

> The main lesson of post-war history is that though the growth rate of the banking sector has varied greatly from year to year, only a modest part of the variation is attributable to the way the authorities have used the instruments of policy at their disposal.

Fig 103 shows the course of inflation, as measured by the retail price index, the money supply (sterling M3), unemployment and interest rates (MLR) between 1970 and the early 1980s. There is no doubt that inflation and the money supply were closely correlated. The size of the public sector borrowing requirement has been deliberately omitted from the diagram on grounds of clarity, but if it had been included further positive associations between the PSBR and both inflation and the money supply would have been apparent.

However, too much should not be read into the historical record in Fig 103. *Statistical association* is one thing; *causality* quite another. Indeed, economists of widely differing persuasions accept the correlation between monetary aggregates and

1 'The Implementation of Monetary Policy in Post-war Britain', Brian Tew, *Midland Bank Review*, Spring 1981.

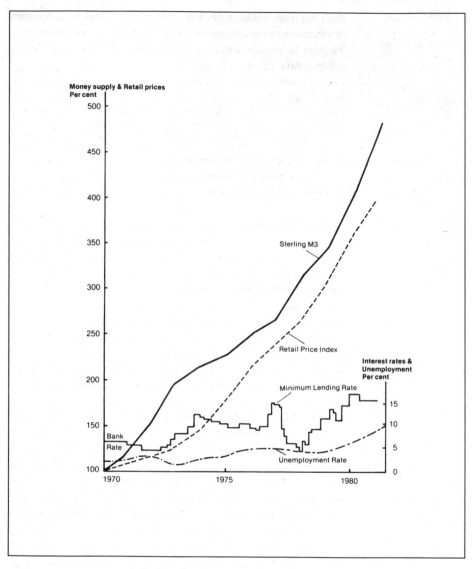

*Fig 103* Money supply, retail prices, unemployment and interest rates 1970–82 Sources: *Annual Abstract of Statistics, Financial Statistics,* and *Monthly Digest of Statistics*

inflation, but interpret the causal forces that give rise to them very differently. Moreover, the series used in the construction of the diagram are simple and selective. For example, the money supply is identified as sterling M3 because the 1980 government declared this to be its prime monetary control variable. There are, however, as we saw in Chapter 8, alternative definitions of monetary supply targets, five of which were described (see pages 174–5).

Furthermore, the statistics used in the construction of Fig 103 are in crude form, whereas adjustments may sometimes be called for to assist in analysis, eg to allow for inflation (by expressing them in *real* terms). The evidence certainly lends itself to more than one interpretation. Economists at the highest levels still disagree profoundly over the explanations of this data.

<table>
<tr><td>

Other
stabilisation
policies

</td><td>

Fiscal and monetary policies are not the only instruments used in connection with the macroeconomic goals with which we are now familiar. Three others will be dealt with here:

- **prices/incomes policies**
- **labour market intervention**
- **indicative planning**

</td></tr>
<tr><td>

*Prices/incomes policies*

</td><td>

The idea behind prices/incomes policies is that of setting targets limiting price and wage increases in an attempt to control inflation. Such policies can be traced back to the late 1940s when the Labour Party was in office and the trade unions were asked to accept a 'wage freeze'. Subsequent governments varied in the extent to which they favoured this approach. The first independent body set up to give advice on these matters was a Council on Prices, Productivity and Incomes, in 1957. A National Incomes Commission and a National Board for Prices and Incomes came and went in the 1960s, but as the pace of inflation accelerated in the 1970s a Price Commission and a Pay Board, operating a pay code approved by Parliament, took their place.

</td></tr>
</table>

The Labour government elected in 1974 abolished the Pay Board while retaining the Price Commission. The government itself then negotiated what was described as a 'social contract' with the trade unions for agreed limits on wage increases. The legal powers of the Price Commission were used to reject requests for price increases from employers who did not adhere to the nationally agreed maxima. With the fall of the government in 1979, the incoming Conservative administration abolished the Price Commission and announced that prices and incomes policies were not to be included in its armoury of weapons for the control of the economy, mainly because of its belief in the merits of a freely working price system for the allocation of resources.

Part of the problem when discussing prices and incomes policies lies in the fact that the circumstances in which these policies have been used have varied greatly. We can distinguish three major uses for incomes policies. First, they may be employed to suppress demand inflation. However, if the excess demand is not removed the inflation is merely *suppressed* and will recur once the restrictions are removed.

The second major use of incomes policies is as an adjunct to restrictive fiscal and monetary policies to help break entrenched inflation. If inflation has been going on for some time and is *expected to continue*, it develops a momentum of its own. If everyone expects the general level of wages and prices to increase, they raise their own wage or price to keep in step, and this causes the very inflation they were expecting. Incomes policies may then be used to interrupt the inflationary process by lowering people's expectations of the future course of prices and wages. If successful, the inflation can then be attacked with new fiscal and monetary policies much faster than by demand restraint alone.

The third and final use of incomes policies is as a *permanent* measure. If it is true, as some economists allege, that the market processes of wage and price determination themselves impart an inflationary bias into the proceedings, because of the predominance of large firms and trade unions, then some form of permanent incomes policy may be needed to restrain inflation.

Incomes policies, particularly those of the third type, have a discouraging past history. First, it has proved much easier to control negotiated *wage rates* than overall *earnings* (take-home pay), although the latter are what affect costs and prices. The phenomenon of **wage drift** refers to the tendency for market forces to push up earnings despite control of wage rates. A second problem is that if union officials cooperate with the government they lose the confidence of their rank and file members, who regard them as having sold out to the other side.

Incomes policies appear to have been most effective in the short term and to have broken down when under pressure for too long. It also seems improbable that they could ever be completely effective in Britain's complex economy. The pay of some groups of workers is relatively easy to control, eg those in the public sector, while that of others may be virtually uncontrollable, eg the self-employed. Tight incomes policies are difficult to enforce and the same can be said of price controls. The black economy (see page 160) and black markets for goods tend to flourish when pressures are applied with great rigour. Finally, it may be said that trade union support is likely to be critical for the success of incomes policies, but the faith of that movement in free collective bargaining is traditionally strong and may be difficult to change.

Some economists believe that unemployment is due to the imperfect functioning of the labour market. Beyond reasonable doubt, the market for labour does not behave like the perfectly competitive markets for some industrial raw materials where prices fluctuate continuously to equate supply and demand. This is an institutional fact of labour markets the world over.

More serious, however, is the contention of many economists that current high levels of unemployment in countries such as Britain and France are due to the fact that the general level of wages has risen too high. On this view wages have absorbed so high a proportion of total revenue that less efficient firms have been forced to close down, causing the level of unemployment to rise. Some of these economists blame the increased power of trade unions for much of Britain's recent economic troubles. As we saw earlier in Chapter 4 (see pages 88–9) the incidence of strikes in support of wages claims mounted in the 1970s well above that of the 1950s and 1960s (though it was still below that of the worst interwar years).

The settlement of wages in the UK has for long been based upon the principle of free collective bargaining. There has, however, always been a public interest in helping to achieve a fair balance between the parties and in avoiding disputes. An early measure was the establishment of **joint industrial councils** for industries which had not by then provided their own negotiating machiney. More recently, in 1974, an independent **Advisory Conciliation and Arbitration Service (ACAS)** was set up, together with a permanent **Central Arbitration Committee (CAC)** to which disputes may be referred by agreement. In the most serious cases the Secretary of State for Employment can appoint a special court of inquiry or committee of investigation. Their recommendations are not legally binding, but often lead to settlements. (For disputes involving individual workers their are tribunals dealing with unfair dismissals, sex discrimination, etc.)

Many and varied attempts have been made to influence the legal and institutional background within which collective bargaining takes place. Invariably they reflect the philosophy of the governments which made them.

In 1971 a Conservative government brought in an Industrial Relations Act which was bitterly opposed by the trade unions. It followed some of the recommendations of a Royal Commission on Trade Unions (the Donovan Commission) which had reported in 1969. The Donovan Report favoured a strategy of non–legalistic voluntary reform but identified so-called unofficial strikes (called by shop stewards at the place of work without official support from the union headquarters) as a major source of trouble in industrial relations. A **Commission on Industrial Relations (CIR)** was also recommended and established.

The Industrial Relations Act of 1971 tried to create a new legal framework for industrial relations. The CIR was retained and given some teeth. In addition the Act set up a registration system for unions, a National Industrial Relations Court with power to order 'cooling off' periods and strike ballots, financial penalties for unions (including damages resulting from strikes) and a new concept of **unfair industrial practices**, covering **closed shops** and the calling of strikes by unauthorised union officials. The Act tried to limit participation in disputes to the unions *directly* involved.

In 1974 a Labour government repealed the Industrial Relations Act and substituted the Trade Union and Labour Relations Act and the Employment Protection Act the following year. These pieces of legislation were less hostile towards the trade unions. Included, for example, was a provision requiring employers to supply unions with certain information during pay negotiations.

A Conservative government was elected in 1979. It did not reinstate the full provisions of its earlier legislation, partly because of opposition from the trade unions but also because management did not take any great advantage of the Act. Instead, the government brought in the Employment Acts of 1980 and 1982, to protect employees against unfair dismissal, eg where a closed shop agreement exists which is not supported by at least 80 per cent of the workers. The Acts also greatly weakened the special immunities for trade unions provided by law and gave employers the right to seek injunctions and damages in the courts against trade unions themselves (as well as union officials) arising from cases involving commercial deals and industrial action—something which had not been possible since 1906. For the first time unions could be sued for unlawful acts unconnected with industrial action, eg libel, negligence and nuisance. Not surprisingly, the trade unions were strongly opposed to the new law which came into effect in 1982.

*Indicative planning* A policy of expanding aggregate demand to foster economic growth and full employment can fail because of unforeseen supply-side bottlenecks. A centrally planned economy might, at least in theory, avoid such problems but for a mixed economy like the UK, where major sectors are in private hands, this is certainly not the case. Moreover, because of the great complexity of the economic network and the high degree of interdependence among its constituent parts, British governments have tried to introduce some machinery which, by coordinating plans for several industries, might assist firms to formulate more realistic plans for themselves.

**Indicative planning** is the term used to describe such combinations of consultative machinery and sectoral projections, eg for labour supply, productivity and import requirements, which might lead to the setting of attainable targets for economic growth and other macroeconomic variables. An important move in this direction was the establishment, in 1962, of the **National Economic Development Council** (**NEDC**, but popularly known as '**Neddy**') together with a number of specialised 'little Neddies' for individual industries. The NEDC consists of representatives of government and both sides of industry and is under the chairmanship of the Chancellor of the Exchequer. The various councils meet to consider problems and obstacles in the way of economic growth.

A more ambitious attempt at indicative planning was made in 1965 after the election of a Labour government. A new government department, the Department of Economic Affairs (DEA), was set up and published a **national plan** aimed at a growth rate of about 4 per cent per annum for the rest of the decade. The plan was abandoned only a year after its introduction, when the economy was faced with a balance of payments crisis. The DEA was disbanded and the plan has not been repeated. Moreover, even countries such as France, which were regarded as having successfully used indicative planning policies in earlier years, have not returned to them.

**International economic policy**[1]

Whether the exchange rate is fixed, as it was prior to 1972, or floating, as it has been since then, determines the importance that must be given to the exchange rate and the balance of payments as targets of economic policy. When we were outlining the goals of macro-policy at the beginning of this chapter, we described balance of payments and exchange rate considerations as secondary goals in contrast to the primary objectives of growth, price stability and full employment. These external goals are of secondary importance because, while the pound is floating (as it is at the time of writing), its external value is determined by the forces of demand and supply. In these circumstances its external value

---

1 The theory and a more detailed factual discussion of what is contained in this section can be found in Lipsey Chapter 45.

can be allowed to change so as to bring the balance of payments into equilibrium.

Unfortunately, however, market-determined exchange rates tend to fluctuate quite considerably. The monetary authorities of many countries worry that the short-term fluctuations in import and export prices create uncertainty among traders, so exerting a depressing effect on the volume of world trade. As a result many governments (operating through their central banks) accept as a goal of policy sufficient intervention to reduce short-term fluctuations in the exchange rate, due primarily to movements of short-term capital, but do not try to resist long-term pressures due to such factors as differing rates of inflation and productivity growth among nations.

In the Bretton Woods system of fixed exchange rates that ruled from 1945 to the early 1970s, and which will be discussed later, an overriding object of policy had to be to maintain a 'satisfactory' balance of payments position for sterling, in the sense that there was no strong pressure forcing the exchange rate up or down. Under fixed rates the need to maintain a satisfactory balance of payments position can seriously interfere with the achievement of one or more primary policy goals. This has happened quite frequently in the past. Expansionary policies aimed at the promotion of economic growth led to pressures on the balance of payments as imports rose with rising incomes, exports declined in the face of rising prices and high domestic demand, and capital flowed out of the country because of adverse expectations among investors. The result, especially in the 1950s and 1960s, was that the government of the day slammed their expansionary policies into reverse in what came to be called 'stop–go'.

## Balance of payments problems

Balance of payments problems arise when there is a tendency for the demand for sterling to fall relative to its supply. This does not necessarily imply a deficit on the balance of visible trade, nor even on the current account (see pages 164–6), though it may happen that adverse movements of either of these can lead to balance of payments problems as capital is frightened away. Large-scale outflows of capital can, however, accompany a strong current account, as occurred in the early 1980s when relatively high rates of interest in the USA were a prime reason for speculators switching funds from London to New York.

In free market conditions the best single indicator of the strength of the forces of supply and demand on the balance of payments is the rate of exchange between currencies. Fig 104 shows the course of the US dollar–sterling rate since 1972 (an alternative index for estimating the pressure on sterling, which is better for some purposes, is the so-called 'effective exchange rate'—a weighted average exchange rate between sterling and the currencies of the UK's major trading

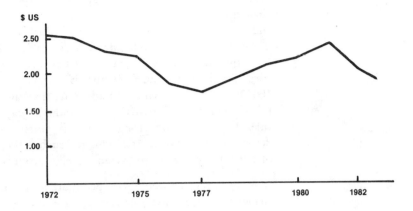

*Fig 104* Exchange rate between sterling and US dollars 1972–82; number of dollars obtained for £1 (annual averages) Sources: *Annual Abstract of Statistics*, and *Financial Statistics*

partners). Fig 104 charts the depreciation of sterling in the years up to 1977, as well as its subsequent strength due to a combination of internal and external influences—government policy, North Sea oil, weakness overseas and high domestic interest rates. The diagram also shows the renewed fall in the purchasing power of the found vis à vis the dollar after 1980, initiated by the relatively high interest rates obtainable in the USA, but which pushed sterling back towards its long-term trend value.

It is instructive to compare the record of sterling's exchange rate in Fig 104 with that of the balance of payments on current account (Fig 83 page 164). Such a comparison confirms that, in the long run, sterling tends to be strong when the current account is favourable to the UK and vice versa.

The instruments of balance of payments policy

Government policies to change the balance of payments or influence the external value of sterling may be directed at either the current account or the capital account, or even both. Those concerned with the current account fall into two categories:

- **expenditure-changing policies**
- **expenditure-switching policies**

The mechanism of expenditure-changing is achieved by the use of the instruments of fiscal and monetary policies discussed earlier (see pages 204 ff). The tools for expenditure-switching are two-fold:

- **commercial policy**
- **altering the exchange rate**

*Commercial policy*

Under the general heading of commercial policy are all the means of reducing imports (or increasing exports) other than changing the exchange rate. The major tools here are tariffs and other import restrictions, both of which were dealt with in Chapter 5. It needs to be added that since the UK joined the EEC these two tools cannot be used against member countries. Similarly Britain's membership of GATT (see pages 106–7) inhibits the raising of trade restrictions against imports from other GATT participants, although ways round the rules have been increasing in recent years, eg non-tariff devices to protect domestic industries such as the artificial use of standards designed to exclude foreign products.

*Changing the exchange rate*

The second technique for expenditure-switching involves changes in the exchange rate. Sterling is said to be *depreciated* (or *appreciated*) when its value falls (or rises) respectively on freely fluctuating exchange rate markets, but it is said to be *devalued*, or *revalued*, when its fixed rate is changed downwards or upwards respectively in a regime of fixed exchange rates. Depreciation of the currency lowers the price of sterling to foreigners. It means that importers in the rest of the world can buy more sterling with their own currencies. This helps to stimulate the UK's exports while at the same time raising the domestic price of imports into the UK and inhibiting the quantity bought. Whether or not such devaluation raises the *value* of exports or lowers the *value* of imports depends, inter alia, on how responsive demand and supply are to price changes.

Prior to 1972 the UK maintained a fixed rate of exchange for sterling, and devaluation was sometimes used to help the balance of payments. The last occasion on which this happened was the 15 per cent devaluation of 1967. Since there are long lags in the adjustment of trading relations to price changes, this did not bring about an immediate improvement in the balance of payments. It was not until 1969 that any substantial benefit was felt. This was aided by the government's adoption of policies of fiscal and monetary restraint. Such supplementation is usual in that it prevents the erosion of any benefits following on from the devaluation, which is in itself expansionary because it increases the demand for domestic output.

When the UK abandoned a fixed exchange rate in 1972 the policy decision of whether or not to devalue was no longer needed, since the external value of sterling was free to be determined on the open market. Since then, however, the Bank of England has often intervened to try to iron out short-term fluctuations in the exchange rate. When the Bank intervenes in a free market to influence the value of sterling, but not to support a pre-announced pegged rate, it is referred to as a **managed** or a '**dirty' float**.

Managing a floating exchange rate (or maintaining a pegged rate) requires reserves of foreign exchange. When the Bank of England is supporting sterling it buys that currency and sells foreign exchange, thereby reducing its reserves; when it is holding down the price of sterling it sells sterling and buys foreign exchange, thereby adding to its reserves. With a dirty float the Bank has to decide whether or not to resist pressures for a depreciation (or an appreciation) when they develop. The Bank will be more likely to resist if it thinks the pressures are short term rather than long term.

As regards the capital account, there are again two policy instruments:

- exchange control
- monetary policy

*Exchange control*

Exchange control, the first technique directed at the capital account, actually aims to restrict the purchase and sale of foreign exchange for *all* purposes, including both visible and invisible transactions and capital movements. The machinery for the operation of exchange control in the UK has been run by the Bank of England, to whom applications for foreign currency used to be made.

Exchange controls may be general, applying to all foreign currencies, or discriminatory, affecting only currencies in particularly short supply ('hard' rather than 'soft' currencies, in the jargon). In the UK, exchange controls were imposed on the outbreak of war in 1939 to limit the use of currencies to essential purposes. They were progressively relaxed after the Second World War, though more quickly for non-residents than for residents. Complete abolition of exchange controls, though, did not occur until 1980, since when it has no longer been necessary to obtain permission from the Bank of England to buy foreign exchange for any purpose.

*Monetary policy*

The second technique for influencing capital movements is monetary policy. Raising interest rates tends to encourage capital inflows (or discourage outflows); lowering interest rates tends to encourage outflows (or discourage inflows). It is important to notice in this context that it is not the absolute level of interest rate in the UK that matters, but UK rates in relation to those ruling elsewhere. (An investor wants to know if he can make more or less by lending his funds in the UK rather than in other countries.) Since there is a large volume of short-term capital in world markets seeking the highest return, interest rate manipulation can be an extremely effective device, though its implications for domestic policy must be taken into account.

## Reserves

Reserves are required, as we have seen, to enable the Bank of England to intervene in the foreign exchange market. The UK's international reserves in the early 1980s stood at a figure of about £12 000 million, representing approximately the value of 3 months' imports. Such a sum may appear small by that standard, although in comparison with potential *deficits* on current account it seems larger. Even so, in some years reserves have been less can current account deficits, eg in 1974. Moreover, investors are liable to notice and respond to any substantial depletion of the reserves and their actions may aggravate the balance of payments position further.

## International cooperation

During the 19th century exchange rates between the major currencies in the world were fixed through a system known as the **gold standard**. Each country's currency was freely convertible into a fixed amount of gold, which effectively fixed the exchange values of the currencies in question in relation to each other.

The gold standard broke down during the interwar years, and in the depression of the 1930s nations resorted to competitive devaluations and exchange controls to try to protect themselves from balance of payments deficits. As time went on such actions tended to cancel each other out, while world trade spiralled downwards. Such 'beggar-my-neighbour' attitudes benefited no one and during the Second World War the representatives of the majority of countries on the 'allied' side met at an international conference at **Bretton Woods**, New Hampshire, out of which grew a system, akin in some ways to the gold standard, which operated during the following 20 years.

## Bretton Woods

The Bretton Woods Agreement of 1944 set up two international institutions, the International Bank for Reconstruction and Development and the International Monetary Fund (IMF). The former was discussed in Chapter 5 (see page 111).

The prime objective of the charter establishing the IMF was to return to a system of fixed exchange rates, with the important proviso that they would be adjusted in the light of long-term changes in economic conditions. Such a system is of the **adjustable peg** type previously referred to. It aims to eliminate short-term instability and competitive devaluations, while incorporating arrangements to accommodate structural changes in the relative strengths of different currencies brought about by differential rates of inflation, economic growth or any other cause.

The Bretton Woods system had to cope with three main problems. First, reserves did not grow as fast as trade. By the late 1960s international reserves were distinctly inadequate. Second, very large speculative movements of capital occurred whenever people believed that a realignment of exchange rates was needed. Capital fled from currencies expected to be devalued, into currencies expected to be revalued. Third, and largely to the surprise of the architects of the system, countries tended, largely for domestic political considerations, to cling to their existing exchange rates. They accepted devaluations and revaluations only when literally forced into them by an irresistible flood of capital away from currencies that were clearly overvalued and into currencies that were clearly undervalued.

During the first postwar years the Bretton Woods system was aided by the very large gold reserves of the USA, but by the late 1960s the United States' balance of payments position had deteriorated to such an extent that she decided to suspend the convertibility of dollars into gold. Confidence in the dollar (and in sterling, the other major reserve currency of the time) lapsed. The dollar was eventually devalued (by 7.9 per cent) in 1971 and again in 1973. Dollar devaluations and the suspension of convertibility were the signal for the virtual collapse of the IMF rules as originally laid down. An agreement signed at the Smithsonian Institute in Washington in 1971 established new parities, but they were not long lived. Within a couple of years most countries had decided to allow their currencies to float (the UK in 1972, as we have seen), although trying to 'manage' them in the interests of short-term exchange stability.

The International Monetary Fund itself did not, however, collapse. It adapted its rules to the new situation, and in 1974 issued three new guiding principles for countries managing their exchange rates:

1 Accepting the need for the avoidance of sudden large movements in the value of currencies.

2 Calling for the establishment of target exchange rates for the medium term.

3 Recognising that exchange rate management involves joint responsibilities (to prevent countries adopting mutually inconsistent exchange rate policies such as occur, for example, when country A wants to lower the value of its currency relative to that of country B, while B is trying to do the same thing relative to A's currency).

*Special drawing rights*

One response by IMF members to the shortage of international reserves was to find ways of increasing them. A major step in this direction was the introduction of so-called **special drawing rights** (**SDRs**) in 1970.

SDRs are drawing rights, fixed initially in terms of gold. They were allocated by quota to member countries who could use them to support their existing exchange rates. In the years that followed the SDR system was extended in several ways, including valuing SDRs in terms of a 'basket' of currencies (1974), reducing the restrictions on the purposes for which SDRs could be used (1978), and raising the rate of interest payable on SDRs to levels comparable to those in world markets (1981). The quotas available to member countries were also increased, in 1974, to aid countries affected by the oil price rise, and again in 1981. The result of these measures was to ease world liquidity problems, though one should not exaggerate their quantitative importance. By 1981 SDRs accounted for only about 5 per cent of total world reserves of gold and other currencies.

*Other international cooperative arrangements*

The IMF was not the only postwar example of international cooperation related to balance of payments problems. A 'Group of Ten' countries, including the UK, France, West Germany and the USA, agreed in 1962 to help each other (actually through the IMF) should such circumstances arise, and a 'Group of Twelve' central banks signed an agreement in Basle in 1968 to assist Britain with its balance of payments difficulties of that year. Then in 1973 five members of the EEC decided to stabilise their currencies against each other, while allowing them to float vis à vis the dollar, which had just been devalued. The arrangement was known as the **'snake'**, and it developed into a **European monetary system** (**EMS**) in 1979.

The EMS was designed to provide a degree of exchange rate stability within the Common Market not too dissimilar from the original IMF arrangements, in so far as members agreed to keep their exchange rates *with each other* within a margin of 2¼ per cent (a 6 per cent margin being allowed for new entrants and Italy). A number of changes in exchange rates have occurred since the inception of the scheme but the UK had not, at the time of writing, joined the EMS, preferring the extra flexibility of remaining outside it.

## Concluding remarks: macroeconomic policy—a perspective

This has been a long chapter. It has touched upon some of the most interesting, complex and controversial issues in modern economics. We cannot, therefore, provide the reader with a neat summary of the chapter's contents. We expect you found it difficult. It is. The best brains in the world have not been able to solve all the problems we have considered and come up with policy combinations for the simultaneous achievement of the multiple aims of full employment, price stability and satisfactory economic growth—especially for a country with a large overseas sector.

It must, moreover, be understood that the division of economic policy into separate micro- and macroeconomic compartments (corresponding to Chapters 6 and 9 in this book) is artificial. We earlier described the goals of micro-policy as efficiency and equity. Yet it takes not great intellectual effort to realise that growth and efficiency are inextricably entwined and that all macro-policies have distributive implications and therefore involve considerations of equity.

Economic policy formation in the real world must, to an extent, be based on normative judgments. The Keynesian–Monetarist controversy of recent years, for example, has been perhaps as much ideological as 'scientific' in base. If we understood better how the economy worked, all of the issues could be quickly settled by recourse to the facts, in the way that some of the issues have been. However, we are still learning (as we always shall be). That may not be very comforting for those who hope for final solutions to all of the economy's problems, but at least it makes economics a fascinating subject, for us anyway and, we hope, for you too.

# Index

*Where references are given in heavy type these indicate the main source*

GDP is the total monetary value of
final gds. & services produced by
country in ae. yr. It has a price
& quantity component es. If GDP
increased by 10% – quantity is
the same – just an increase in prices